Landis

W9-CZX-882

stages of development:
pp. 210-

✳ inner (lowman) & outer bdries — p.199

INTRODUCTION TO THE
SZONDI TEST

INTRODUCTION TO THE
SZONDI
TEST

THEORY AND PRACTICE

By SUSAN DERI

With a Foreword
By Dr. LIPOT SZONDI

GRUNE & STRATTON
NEW YORK   1949

Library of Congress Catalog Card Number 49-8788

Copyright, 1949

GRUNE & STRATTON, INC.
381 Fourth Avenue
New York City

Second Printing, 1950
Third Printing, 1954

Printed in U.S.A.

Contents

v

CHAPTER VII

CHAPTER VIII

CHAPTER IX

CHAPTER X

CHAPTER XI

Foreword

My student and former co-worker, Susan Deri, modestly entitles her book *Introduction*. Its substance shows, however, that her work goes beyond a simple introduction. It is, in three different respects, a definitely needed and splendidly executed supplement to and elaboration of my book *Experimentelle Triebdiagnostik*.

In the first place, Mrs. Deri has succeeded in presenting the dynamic thought processes in the interpretation of the test. Neither myself nor any of my collaborators had been able to do so.

Secondly, the author supplements the *Triebdiagnostik* with a complete and living presentation of the eight factors of my drive system.

When Mrs. Deri visited me in Zurich recently and read to me from her manuscript the chapters on the drive factors, I saw clearly what I myself omitted in my book.

From the very first minute of the birth of the drive system to the final unfolding of the drive diagnosis, Mrs. Deri participated personally in all my worries and elations. She knew the tribulations of research until finally and laboriously the right way was found. Only because of this personal experience could Mrs. Deri understand the eight drive factors so deeply. She assimilated the concept, as though the eight factors were in reality eight living beings to whom she is eternally bound in friendship.

In the third place, she took upon herself the important task of making American psychologists understand the fundamentally different aspect of European *Seelenkunde*. We Europeans still pursue an "epic" form of psychology of a kind that we learned from Dostoevski and Freud. The story of the *soul* of man to us is still a heroic novel that we like to tell unhurriedly in long sentences. This epic form of presentation is inadequate to the American tempo of thinking. Therefore, a book like Mrs. Deri's appears to me indispensable for bridging these differences in scientific thinking and presentation.

Psychologists in America who work toward a new conception of psychologic depth diagnosis will, I hope, value and benefit from the sincerity of these scientific efforts and the extraordinary facility of a born teacher.

L. SZONDI

Preface

This book is the outgrowth of almost eleven years of clinical experience with and teaching of the Szondi test. This time span actually coincides with the life span of the test. Having worked intensively with the originator of the method for four years, which included the very first attempts to use this test as a method of personality investigation, necessarily resulted in a strong subjective identification with the test, a personal concern about every step in its development and in regard to its reception by psychologists and psychiatrists.

Most probably it was just this concern which kept me from writing a "manual" for this test sooner. I knew that the rationale for this method is much more involved and more difficult to prove—with the exception of proving it pragmatically by the use of the test—than it is for any of the other projective technics. I also knew, or rather I have noticed gradually, that the general interest in this method, as one of the new projective technics, is increasing rapidly, almost at a rate which alarmed me because I knew how easily this test can be misused in the hands of persons not adequately trained in its use, and that the misuse can harm the further development of the method, as well as those individuals who serve as subjects for misinterpretation. However, since there was practically no literature in English on the Szondi method, and the picture set became available commercially, there was no way to stop those who felt like experimenting or playing with the pictures. The fact that the stimulus pictures are labeled with the initials of well-known diagnostic entities only enhanced the impression that this is a test which can be used rather easily because the interpretation in terms of the diagnostic categories is practically self-evident.

In actuality, however, the fact that the photographs of
the test represent psychiatric patients with well-known diagnoses, is exactly what makes interpretation, and the formulation of satisfactory rationales for interpretation, so difficult. The problem is how to account for the fact that we
use various psychiatric categories as a "measuring stick" for
"normal" or "abnormal" psychologic characteristics alike.
The attempt to formulate such a coherent framework of psychologic rationales which would give a theoretical basis to
our pragmatic knowledge of interpretation was the purpose
which spurred me in the writing of this book. I have tried
to present the dynamic thought-processes implied in interpretation, pointing out the complexities and the manifold
meaning of any single factorial constellation depending on
the positions of all the other factors, rather than to present
the interpretation in a simplified form. It is conceivable
that, after having read this introductory book, some psychologists or psychiatrists will withdraw their interest from
the Szondi test following their recognition that instead of
its being a "streamlined" new instrument which can be
administered in a few minutes and interpreted in an additional few minutes, it is a time-consuming method which
has to be administered at least six times to the same subject,
and which requires a lengthy process of interpretation. I
have been asked whether the Szondi test is a "really" scientific instrument which determines mental traits with the
same ease and exactness as the amount of hemoglobin can
be determined in a blood analysis, and not the same kind
of "worthless and vague instrument as the Rorschach and
psychoanalysis." The answer in this book will be found
in the form of a definite "no." This means, of course, that
anybody who finds the Rorschach and psychoanalysis "worthless and vague" also will be dissatisfied with the Szondi
test, and for his own sake as well as for the sake of the

test, it might be more advantageous if he turns his interest to other fields than projective technics.

However, that does not mean that I am not aware of the shortcomings of this introductory book as well as, to some extent, of the present state of our knowledge of the test, in regard to the lack of rigorous quantitative validating data. Were it not for the pressing circumstances mentioned above, I would have preferred delaying to write a comprehensive book on this method until I had secured more strictly quantitative data with "up-to-date" statistical treatment of them to support my statements. As it is, the acceptance of practically any of my statements about the meaning of the various factorial constellations is left to the good-will of the reader. I have to trust, just as I have to trust at the outset of my beginners' course, that the inner consistency of the reasoning involved in interpretation will help to keep the reader's or the learner's judgment suspended until he can convince himself about the clinical validity of the statements by the actual use of the test. If interest can be held up to this point, then I am rather optimistic because the coincidence of students' interpretations with independent clinical evidence is a constant source of validation for myself as well as for the students. Also the fact that those who spent sufficient time with the studying of this method always find it one of their most useful diagnostic tools, and remark on the increasing demands for "Szondi reports" after having sent the first ones to clinicians or psychiatrists, can be regarded as a validation although it cannot be reported in quantitative terms. I am fully aware of the autistic nature of this reasoning since actually in this manner I am the only one who received the accumulative evidence of all these individual clinical validations. Yet these experiences were of great importance to me because they proved that the theory of the test interpretation has reached that stage in development at which it can be taught successfully without much difficulty to any advanced student in clinical psychology or psychiatry, requiring only a basic knowledge in these fields, some actual experience with patients and a general "feeling" for projective technics. Six or more years ago I would not have been able to enumerate the various background and personality qualifications which were thought necessary for learning the test in the form of a course in contrast to the way we, the immediate students and co-workers of Szondi, have learned it by growing up with the test and learning from Szondi by daily long discussions of every single test we made in the psychologic laboratory and out-patient clinic of which he was the head. In the course of this continuous and gradual learning process, much has been observed empirically for which the conceptual explanation was still lacking and therefore could not be transmitted by means of more formalized teaching.

The successful clinical work of those psychologists who have learned this method more recently has encouraged me to organize my usual course material in the present book form, and I can only hope that it will serve its purpose by giving the basic knowledge for interpretation and thereby helping those who plan to do actual work with this test. The presentation of the numerical data, even those which are available, is completely omitted, partly because it can be found in the appendix of Szondi's book *(Experimentelle Triebdiagnostik)* partly because the data are not treated with the statistical methods generally used in this country. However, the trends of the frequency distributions in regard to various age and clinical groups are always mentioned and, if possible, accompanied by hints in regard to the underlying psychodynamic process which might account for the particularly high or low frequency of a given constellation in a certain group of subjects. The temptation to elaborate on possible hypotheses of psychodynamic explanations was great, yet I tried to limit myself to what I thought was absolutely necessary for the sake of making the empirical findings psychologically meaningful and also for the sake of stimulating further research which will throw more light on these basic problems of psychodynamics. I also wanted to illustrate what—to my mind—is the most specific and the most interesting potentiality of the Szondi test, namely its use for the purpose of making visible the hidden dynamic processes which lie behind the generally used one-word diagnostic labelings.

What I mostly hope is that this introductory book will at least point out a number of possible avenues for more specific research studies and can serve as a guide in interpretation, and also help to differentiate between the adequate methods of handling such complex data and those which are not appropriate for handling the data of this method.

To express any form of thanks to the person who originated the test, and without whose teachings I would have never been able to learn the interpretation of a profile, seems rather out of place. Also I feel that no conventional form of expressing gratitude could do justice to my actual indebtedness for the absolutely untiring and unlimited efforts, enthusiasm and time Szondi has spent for years in explaining and discussing his ideas with the few of us who were fortunate enough to work under his personal supervision. The unique atmosphere of enthusiastic work, this closely-knit group of co-workers around Szondi, which due to Szondi's personal inspiration and to the common interest of all of us, continued almost fanatically for years during which we forgot the existence of official working or office hours and argued theoretical or practical points until late in the night or even early morning, can not be described to anybody who has not experienced it personally.

In organizing my material, I was helped by several psychologists who were kind enough to let me use the notes they wrote on the basis of my courses. In the first place I want to express my thanks to the "Chicago group" whose mimeographed notes were the most extensive and who were the first in this country to organize a regular weekly "Szondi Seminar," under the direction of Mrs. Ruth L. Bromberg, for all those psychologists who were already trained in the use of the test. Ruth L. Bromberg, Dr. Hedda Bolgar, Dr. Ann Elonen, Dr. Erika Fromm, Dr. Mary Grier-Jacques, Harriette Moore and Elleva Patten have worked most on the collective organization of their Szondi notes, which resulted in a most useful fourteen page syllabus. Later I was helped by the notes of Mr. Stanley Friedman, Mr. Jerome Himmelchoch and Mrs. Nina Diamond-Fieldstiel, for which I want to thank them here.

Mr. Henry Stratton I want to thank for his ready encouragement, and Mr. David Spengler for his understanding effort in editing my manuscript.

SUSAN DERI

CHAPTER I

Introduction

MORE THAN ten years ago, Dr. Lipot Szondi, Hungarian
psychiatrist, constructed a picture test, consisting of photographs of mental patients. The original purpose of this test
was to prove experimentally his theory about the role of
latent recessive genes in influencing our psychologic reactions. According to his theory, the mental disorders represented in the test are of genetic origin and the subject's
emotional reactions to these photographs were believed to
depend upon some sort of similarity between the gene-
structure of the patient represented by the photograph and
that of the subject reacting to the photograph. The subject
was asked to choose those pictures he liked most and those
he disliked most. The validating data in regard to the
genetic origin of the choices were expected from the subject's
family tree.

Detailed presentation and critical evaluation of the theory
will not be found in this guidebook. For this material the
reader is referred to Szondi's books: *Schicksalsanalyse* * and
Experimentelle Triebdiagnostik.† *Schicksalsanalyse,* especially, gives a most detailed presentation of Szondi's theory
in regard to the psychologic function of the latent recessive
genes, with a great number of concrete genealogic examples
and family trees.

In his second work, Szondi describes his test as an experimental method for revealing the psychologic effects of the
latent genes as they direct us in our spontaneous choice
reactions.

* Szondi, L.: Schicksalsanalyse. Basel, Benno Schwabe, 1948.
† —— Triebdiagnostik. Bern, Hans Huber, 1947.

Irrespective of whether or not one accepts Szondi's gene-theory, and whether or not one can agree with him in considering his test as being the proper methodology for proving or disproving this theory, the test has proved itself empirically to be one of the most useful projective technics. It is solely from this point of view that the present manual has been written. In the following chapters, the test will be described as a projective technic and the basic processes of interpretation will be discussed from a purely psychologic point of view. It was this attempt to construct a consistent and purely psychologic set of rationales for interpretation which made me decide to write this manual, which is intended to supplement, and not to replace, the reading of *Experimentelle Triebdiagnostik*.

Having had the privilege of working with Dr. Szondi, first as his student, later as his co-worker, from the beginning of his experimentations with the test, I was in the fortunate position of being able to assimilate his way of thinking in the years when no day could pass without intensive discussions about general and specific problems of interpretation. Only Szondi's unparalleled enthusiasm was able to hold together without the least formal organization a group of almost equally enthusiastic co-workers and students for all of whom "the test" was the most vitally important problem in all those years, the end of which was marked by the outbreak of World War II. The war caused the disruption of the group, and soon after I arrived in this country in 1941, there were no more means to communicate with Dr. Szondi in regard to further developments of the test. During these years he has worked in the direction of establishing new, more formalized ways of interpretation, his gene-theory still holding its central position. All these more recent developments in formal methods of interpretation are contained in Szondi's *Experimentelle Triebdiagnostik*.

During the same years my thinking about the test developed more and more in the direction of considering it one of the projective technics. The extent to which the principles usually underlying projective technics apply to the Szondi test will be discussed later. My object in writing this book is to construct and present a series of psychologic assumptions from which the interpretation of the test profiles can be derived. Emphasis is on the attempt to make verbally explicit the basic psychologic assumptions implicit in the interpretation of the single test factors. This work of interpolating certain links in the process of psychologic interpretation had to be done in order to fill out the gap existing between the original stimulus situation of looking at certain photographs and the final step of interpreting the personality, which many times was based on pragmatic knowledge. Without trying to fill out this gap, and to retrace our interpretative statements step by step to their origin in the actual stimulus material, much of the interpretation may sound purely intuitive and mystical. Actually my experience in teaching this method has convinced me—more than I was before—that this is not the case. I would not say that there are not certain personality types who have more spontaneous understanding and "feeling" for interpretation than others, but some basic aspects of interpretation can be definitely taught to any advanced student of clinical psychology or psychiatry. The ability to interpret finer nuances, and to perceive the interdependence of complicated configurations in the test profiles, will always depend upon the general psychiatric knowledge of the interpreter. Psychoanalysts or psychologists with broad background of psychoanalytic knowledge, find it—according to my experience—easiest to familiarize themselves with the way of thinking necessary for "depth"-interpretation.

In my attempt to describe the basic psychologic processes involved in interpretation, I am going to use, besides Szondi's own theoretic concepts concerning the basic personality structure, many explanatory concepts borrowed from Freudian psychoanalysis and Lewin's vector-psychology. I found

the genetically noncommittal yet dynamic concepts of the
Lewinian theory of personality organization extremely helpful in describing certain assumptions underlying the functioning of the Szondi test. My conceptual thinking about
the test has been greatly influenced by two years of research
work with Dr. Kurt Lewin in this country, not so much in
specific discussions with him about the test, as in the general
"conceptual atmosphere" around him and his co-workers
which helped me to see certain problems in connection with
the test from a new angle. On the other hand, besides
getting better acquainted with certain psychologic theories,
I also recognized more than before the agreement or rela
tionship between the results of some experiments and tests,
other than the Szondi test, and conclusions reached on the
basis of the Szondi test. This manual is the result of all these
experiences briefly mentioned above and slowly taking the
shape of a more or less integrated whole during the course
of teaching this method at various schools.

There is necessarily some overlap in the material of this
book and Szondi's *Experimentelle Triebdiagnostik,* although
I tried to keep this overlap at a minimum. As I said before,
my goal was to make the Szondi method more comprehensible
for psychologists who prefer a purely psychologic frame of
reference for interpretation. Accordingly, the main differences between Szondi's book and my manual will be the
following:

1. As mentioned above, the theory about the genetic
origin of instincts and the role the latent recessive genes
are supposed to play in our reaction to the stimulus material
of the test, is presented only in Szondi's book.

2. Szondi centers his reasoning in interpretation around
his more recently developed formalized categories. This
method will be only touched upon in my manual; the respec
tive tables can be found in Szondi's book.

3. As a general principle, I am going to present the qualitative way of thinking underlying the interpretation and then mention the trends characteristic for various groups of subjects, without using the numerical data contained in the appendix of Szondi's book.

4. Finally, I am going to include several examples of individual case interpretations.

CHAPTER II

Test Material and Technic of Administration

1. GENERAL NATURE OF THE TEST

BEFORE going into the description of the test material and technic of administration, something general ought to be said about the test, such as What aspect of the personality does the test intend to "measure"? What are its fields of application? How does it compare with other projective technics?

In spite of being aware of the fact that logically one could expect to have these general questions answered before the presentation of specific technical details, I am going to postpone the detailed discussion of these problems until more has been said about the test. Out of this order of presentation—from the more specific to the general—answers to many questions will emerge naturally from the discussion, while references to aspects of the test not yet discussed will be avoided.

A most general idea in regard to what the test intends to reveal is indicated by the name "projective technic." Today, when there is such a rapid increase of interest in this type of personality investigation, it seems almost redundant to repeat the goal which is common to all of these methods. It is known that the purpose of all the projective technics is to establish a testing situation where, due to the ambiguity of the stimulus material and the general nature of the instructions, the subject is enabled to express his "private world," without knowing what he really reveals. What the exact content of this "private world" is would be hard—if not impossible—to define, but we know that, depending on the specific nature of the stimulus material, it varies somewhat in its meaning. As an attempt to bridge over this embarrassing conceptual uncertainty, a number of rather vague and all-inclusive concepts were developed in the recent literature about projective technics. The most frequently used concepts to denote the object the various projective technics reveal are, besides "the subject's private world," "basic personality structure" or "dynamic aspects of personality." Actually—even though vague—these expressions are quite adequate to emphasize the tendency that all these methods aim at reflecting the personality as a complex organism not divisible into separately functioning faculties or traits. These concepts also reflect our present state of knowledge—or rather our lack of exact knowledge—in regard to what personality really is. The fact that by now we know what it is *not*—that it is not the conglomeration of separate, well defined "traits" which can be independently measured on strictly quantitative scales—marks the most important step in the development of "human" psychology. In the realm of testing, the projective technics are the only instruments doing justice to this holistic and dynamic conception of personality.

In the light of these considerations, we can say that the purpose of the Szondi test is to reflect the personality as a functioning, dynamic whole. More specifically, it conceives of the personality as consisting of a number of need-systems (or drives) and reflects the quantitative distribution of tension in these specific need-systems plus the way the person handles these need-tensions. Its field of application is again similar to that of other projective technics; in other words, as a diagnostic instrument for clinical use or for the interpretation of the so-called normal personality, vocational guidance, experimental social psychology and a variety of fields of research. Because the Szondi test—more than any of the other projective technics reflects the personality as a dynamic process undergoing constant fluctuations through the accumulation and discharge of the various need-tensions, the test is particularly apt to follow up and make visible certain psychodynamic changes, such as the psychologic changes during a paroxysmal cycle of epilepsy, or the effects of various therapeutic procedures. A comparison of the Szondi test with other projective technics cannot be drawn at all before more about this test has been said.

2. MATERIAL AND ADMINISTRATION

The test material consists of 48 photographs, 2 by 3 inches in size. Each photograph represents the face of a mental patient. The pictures are divided into six sets, each containing eight photographs. Each set contains the picture of a homosexual, a sadist, an epileptic, an hysteric, a catatonic schizophrenic, a paranoid schizophrenic, a manic-depressive depressive and a manic-depressive manic. Thus, in the total test each disease entity is represented by six pictures.

On the back of each card there is a Roman numeral, indicating the series number, an Arabic numeral indicating the rank number of the picture within the series, and an initial for indicating the specific type of mental disorder represented by the photograph.

The series, each containing eight pictures, are presented to the subject consecutively, the cards of each series layed out in front of the subject in two lines of four pictures, so that the Arabic numerals 1 and 8 are in a vertical line. In order to save the cards from getting soiled, several psychologists working with the Szondi test suggested that the photographs be covered with cellophane. This is not advisable because the insertion of cellophane between the photographs and the subject might result in some distortion of the visual effect, due to the reflection caused by the shiny surface.

The subject's task is to choose from each series the two

pictures he likes most and the two he dislikes most. It is impossible to give the exact wording of the instructions, since in administering a projective technic one always has to allow for some individual variations as the case might require. Nevertheless, some suggestions in regard to verbal directions can be given. As an introduction the examiner might say, "I am going to show you some pictures of various people, and all you have to do is to tell me which are the ones you like most and which are the ones you dislike most (or like the least). Of course there are no right or wrong choices, since liking or disliking any of these faces is completely a matter of individual taste."

After this introduction the examiner lays out the first series of eight pictures in the order indicated above. After all the eight pictures are layed out the subject is told, "Now look at all these faces and pick out first the two you like most and then the two you dislike most. Don't think long, just do it spontaneously (or quickly), you don't have to give any reason for your choice." Exact timing of the choices is not usually done, except for some specific research purpose, but if the case requires, the subject is prompted several times to choose the pictures without hesitation and without much delay. The subject is not allowed to change the order of the pictures or to pick up any one of them to hold it closer to his eyes. In other words, the order of the pictures, once layed out on the table, should never be changed. After verbal directions have been given, some subjects start out asking an array of questions in regard to "what do you mean by liking or disliking?" (This is particularly true for intellectuals, especially psychologists.) These questions should not be taken too seriously, and by no means should the examiner give in to the temptation of starting lengthy philosophical or psychological arguments about the concepts of "liking" or "disliking" in general. Any such attempt on the part of the subject has to be interpreted (but not verbally)

as resistance, taking the form of escaping into intellectualization. The test profiles of such subjects usually reveal compulsive features. In case the subject asks for more precise
qualifications of the directions, or contends that all the pictures look so "horrible" that he cannot possibly like any
of them, or that they all look like "good" people and he
cannot dislike any of them, the examiner has to reword in
a noncommittal way his original instructions. In such cases
I usually get satisfactory results by saying that "imagine that
you are closed in a room with these eight people and nobody
else, who are the two you would like to sit next to you
for a chat? Who are the two you would like the least to sit
close to you?" According to my experience, more directions
are not needed, unless one is forced to repeat the same
direction in a different tone of voice, with increasingly
obvious indications that we expect to get through the whole
procedure quickly. Usually these variations are not needed
at all, and most subjects pick out liked and disliked pictures
without much difficulty, even though they often make dis-
paraging remarks about the "silliness" of such a test. Most
of the difficulties are encountered in compulsive neurotics,
and in cases of psychotic depression, especially if there is a
strong paranoid component. These are the subjects who
do not want to "judge" anybody by face, or who feel that
all people are "basically good." The ways of relieving such
guilt feelings have to be left to the ingenuity of every well
trained examiner. However, the fact that the examiner
has to be well trained is important. The administration of
the test should never be left to psychologically untrained
personnel; neither should the test material be handed to
the subject for the purpose of self-administration. This
point has to be stressed because the apparent simplicity of
the administration is misleading, and I was surprised to hear
that even well trained psychologists sometimes resorted to
the above methods. As a matter of fact it would not be an

easy task to give a logical explanation why self-administering the test, in case of intelligent subjects, should not work; still there are indications that the presence or absence of an examiner does influence the results to some extent. There are no systematic experimental results to throw more light on this question; however, I base my hunch in this respect on several individual test profile series which I was able to single out from a number of series because of the unusual types of changes occurring from one testing to the other. These "atypical" series, in which cases the usual interpretation of sudden changes did not seem to coincide with the actual personality description, were all self-administered. These rather accidental observations suggest that the more systematic exploration of the role of the examiner would be desirable. One conceivable theory would be that the presence of another person effects in some way yet unknown the mechanisms of control in reinforcing the function of the superego. Whether or not the self-administered profiles give a "truer" picture of the personality cannot be decided yet, but what we know is that our present empirical knowledge of interpretation has been based on thousands of test profiles not self-administered.

Now that we have discussed the difficulties one might encounter in connection with giving the directions to the subject, let us proceed to the description of the administration proper. After the subject has chosen the two pictures he likes most, we place them on the table in front of us, with the photograph side up, so that the subject cannot see the initials on the back. After the subject has handed us the two he dislikes most, we start to pile them up next to the *liked* ones, again picture side up. The remaining four pictures are put back to the corresponding box of the case. The same procedure is repeated with all the six series; thus finally we have two piles of pictures in front of us, one containing the twelve most liked, the other one the twelve most disliked. The next step is to lay out in front of the subject the twelve *likes* and ask him to choose the four he likes the most. The instruction is usually: "Now I am going to show you again the twelve pictures you liked most, and now pick out in order the four you like most among these." The twelve pictures are lined up in three rows of four in each. The same "final choice" procedure is repeated with the twelve *dislikes,* with the instruction of choosing now the four most disliked ones. After having finished the administration of the test, the examiner should immediately record the choice-reactions on the scoring sheet. On the upper half of the scoring sheet the choices are recorded graphically in the form of a test profile.

On the test profile the eight vertical columns headed by the small initials, stand for the eight diseases represented in the test. These eight categories will be referred to from now on as the eight factors. (h = homosexual, s = sadistic, e = epileptic, hy = hysteric, k = catatonic, p = paranoid, d = depressive, m = manic.) Each square above the zero-line stands for a *like* choice in this particular factor, and each square below the zero-line represents a *dislike* choice. In each factor we mark the number of *like* choices by filling in the appropriate number of squares above the zero-line with red pencil (shown in our profiles here by shaded squares) and the *dislikes* by filling in the appropriate number of squares under the zero-line with blue pencil (shown here by solid black squares). Thus each profile after it has been drawn out consists of 12 red and 12 blue squares. The final choices of four most liked and four most disliked can be drawn out either on the separate profile on the same scoring sheet or else one can mark these final four and four choices with heavy shading on the original test profile so that the eight final choices stand out with their darker shading on the background of the 24 original choices.

Name: Alter: Beruf:

Szondi-Test
Blatt mit zwei Triebprofilen

	Trieb — Profil							
	S.		P.		Sch.		C.	
	h.	s.	e.	hy.	k.	p.	d.	m.
+6								
+5								
+4								
+3								
+2								
+1								
0								
−1								
−2								
−3								
−4								
−5								
−6								

Sympathie   Antipathie

I.			
II.			
III.			
IV.			
V.			
VI.			

	Trieb — Profil							
	S.		P.		Sch.		C.	
	h.	s.	e.	hy.	k.	p.	d.	m.
+6								
+5								
+4								
+3								
+2								
+1								
0								
−1								
−2								
−3								
−4								
−5								
−6								

Sympathie   Antipathie

I.			
II.			
III.			
IV.			
V.			
VI.			

Copyright 1947 by Verlag Hans Huber. Bern

FIG. 1. TEST PROFILE RECORDING FORMS

The lower half of the scoring sheet allows space for marking down the 24 choices by their initials. The 12 *likes* are recorded under the heading of *sympathie* and the 12 *dislikes* under the heading *antipathie*. The Roman numerals on this part of the scoring sheet indicate the number of the series from I to VI, so that all we have to write down in the respective box is the initial indicated on the back of the picture. The eight final choices are recorded by encircling the initials of those pictures which were chosen in the "final" phase of the testing. The rank order of the final choices should be indicated by attaching small Arabic index numbers to the encircled initials.

The examiner should *never* rely on the graphic representation of the test profile alone, without also marking down the initials of the chosen pictures. The marking of the initials should be carried out during the course of the test administration, and the graphic representation of the test profile should be based on the counting of the choices marked by initials, and always carried out after the actual test administration has been finished. This procedure should always be followed not only as a checking device but also in order to keep records of the specific pictures chosen in each series. These data might be valuable for later research purposes in regard to the significance of the succession of choices. Something is already known about the specific significance of the first choices.

The administration of the test has to be repeated at least six, preferably ten, times, with at least one day intervals between administrations, to be able to give a valid clinical interpretation of the personality. As a rule the one day, as a minimum interval, should be kept, unless some specific experience occurs (epileptic seizure, introduction of some drug, hypnosis, etc.) in which case the interval can be shortened.

Some experimentation with administering the test twice

within a few hours is carried out at present by Molly Har-
rower, who gives the Szondi test at the beginning of a long
testing session, consisting of a number of projective technics
and an intelligence test, and again at the end of the session.
The results are not evaluated yet in regard to whether the
changes occurring from first to second testing under these
conditions can be interpreted according to principles followed, when the interval between the two administrations
is at least a day. At any rate, the fact that there are changes
even within such a relatively very short period of time, points
to the necessity of investigating more the psychologic meaning of these "short-range" changes. On the basis of my
very limited experience with such brief repetitions, I am
inclined to think that the dynamics underlying these changes
and those occurring after a longer interval are not identical.
One conceivable hypothesis is that the changes taking place
after a few hours are due to the immediate psychologic effect
of having been exposed to the same stimulus material an
hour or two earlier. Factors such as satiation, or some immediate superficial release of tensions through the act of reacting
emotionally to the test material, might account for the
changes. Having been subjected to other projective tests
immediately before the second administration of the Szondi
test might affect the results in a similar way.

When we repeat the test, the instructions have to be somewhat modified. The purpose of this modification is to eliminate the effect of memory. The subject has to understand
that the purpose of readministration of the test is *not* to
check on the consistency of his reactions; we have to make it
explicit that this is *not* a disguised memory test but that what
we are interested in is to see "how he feels today in regard
to these pictures."

I usually introduce the second administration by saying
that "I am going to show you the same pictures you saw the
other day. Choose again the two you like most and the two

you dislike most of each series, but do not think that you have to choose the same ones you did the other day. Sometimes when we are in a different mood we like a different kind of person. So go ahead and pick out the ones you like most and the ones you dislike most, and never mind if they are the same or not as last time."

Besides the type of scoring sheet reproduced above, another type is available * (fig. 5), on which the examiner can record a whole series of ten test profiles on one sheet. For individual case interpretations it is advisable to use this type of scoring sheet not only because of the ten test profiles but also because it allows room for certain formal categorization and computations on the basis of the ten profiles. (Directions in regard to how to fill out this part of the scoring sheet will follow in the discussion of methods of interpreting a series of ten profiles.)

The scoring sheet with two profiles is used whenever we know that we are not going to administer a complete series. For various research purposes, where the single profiles are considered only as members of a group, and the data are used for statistical group analyses, the use of one or two profiles for each subject is permissible.

* Published by Hans Huber, Bern, Switzerland; American distributor, Grune and Stratton, New York City.

CHAPTER III

Experiment of Factorial Association

BEFORE we discuss the basic principles of interpretation, I want to mention an additional use of the Szondi test. This is the so-called "factorial association experiment." It consists of asking the subject to tell us stories about the pictures chosen in the "final test" as the four best liked and four most disliked. Whether or not one is able to administer this part of the experiment usually depends on the amount of time at the examiner's disposal. Whenever feasible, the subject should be asked to associate freely to the eight pictures chosen in the final test or—ideally—to all the 24 pictures chosen in the main experiment. The associations thus obtained are highly valuable not only because in this way we gain verbally projected material useful for detailed personality interpretations, especially in cases where the differential diagnosis between neurosis and prepsychosis or psychosis is questionable, but also because the associations allow us to gain insight into the specific ways in which the stimulus material affects the subject. Experience has shown that the pictures representative of the eight diagnostic categories included in the test elicit different kinds of associations. Associations given to pictures of the same factor have usually something in common and in some way reflect the special psychologic characteristics of the respective disease category. A few examples are quoted here:

Subject: 46 years old, male; diagnosis: paranoid schizophrenia; stimulus: picture Vh. "Young boy, about sixteen to eighteen years old. Goes to school. He still is under his parents' care. Everybody likes him. When people get in my age, then love is missing. Maybe he (the boy on the picture) is in love, but if so I am sure he is in the beginning stage."

The same subject's association to picture IV*e*. "An older man, looks like to me sort of a professional man, intelligent. Many things could be told about him. Sinister but not rude. I am positive that he does not want to be rude." The same subject's associations to picture II*hy*. "Middle-aged woman, sulking face. Maybe married but she is indifferent to her family and neglects them. The half-closed eyes also show that she does not want to see her family. She is lacking sincerity; she is a hypocrite." The same subject's association to picture V*m*. "An older man, could be a businessman. He is married by all means and lives very happily with his family. Probably he has a warmer family life than people usually. In spite of his smile his facial expression also reflects some worry."

The following are examples from the associations of a catatonic schizophrenic patient who refused to take any other test. Even though his verbal associations are scanty, they reflect the specific character of the various factors which served as stimuli: The subject was a 21 year old male patient in a state hospital. Diagnosis: catatonic schizophrenia:

Association to IV*h*. "A college student. Not married. Definitely not married. One can see on his face that he is not married." To picture VI*s*. "I don't know him. He could be a boxer. A serious person. Healthy. I am sure this one wants to get married. He is in love. May be about 31 years old." To picture I*s*. "Vicious looking, capable of anything. A tramp, a deserter. He is hiding from the police. A wrestler, an international wrestler." III*hy*. "He is either Chinese or Japanese. Either a spy or a priest." VI*hy*. "A spy. Old and worried. Could be an Eskimo or a Russian." V*p*. "This one has college education, for sure."

Association to picture IIId. "Poor working woman. Has many financial troubles. She is under the spell of the devil. She had much grief and sorrow in her life. Otherwise she is an industrious woman."

The following are a few examples from the associations of a more or less well-functioning 53 year old woman (a woman who never felt the need to get psychiatric help, which can be taken as an operational definition of health). Vs. "Could be a German college professor but also could be a sportsman. Maybe I only think of sportsman because of his muscles, if dressed (on the picture one can see the face in profile and the bare shoulder of a man) he could look like a professor, a teacher, a pedagogue. IIs. "This hair on his chest is disgusting. Could be a surgeon." VIs. "Oh, I didn't like this one. A villain, violent, brutal, uneducated, criminal. He has an evil look. He might even knock somebody down, he would rather do something physically violent than steal." IVp. "I liked this one. Could be a professor. Strictly intellectual." IIp. "Seriously psychotic. Maybe he has delusions and had to be institutionalized." VIhy. "This one reminds me of a seamstress who used to work in our house. She was an embittered old maid. This one isn't normal either but not institutionalized. She is frustrated, sad and bitter." Association to picture IVm. "This one is some kind of a singer, not of the real good ones, though. For that she ought to be prettier. She is some sort of a night club entertainer, in a cheap night club."

The last group of examples are taken from a well-functioning college professor, a 58 year old man, a professor of chemistry.

VIe. "This one looks like an idiot. I wouldn't hire her for the lowest kind of work. She is so stupid that she might do anything unexpected, she even might kill in a sudden outburst, though she is not schizophrenic." Ik. "She is crazy. I can imagine her just sitting and sitting and getting excited from time to time. She looks like a moron. I would be afraid of her." III*k*. "Isn't as scary as the other one. She is not particularly evil, but quite stupid. In a city one cannot see such persons. She lives in a village, caged in, never getting together with people." IV*d*. "Shrewd, calculating and fanatic at the same time. Quite an unreliable person."

These examples were inserted here to illustrate the types of associations evoked by the pictures; however, their full psychologic implication probably cannot be appreciated until after the discussion of the interpretative meaning of the single factors. A few interesting trends in the above examples can be pointed out here. There were two associations to *h* pictures (V*h*. and IV*h*.) given by two different subjects. One could express the common feature of the two associations as the emphasis on the heterosexual immaturity of the person represented on the photograph. ("Definitely not married," ". . . if in love definitely in the beginning stage.") According to our theory, it is just the emphasis on the tender pregenital love as against the real goal-directed heterosexual love which is characteristic of the *h* factor and reactions to *h* pictures have to be interpreted according to this theory. "Still under the care of the parents," "everybody likes him," and the subject's expression of longing for this kind of love himself, are all in line with our above interpretation of the *h* factor.

Five associations to four different *s* pictures, given by two different subjects, were quoted literally. The common features in the associations were the stress on physical force, and aggression. It is interesting that in these five short examples practically a complete list of the various outlet possibilities for aggression at different levels of sublimation has been listed. In order, these were the following: "violent, brutal . . . criminal," ". . . might knock down somebody," "rather physical violence than stealing." (We always interpreted stealing as rather an *h* than an *s* type of crime.) Then the first step in socializing physical aggression: "a wrestler," "a boxer," "a sportsman." Then the most sublimated forms of aggression: "a teacher, a pedagogue, a German college professor," "a surgeon."

The various possibilities in interpretation of the s factor are exactly in line with these associations. There were two associations to two different e pictures, given by two subjects. The basic duality in regard to how to deal with aggressive impulses—which according to our theory is underlying the psychologic meaning of the e factor—is nicely reflected in the two associations. The overemphasis on the aspect of forced emotional control is reflected in "sinister but not rude," and the additional insistence that "I am positive that he does not *want* to be rude." Similarly, the other e picture (VIe) is perceived as "stupid" and calm at the moment but potentially dangerous: "she might do anything unexpected . . . even kill in a sudden outburst. . . ." This description coincides exactly with our theory about the underlying psychodynamics of an epileptic seizure.

Four associations to three different hy pictures, given by three different subjects, were quoted above. The common elements in these associations were the following: the faces seen on the hy pictures were described as expressing some sort of strange role-playing, or else they refer to some disturbance in the sphere of emotional expressiveness; however, not in regard to violent, aggressive emotions (as in the e factor) but rather referring to the ability of expressing love-object oriented emotions. Examples: "May be married but indifferent to family and neglects them"; "does not want to see her family"; "lacking sincerity"; "hypocrite"; "Chinese," "Japanese," "Eskimo," "Russian." The latter associations are most probably meant to indicate the impression of some sort of unusual role. Similarly, the associations of "spy" and "priest" are most probably expressions of the feeling that the person is acting out or hiding behind various roles.

The meaning of the *hy* factor will be described as indicating the need for exhibitionistic activities which, depending on the subject's attitude toward this need, can result either in direct display of affection or in hiding the real affection behind a role.

Two associations to two different *k* pictures were quoted from the same subject. Both express the most important psychologic characteristic of catatonic; namely, the lack of emotional communication with the environment. This quality of the catatonic schizophrenics forms also the central core of the interpretation of the *k* factor. In the above associations this quality is expressed by the description of the person whose face is represented on the photograph as "just sitting and sitting . . ." or by the statement that "in a city one cannot see such persons. She lives in a village, caged in, never getting together with people."

Associations to *p* pictures were illustrated by three examples given to three different *p* pictures by two subjects. All three associations—brief as they are—contain typically paranoid elements, one directly on the pathologic level, describing the person as having "delusions" and "institutionalized," the other two mentioning sublimated forms of paranoid characteristics by emphasizing the "intellectual" quality of the individuals represented by the *p* pictures. The interpretation of the strong drive for intellectual sublimation per se, as a "normal variation" of paranoid tendencies, will be more fully discussed in connection with the interpretation of the *p* factor.

There were two associations quoted to two different *d* pictures, by two subjects. Both are in line without interpretation of the meaning of the *d* factor, although, in this case it is even more difficult than in the previous cases to point out the basic common "denominator" of the two associations. The preoccupation with materialistic values and emotional reactions, negative as well as positive, to the loss of such values, is reflected in both associations. The psychotic subject describes the woman whose face is represented in picture III*d* as "poor," having "financial difficulties," "having many sorrows and worries," but "industrious." The other subject described the man seen in picture IV*d* as "Shrewd and calculating" and "unreliable." These characteristics fit well into our interpretation of the *d* factor which is linked with what psychoanalysts usually refer to as "anal" character.

Associations to *m* pictures are illustrated by two examples given by two subjects to two different *m* pictures. The common feature in both associations is the stress on "worldly" characteristics, the tendency to associate types of individuals who try to enjoy things. "Business man who lives very happily with his family," "has warmer family life than people usually" or the other subject's description of the woman represented in IV*m* as a "nightclub singer, entertaining people" are typical examples of association to *m* pictures. They reflect the basic interpretation of the *m* factor which centers around what is usually referred to as "oral" character.

These illustrative examples of verbal associations are of course not "proof" in the strict sense of the word; yet they throw light on the specific ways in which the stimulus material of this test affects the subject. It is most probably justified to assume that the same perspective and projective processes which are expressed in the verbal associations are operating when choosing *likes* and *dislikes* from the pictures, not accompanied by explicit verbal associations. In other words the verbal material gained by the experiment of "factorial association" supports our theory in regard to the specific valence character of the eight factors in a rather direct way. The fact that the test "works" has to be accepted anyway as a pragmatic proof that something essentially characteristic is expressed and reacted to in the pictures used as stimulus material. However, this is a more indirect way of reasoning than lies in an ability to point to verbal associations evoked by nothing but the corresponding stimulus photograph, and consistently reflecting some aspect of what we assume to be the basic underlying psychodynamics of the particular diagnostic category, or in the terminology of the test, of the particular factors.

The twenty-two sample associations alone are not convincing for the validation of our hypotheses in regard to the meaning of the eight factors, especially not for those who have not yet started to work with the test and to collect associative material themselves. Actually, the above examples were selected practically at random from several hundreds of associations, and they are representative of the type of material we usually obtain through the experiment of factorial association. Just because this type of material is extremely valuable for the purpose of validating various aspects of the hypotheses underlying interpretation, a more systematic study of such material would be desirable. If proper categories are used in analyzing the verbal material, the quantification of the results should be feasible, and once we are in possession of such data, much of the still somewhat mystic sounding suppositions underlying interpretation will be elevated to "experimentally proved" theory.

On the basis of the above examples, I tried to illustrate at least one possible way of analyzing factorial associations, and there is no reason why the same principles could not be applied to the analysis of much larger samples. The thorough knowledge and understanding of the psychodynamic interpretation of each factor is naturally an essential prerequisite for undertaking this type of research.

Besides illustrating a methodology, our purpose for including this scope of analysis of the associations is to give an earliest over-all approach to the interpretation of the eight factors. It is hoped that these concrete examples will facilitate the understanding of some of the propositions implied in interpretation and discussed in later chapters.

Chapter IV

General Principles of Interpretation

1. Basic Meaning of the Factors

AS HAS been said before, the objective of this manual is to present a series of purely psychologic assumptions from which the interpretation of the test profiles can be derived. Our first task is to find a general principle which explains the meaning of choices, irrespective of the specific meaning of the various factors. In other words, we are looking for a general interpretation valid for all eight factors. Such an interpretation can be found in the concept of need-tension, or tension system, or driving force. Actually, all of these terms can be used to convey the basic meaning common to all the eight factors, since these factors correspond to dynamic needs in the organism which act as driving forces, in the sense of directing the person to perform certain acts and to choose or avoid certain objects. The function of these actions, object-choices, and avoidances is to reduce the tension originally existing due to unreleased need. Accordingly, the degree of tension in a certain need-system depends upon the existence or nonexistence of appropriate ways to discharge the tension through specific activities. The specific type of activity and the specific type of goal-objects which will be needed in order to release the tension will be determined by the quality of the particular need-system which, due to its high tension, acts as a driving force. Lewin has formulated this dynamic theory of need-systems by stating that, depending upon the state of tension in the various need-systems of the organism, various environmental objects acquire valence character.

The concept of need-tension is a theoretic explanation which can be induced only from the presence of certain goal-directed activities. Goal-directed activity in this general sense can mean a positive attempt to reach for a certain goal-object as well as a directed avoidance of a certain object. In the first case, we talk about the object as having a positive valence; in the second case, we refer to the avoided object as representing a negative valence.

This much of Lewin's dynamic theory of action had to be recapitulated because the action of choosing certain pictures in the Szondi test has to be interpreted on the basis of the same dynamic principle.

2. The Meaning of "Loaded" and "Open" Reactions

We assume that the eight factors (diagnostic categories) in the test correspond to eight different need-systems in the organism. Thus we have an eight dimensional concept of the personality, where the eight need-systems form a dynamically interdependent whole. The eight types of mental and emotional diseases represented in the test have to be thought of as expressing certain psychological needs in extreme form, which to some degree exist in everybody. That is the reason the choice reactions from pictures representing actual mental patients are indicative of the personality structure of psychologically well-functioning subjects, as well as for patients with any type and degree of emotional disturbances. Depending on the degree of (or intensity of) the state of tension in each of the eight need-systems, the pictures representing the corresponding needs will assume valence character in various proportions. In this case the subject *chooses* pictures from the factor corresponding to his own need in tension. The *absolute* number of choices within one factor has to be interpreted according to this principle. Relatively great numbers of choices (four or more) from one category means that the corresponding need is in state of strong tension.

On the test profile, the dynamically strongest need-tensions are indicated by the so-called *loaded* reaction, which means factors with four or more choices. (Three would be the expected average and six are the maximum number of choices in each factor.)

On the other hand, lack of choices in a certain category means that the corresponding need is *not* in state of tension. Theoretically, this state might be due to two reasons. It might be due either to an original weakness of the particular need, or else it might mean that the tension in this need-system has been released by "living out" the drive through adequate activity. At any rate, the so-called *"open"* or "drained" reactions on the test profiles are important diagnostic signs because they indicate the areas in which there is the *least* resistance to discharge of a corresponding need. That is the reason observable symptoms, together with other forms of manifest behavior, can be interpreted on the basis of the "open" or "drained" reactions. On the test profile, those factors are called "open" in which the number of choices is zero, or one, or maximum two, but in this case only if the two choices are distributed as one *plus* (liked) and one *minus* (disliked).

At this point, more specific interpretation of the "open" reactions can not be given because, depending on the configurational pattern of the total test profile, and on the patterning of the total series of test profiles, the interpretation of "discharging a particular need-tension" varies. Since all eight of these basic psychologic tendencies—represented on the profile by the eight factors—have a wide range of potential manifestation ranging from normal psychologic phenomena to neurotic, psychotic or antisocial symptoms, one has to be cautious with the interpretation of the "open" reactions. This point has to be stressed because experience shows that it is in this respect that beginners in the Szondi method are most likely to make gross mistakes, usually in the direction of tending too quickly toward interpretations of serious pathologic symptoms. This is probably a usual danger for beginners in the use of any projective technic; however, because the pictures in the Szondi test are labeled with the initials of well-known pathologic categories, the danger of tending rather toward pathologic interpretations is increased. This is true for interpreting any types of reaction in the test, but mostly for the "open" factors. The misunderstanding is usually caused by the ambiguous meaning of the terms "open" or "manifest." These terms mean only that in the area to which they relate there is a possibility for some sort of a continuous discharge; or in other words, there are no psychologic or other barriers causing a damming up of the original drive. What form and intensity of discharge is already sufficient to prevent such a damming up of the need-energy depends, among other factors, on the original intensity and quality of the particular need in question. (And what this original intensity and quality of the needs depends on, we probably do not know. That is the point in our casual thinking where we have to resort to explanatory concepts such as "constitution" or "genes.") One person can discharge aggression in a continuous way and give a characteristic "open" reaction in the s factor by "living out" this need through highly sublimated and socially most acceptable forms of intellectual aggression, for instance in scientific work, while the meaning of "open s" in another individual might be actual criminal activity.

The following two profiles illustrate the above example. Figure 2 is the profile of a 40 year old woman, most active in the field of social sciences and "fighting" for the right of underprivileged minorities, while Figure 3 is the profile of a 17 year old murderer. The open s reaction is common in both; however, the difference in the rest of the test-patterns is obvious; i.e., all the other seven factors show opposing tendencies.

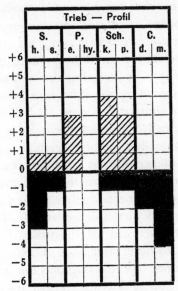

FIG. 2. SOCIAL SCIENTIST; A 40 YEAR OLD WOMAN

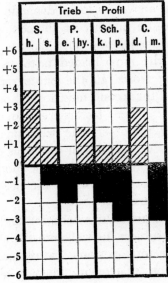

FIG. 3. A 17 YEAR OLD MALE ACCUSED OF MURDER

To summarize what has been said about the interpretation of the "loaded" and the "open" factors: when interpreting a test profile, the first thing we have to do is to determine the relative dynamic strength of the eight factors. This is done simply by counting the number of choices in each factor, disregarding the difference between the "plus" or "minus" directions. The most loaded factors will indicate the dynamically strongest needs in the person, those needs which either due to their original extreme intensity, or due to the existence of some sort of an external or internal barrier, were not able to release their dynamic energy. That is the reason why these needs operate as the underlying *causal* determinants of the observable behavior. While the underlying psychodynamics can be diagnosed from the loaded factors, the actually observable form of behavior or the actual form of the manifest clinical symptoms can be interpreted on the basis of the "open" factors. These are the areas where "kinetic" energy can be discharged.

With the presentation of a concrete example (Figure 4) to illustrate the above outlined dynamic theory of interpreting the absolute number of choices, we will close the discussion of the loaded and open factors.

In Figure 4, the most loaded factor is the *k* with six choices (in other words *all* the photographs of catatonics were chosen) and the second most loaded one is the *h* factor with five choices. "Open" factors are the *s, e* and *m*. According to our theory, the observable behavior of this man must display characteristic features in the areas corresponding to the *s, e* and *m* factors, while the basic motivational sources of his behavior must be found in the needs corresponding to the *k* and *h* factors.

What is known about the behavior and the personality problems of this subject fits well into the above theory. As to the "open" factors: periodic paroxismal (*e* factor) outbursts of aggression (*s* factor) are his most obvious symptoms of maladjustment. At these occasions of outburst he loses practically all control in a rage of yelling and shouting (*m* factor) at the least provocation—or rather, what seems like provocation to him. The present profile was taken not long after such a paroxismal outburst, hence the draining in the *s, e,* and *m* factors.

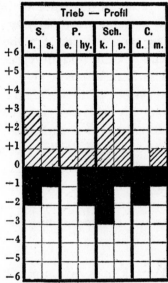

FIG. 4. TWENTY-EIGHT YEAR OLD MALE MATHEMATICIAN

However, these spectacular temper tantrums were only surface symptoms and seemed to serve the purpose of releasing his accumulated irritability which was caused by his conflicts in the areas corresponding to *h* and *k* factors. Indeed, he experienced painful conflicts in the sexual area, and fought almost consciously against his own tendency toward passive feminine identification (tension in the *h* factor). The periodic overemphasis on aggression was most probably due to a compensatory defense mechanism. However, a more forceful defense mechanism against the danger of allowing himself any emotional attachment of a passive feminine nature was the attempt to withdraw his object-libido and to try to barricade himself behind a rigid wall of narcissistic pseudo self-sufficiency. This narcissistic withdrawal (tension in the k factor) is actually his main mode of defense and the main reason for his inability to adjust to new situations satisfactorily. Yet, only those who know him very well are aware of the existence of this fight for emotional detachment as being an underlying cause in his difficulties to get along with people. For the more superficial observers, he seems a calm and quiet person whose only personality problem is an unpredictable and uncontrollable temper, which breaks out periodically and does not seem to fit in to the rest of his otherwise apparently peaceful personality. Professionally he is a mathematician, but not successful in his career despite his brilliant intellectual abilities.

I think this description of the subject's personality and behavior is enough to illustrate the meaning of the loaded and the open factors and their use as indicators helping to differentiate between surface symptoms and underlying psychodynamics.

3. The Four Modes of Choice Reactions

Until now we were concerned only with the absolute number of choices within any one factor. Now something must be said about the meaning of the various directions of choices in general; in other words, the task is again to find a principle which explains the meaning of the difference between choosing pictures as *likes* or as *dislikes*, holding equally for all the eight factors.

In the following, by the term "direction" we will refer to the four main possible *modes* of reaction in each factor. The "direction," or mode, of choice-reactions within each factor can be: *(a)* positive; *(b)* negative; *(c)* ambivalent; or *(d)* open.

a. We call a factorial reaction *positive* if two or more choices in any one factor fall in the *likes* category and the *like* choices are at least twice as numerous as the *dislike* choices in the same factor. Concretely, we call a factor positive, or plus, if the choices are distributed in any of the following manners:

2 Likes	2 Likes	3 Likes	3 Likes
0 Dislikes	1 Dislikes	1 Dislikes	0 Dislikes
4 Likes	4 Likes	4 Likes	
2 Dislikes	1 Dislikes	0 Dislikes	
5 Likes	5 Likes	6 Likes .	
1 Dislikes	0 Dislikes	0 Dislikes	

b. We call a factorial reaction *negative* if two or more choices fall in the *dislike* category and the *dislike* choices are at least twice as numerous as the *like* choices. Concretely, negative or minus reaction in any factor must show one of the following distributions of choices:

0 Likes	1 Likes	0 Likes	1 Likes
2 Dislikes	2 Dislikes	3 Dislikes	3 Dislikes
0 Likes	1 Likes	2 Likes	
4 Dislikes	4 Dislikes	4 Dislikes	
0 Likes	1 Likes	0 Likes	
5 Dislikes	5 Dislikes	6 Dislikes	

c. We call a factorial constellation *ambivalent* if the choices within one factor show any of the following distributions:

2 Likes	3 Likes	2 Likes	3 Likes
2 Dislikes	3 Dislikes	3 Dislikes	2 Dislikes

d. Open reactions have been discussed in connection with the factorial loadings and drainings. We refer to a factor constellation as open if the choices are:

o Likes	o Likes	1 Likes	1 Likes
o Dislikes	1 Dislikes	o Dislikes	1 Dislikes

4. INTERPRETATION OF THE FOUR MODES OF FACTORIAL REACTIONS

We know that the absolute number of choices within one factor depends upon the dynamic strength of that particular need tension system. The *mode* of the factorial choice-reactions depends upon the subject's conscious or unconscious attitude toward the particular need.

A *positive* response for pictures of a certain factor indicates a conscious or unconscious identification with the motivational processes as depicted by the photographs of the respective factor.

Negative response indicates the existence of a counter-identification with the psychologic processes as depicted in the respective stimulus pictures.

The wording of the general interpretation of positive and negative reactions had to be cautious because it is usually tempting to identify plus reactions with acceptance and minus reactions with the repression of the particular need corresponding to the factor. However, this would be over-simplification of the actual processes involved, especially if we use the term repression in the strictly psychoanalytic sense of the word.

Nonacceptance of a particular drive does not necessarily mean repression, although repression does presuppose the unconscious attitude of nonacceptance of the particular id drive in question. However, in the Szondi test, the interpretation of the psychologic processes corresponding to the single factors cannot always be equated with various id drives.

In certain factors we have to assume that what the stimulus material represents is already a psychologic mechanism produced by the modifying influence of the ego or superego. For example, we will see that the interpretation of the *e* factor presupposes the assumption that the pictures of the *e* factor represent a state of constrictive control over hostile emotions. Consequently in the *e* factor "repression," in the psychoanalytic sense, is certainly not associated with a negative reaction toward pictures which themselves represent something similar to repression. To the contrary—if at all—repression in the *e* factor is indicated by a plus reaction. (The fact that compulsion neurotics characteristically give positive *e* reaction supports this statement.)

As a general principle one should keep in mind that the psychologic mechanisms interpreted on the basis of various configurations in the Szondi test profiles cannot be directly equated with psychologic mechanisms well known from psychoanalytic literature. Of course there are similarities, and in the following chapters psychoanalytic concepts will be used freely in the course of factorial interpretations, always being conscious, however, of the fact that there is no hundred per cent coincidence between any one Szondi factor constellation and the psychoanalytic concept used for its explanation.

The example cited above of the interpretation of the *e* factor is the clearest example in the test to illustrate the point that negative reaction is not always equal to repression. The interpretation which is valid for positive or negative reactions in either factor is identification, or counteridentification, respectively, with whatever psychologic processes are represented by the stimulus pictures.

The meaning of the *ambivalent* reaction in any of the eight factors can be deducted from the foregoing. It implies that both identification and counteridentification are present simultaneously in regard to the same psychological

need.* . The basic ambivalence toward a given emotional
need as indicated by the plus-minus reaction is subjectively
experienced as conflict, and has a very special significance
in interpretation. Experience has shown that ambivalent
reactions indicate areas where the conflicting, contradictory
tendencies corresponding to the plus and minus reactions
are subjectively experienced, almost to the extent of forming
a conscious source of a psychologic dilemma. The plus-
minus reactions always represent a certain amount of self-
imposed control against the direct discharge of the particular
need in question. That is the reason why ambivalent reactions are sometimes referred to as "subjective symptom
factors" as against the open reactions which can be referred
to in this context as "objective symptom-factors." On the
basis of the foregoing it is understood that by "symptom"
we do not necessarily mean pathologic, clinical symptom,
but any form of observable behavior which serves the purpose of discharging a specific need-tension.

Similarly, the term "subjective symptom" implies only
the subjective experiencing of the simultaneous existence of opposing drives which, under certain conditions,
might even represent a satisfactory synthesis just *because* of
being aware of both aspects of the same basic drive, while
in other cases the same factorial constellation can result in
actual clinical symptom, or rather, become the *source* for an .
overt clinical symptom. Of course on the basis of the total
pattern of a particular test-series we can judge in any individual case whether a particular plus-minus reaction has
to be interpreted as a well-functioning synthesis or as the
symbol of a neurotic ambivalence. In certain factors it
seems easier than in others to find a satisfactory solution for

---

* In the framework of the Szondi test we will refer to "needs" in a
broader sense than is usually done in dynamic psychology. For example,
we will refer to "needs" to control or to inhibit certain open emotional
manifestations as well as to needs to live out drives in an uninhibited
way.

this duality inherent in the plus-minus reaction. (More will be said about this problem of interpretation in a discussion of the eight factors individually.) Besides the evaluation of the individual plus-minus reactions in regard to the particular factor in which it was given, one has to evaluate the ratio of the sum of *all* the open reactions over the sum of *all* the plus-minus reactions within the complete test series of a subject. This ratio: $\dfrac{\Sigma \bigcirc \text{ reactions}}{\Sigma \pm \text{ reactions}}$ informs us approximately about the relative proportion of the amount of available channels for discharging tensions, as against the amount of conscious (at least many times conscious) self-control to restrain drives from overt manifestation. Accordingly, the value of this ratio can serve as an approximate indicator to differentiate between individuals who tend to act out their needs in an uninhibited way and those who rather tend to use mechanisms of control. However, this ratio is not the only sign in the test profiles to indicate uninhibited or restrained behavior; therefore one has to be cautious with the use of its interpretation. (To attempt to attribute definite interpretations to certain numerical values obtained from the scoring of the responses to various projective technics is many times misleading.) In regard to this ratio of the sum of open reactions over the sum of ambivalent reactions it is safe to say that in cases where this ratio is smaller than 1, we are dealing with a subject who is overcontrolled in his behavior. Compulsive characters give characteristically low ratio; in other words, it is characteristic for them to give more ambivalent than open reactions. On the other hand, if the value of this ratio is 5 or larger than 5, we can assume that we are dealing with a person who exercises too little control in regard to living out his drives. Restless, agitated, and erratic behavior can be interpreted from a ratio-value larger than 5. Impulsive characters, certain types of unpredictable psychopaths and agitated psychotics fall into this category.

If the value of the ratio falls between 1 and 5, then only very little use can be made of it for interpretation. It still can be used as supportive evidence for or against a hypothesis estimating the amount of control or rigidity in the subject's behavior, but only in conjunction with other signs.

At this point the meaning of the open reactions does not have to be discussed separately since this has been done in connection with the loaded and open reactions and the ratio of the open over the plus-minus reactions.

Thus we finish our discussion of the general principles to interpret (1) the absolute number of choices in one factor, and (2) the four main modes of factorial reactions.

5. Significance of Constancy or Changes in the Factorial Reactions

A third group of general assumptions underlying inter-pretation of a series of test profiles deals with the meaning of constancy versus changeability of the factorial reactions within a series of profiles. This aspect of interpretation may be included in this main section of general principles of interpretations because it does not presuppose the knowledge of the specific meaning of the eight factors. Clinically, prob-ably this is the most important point of view in the inter-pretation because the various degrees and types of changes are the first indicators which help to discriminate between the main diagnostic categories of "normal" or pathologic behavior. Just because the diagnostic importance of changes varies with the different kinds of changes, we will have to grade the various types of changes according to their diag-nostic significance.

In classifying changes, obviously, we will always refer to variations taking place in a factor-constellation from one testing to another. In order of their increasing patho-

diagnostic importance, such changes can be classified the
following way:

a. The absolute number, as well as the direction of the
choices, within the particular factor does not show any
change, but the actual pictures chosen from the same factor
are not the same; i.e., there are three plus *h* reactions in
both profiles, but the three *h* pictures were picked out a
second time from sets different from the first.

This type of change practically does not involve any
change in interpretation, because the dynamic strength of
the particular drive, as well as the subject's attitude toward
this drive, has not changed.

b. The direction of the factor remains unchanged, but
there is some change in the loading or the distribution of
the factor; for example, a "plus three" reaction changes to
a "plus four," or to a "plus two and minus one" reaction.
The diagnostic importance of such changes depends on the
number of squares which were added to or subtracted from
the reaction in the first set. This type of change has to be
interpreted according to the principle discussed under (1) in
the previous chapter (The dynamic significance of absolute
number of choices).

The appearance of one "minus" reaction in an otherwise
"plus" factor, or of one "plus" reaction in an otherwise
"minus" factor, has a special significance. These single
squares in the opposite direction from the majority of choices
within the same factor express that the subject is able to
divide his attitude toward this particular need without, however, expressing real ambivalence. This mode of reaction
expresses a certain desirable degree of flexibility in regard
to handling the particular drive, and therefore the appearance of such "counteracting" single squares has to be interpreted as a favorable sign in diagnosis. The lack of such
"balancing" squares generally, in either factor, is a characteristic reaction in profiles of psychotics. On the other hand,

the presence of such slightly divided reactions is characteristic
for well-functioning individuals.

   c. In the third degree of change we include those shifts
which already involve a change in the direction of the factor,
but only of the type of changing from "plus" or from "minus"
into "plus-minus," or from a "plus-minus" into either "plus"
or "minus." In other words, these changes always imply
some change in the subject's attitude toward the particular
drive; however, never a complete reversal of the attitude
(from *like* to *dislike* or reverse); nor do these changes ever
indicate a great change in the dynamic strength of the need,
since the maximum change in this category with respect to
the absolute number of choices is a change from an average
(two or three choices in one direction) to a loaded constellation (by definition every ambivalent reaction is at the same
time a loaded reaction since four choices are the minimum
to form a plus-minus reaction) or the reverse.

   This type of change, and those in the previous two categories, are the most frequent changes in the so-called
"normal" population. It can be mentioned in this context
that in the Szondi test we do not assume that the maximum
degree of test-retest reliability is also the most desirable
degree. Since the Szondi test reflects the personality as a
dynamic process, and not as a static entity, some fluctuations
in the reactions, from one testing to the other, is expected
in any well-functioning individual. The maximum degree
of constancy is usually obtained not from the psychologically
best functioning subjects but from compulsive neurotics, or
from compulsively rigid characters.

   d. In the next category of change, we find the shifts from
"plus," or "minus," or "plus-minus" to "open"; or we find
the reverse, from "open" to "plus" or "minus" or "plus-
minus." The function subject to interpretation, common
to all these changes, is significant change in the dynamic
strength of the particular need in question. Depending on

whether the change occurred "towards" the open reaction or "away" from the open reaction, one has to interpret a sudden discharge of tension or a building up of a need-tension. Whether or not a sudden discharge of a need-tension involves a clinical symptom must be decided partly on the basis of the original strength of the tension (i.e., the number of squares in the factor previous to the open reaction), and partly on the specific type of "open" reaction. Even though the constellations $\frac{0}{0}$ or $\frac{!}{!}$ are both called open, still in a qualitative clinical analysis one has to remember that the $\frac{!}{I}$ constellation is "less" open (since there is still residual tension) than is the $\frac{0}{0}$ constellation. The greater the discrepancy in the dynamic strength of the factor from one testing to the other (especially if the time interval between testings is not more than a day), the more likely it is that the discharge of the tension occurred through "living out" the need by some clinical symptom. This is practically always the case if a strongly loaded factor suddenly opens up completely. Sudden drainings of factors with two or three choices, or even four if the draining takes the form of $\frac{!}{I}$, occur quite frequently even in individuals without any known clinical symptoms.

e. In the fifth type of change belongs the so-called factorial reversals: that means shifts from "plus" to "minus" or from "minus" to "plus." The pathodiagnostic significance of this type of change depends again on the number of squares which actually changed their position from plus to minus, or reverse. Obviously the diagnostic significance of a $\frac{2}{I}$ constellation changing into a $\frac{!}{2}$, is much less than change of a $\frac{5}{I}$ or $\frac{6}{0}$ to a $\frac{0}{6}$ or $\frac{!}{5}$. When a "loaded plus" changes into a "loaded minus" or reverse, in the course of 48 hours, one always has to suspect pathologic mechanism in that particular area. This is particularly true in cases where such an intensive reversal in a factor is repeated several times in the course of a series of ten profiles. Such repeated reversals are characteristic for manifest psychoses or certain types of unstable psychopaths.

In evaluating a series of test profiles it is advisable to translate the single graphic profiles into symbols of directions of the eight factors $(+, -, \pm, \bigcirc)$ and then to write the profiles expressed this way, one under the other, consecutively. This procedure helps us to perceive the trends of changes (or constancy) in each factor quickly, since a whole series of ten or more profiles can be recorded in a relatively small space which facilitates quick recognition of trends. However, one should never rely solely on the interpretation of such a "symbolized," abbreviated record, because many of the quantitative and qualitative details can be seen only on the original test profiles. The purpose of converting a series of profiles into symbols of factorial directions is to help us in evaluating quickly the trends in each factor.

To recapitulate the main points in regard to what trends to look for when we first inspect such a symbolized representation of a test profile series:

1. We have to look for the factors which show *open reactions most frequently* because these are the areas with possibilities of steady discharge of the corresponding need. Manifest behavior patterns or observable symptoms are indicated by these factors.

2. We have to look for factors which show *ambivalent reactions most frequently* because these are the "subjective symptom factors," the areas where conflict is actually experienced.

3. We have to look for those *factors which show a steady plus or minus direction* because these factors, where open discharge is not possible nor experienced consciously as conflict, are most likely to act as unconscious driving forces underlying actual behavior or actual clinical symptoms.

4. Finally, coming back to our present topic of discussion, we have to look for the kind of change occurring in each

factor. The meaning of the various types of change need not be repeated here. In inspecting the trends of changes we should never forget to check the intensity of changes from the graphic profiles. The areas where actually the most pathologic processes are taking place can be detected from the *factors which show most frequent complete reversal of direction* (plus to minus or vice versa).

f. For the sake of completeness, one more type of change has to be mentioned. This is the so-called *"mirror reaction" in the vector as a whole.* This type of change implies that both factors of a certain vector change their direction simultaneously in such a manner that on the second profile the *vectorial* configuration is a complete mirror picture of the constellation of the first profile. For example, changes of plus *h* and minus *s* into minus *h* and plus *s,* or of open *e* and minus *hy* into minus *e* and open *hy,* belong to this category.

This is the last category in our classification of changes according to their diagnostic significance because these vectorial "mirror reversals" are the strongest diagnostic signs for the existence of a pathologic process in the respective area. The specific kind of process has to be diagnosed on the basis of the vector in which the mirror reversals occur. Mirror reversals in the *Sch* vector are characteristic for an actual schizophrenic process. This reaction is especially frequent in the beginning stages of the psychosis; in other words, before some sort of stabilization of the personality—even though on a regressed level—took place. Similarly, vectorial mirror changes in the *C* vector are characteristic for cyclic type of mental disturbances; the same type of change in the *S* vector indicates a basically disturbed unstable sexuality, and in the *P* vector, a serious disturbance in the sphere of emotional control. As can be seen from the examples, these types of change—especially if they occur more than once in a series of ten profiles—are interpreted in a primarily pathologic frame of reference. In cases of well-functioning individuals, we rarely find such mirror changes. It might occur, however, that in the course of ten profiles a complete reversal in the configuration of any vector does take place, even in individuals without any obvious clinical symptoms. However, in these cases the complete reversals usually occur gradually; i.e., a plus k and minus p first changes into plus-minus k, minus p, then either directly or through more transitions it reaches the minus k and plus p constellation. Such constantly changing vectors still indicate that the particular area is a potential "danger point" in the personality, because of the lack of consistency in control of corresponding drives; but if the immediate changes from one testing to the other are not of the type described under headings e and f above (pp. 41, 43), then solutions within a socially acceptable and not overtly pathologic framework are still possible.

Thus we finish the classification and the discussion of the psychologic meaning of factorial and vectorial changes. This structural aspect of interpretation should always take place before one proceeds to interpret the meaning of the individual factors or correlation of factors according to their content.

6. General Vectorial Configurations

There are two more "structural" characteristics of the test profiles which are significant for diagnosis. Because these are the last two points which have to be considered in interpretation *before* the qualitative analysis of the factors, their description will be included in this part of the chapter although they have nothing to do with changes.

Both of these formal characteristics concern the relative position of the two factors within the same vector. One aspect pertains to the relative direction of the two factors, the other to the relative loading of the two factors.

Since the two factors of the same vector are always considered to represent two opposing tendencies of the same main psychologic sector of the personality, one can expect that under normal conditions these two related tendencies are not handled in too different a manner. Just because the two related factors represent some basic similarities and contrasting tendencies at the same time, we assume that their simultaneous functioning—if both are in the proper proportion—has some sort of a self-regulatory effect, in the sense of opposing forces balancing the effect of each other. The assumption underlying this statement is that actually both tendencies of a vector are integral parts of a well-functioning organism.

On the other hand, from this assumption it follows that great discrepancy in the manner in which the two closely linked, yet opposing, tendencies are handled indicates lack of balance in the respective main area of the personality. This lack of balance is due to the lack of self-regulating effect of the two opposing factors.

The two structural aspects of the profiles which indicate the presence or the lack of such self-regulated balance in the four main areas in which the Szondi test "measures" personality, are the relative direction and the relative loading of the two interrelated factors of a vector. In well-functioning, "psychologically balanced," individuals, we expect that, in at least two of the four vectors, the factors do not point toward diametrically opposing directions. Typically "dissociated" profiles with factors pointing into opposing directions in all four vectors are characteristic of schizoid individuals. By diametrically opposing directions, I mean a direction of absolute positive reaction in one factor and a direction of completely negative reaction in the other factor in the same vector. The presence or lack of those single "balancing" squares in the opposite direction from the majority of choices within the same factor have special significance in this connection. The presence of such squares in both factors have themselves the effect of regulating somewhat the balance of forces within the same area. That is a good example to illustrate why one should never rely on interpreting the structural trends from the abbreviated (symbolized) record alone. If we see the symbols $+$, $-$ in one vector, that can mean the constellation $\frac{2}{1}\ \frac{1}{2}$, as well as $\frac{5}{0}\ \frac{0}{5}$. The differences in the interpretation of these two variations of $+$, $-$, vectorial reactions, is clear from the foregoing.

The relative loading of the two connected factors is another indication whether or not the two corresponding and counterbalancing drives are dealt with about the same way. The absolute number of squares should be about the same if there is no great discrepancy between the dynamic tension of the two factors. As a general principle, one can say that great difference in the loading of the two factors of a vector is never desirable. Simultaneous tension in both factors has a mutually modifying effect on the manifestation of the two related drives, while tension in one factor with simultaneous discharge of the tension in the "twin" factor results in unmodified, unrestrained attempts to release the particular drive in state of tension. In such a constellation the meaning of both the factor which is *not* open as well as the meaning of the open factor is more likely to imply some sort of pathologic interpretation. This is particularly true if there are more than two such disproportionately charged vectors.

CHAPTER V

Formalized Analysis of a Series of Ten Profiles

IN THIS last chapter concerning structural interpretation, Szondi's new scoring sheet, which summarizes the results of a series of ten profiles, will be presented and discussed. The upper half of the scoring sheet allows space for the graphic representation of the ten profiles, the lower half of the sheet serves for recording the single profiles in symbols of factorial directions. In addition, there is room left for various computations, all of which are based on those aspects of interpretation which were discussed in the previous chapter. Instead of describing and discussing theoretically this scoring method, we will illustrate its use by a concrete example.

Figure 5 represents the complete scoring of ten profiles of a 32 year old man. First we are going to follow the procedure of constructing the complete record step by step, and then we will interpret the results in the light of what has been said about the most important aspects of structural, or "formal," interpretation. By these adjectives it is meant that we will go as far in interpretation as we can without the consideration of the specific meaning of the eight factors. In other words, the points to be considered will be the specific trends of the factors with respect to symptomatic factors ("objective" symptom factors: open; "subjective" symptom factors: plus-minus reactions) and underlying or "root" factors (steady plus or steady minus reactions), and the type of changes taking place in the single factors and vectors.

47

Name: **T. F.**   Alter: **32**   Beruf:

Szondi-Test
Blatt mit zehn Triebprofilen

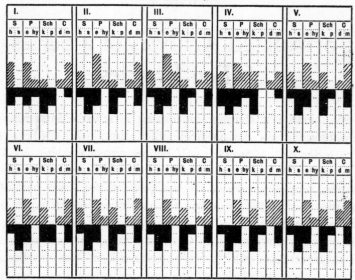

1947	S		P		Sch		C		Σ 0	Σ ±	Σ 0 u. ±
Nr.	h	s	e	hy	k	p	d	m	0	±	0 u. ±
I.	±	O	±	O	–	–	O	+	3	2	5
II.	+	–	+	O	–	O	O	±	3	1	4
III.	+	–	+	+	–	O	O	±	2	1	3
IV.	±	–	±	+	±	O	O	+	2	3	5
V.	+	–	±	O	±	O	O	±	3	3	6
VI.	+	–	±	O	±	–	O	±	2	3	5
VII.	+	–	±	O	±	O	O	±	3	3	6
VIII.	+	–	±	O	±	O	O	±	3	3	6
IX.	O	–	±	O	±	O	+	±	3	3	6
X.	O	–	±	O	±	O	+	±	3	3	6
Σ 0	2	1	0	8	0	8	8	0	27		
Σ ±	2	0	8	0	7	0	0	8		25	
T. sp. G.	4	1	8	8	7	8	8	8			52
Latenzgrösse	S = 3 S_-		P = 0 $e±, hy_0$		Sch = 1 k_-		C = 0 $d_0, m±$				

1. Tendenzspannungsquotient $= \dfrac{\Sigma\, 0}{\Sigma\, \pm} = \dfrac{27}{25} = 1.08$

2. Triebformel:

Symptomatische:	$e±, hy_0, p_0, d_0\ m_+ k_±$
Submanifeste bzw. sublatente:	h
Wurzel-Faktoren:	s_-

3. Latenzproportionen:

$$\underset{S_{s_-}}{3} : \underset{Sch_{k_-}}{1} : \underset{P_{e±, hy_0}}{0} : \underset{C_{d_0, m±}}{0}$$

4. Triebklasse: S_{s_-}

FIG. 5. TEN PROFILES OF A 32 YEAR OLD MALE

After the graphic representation of the ten profiles, the profiles are recorded according to the direction of the factors. In this second half of the scoring scheme, the first column with the consecutive Roman numerals (I to X) denotes the number of the profile in the series of ten. One horizontal row corresponds to one complete profile. The eight initials heading the eight vertical columns indicate the respective boxes for the eight factors. Thus, after all the ten profiles have been "translated" into directions, we can easily follow up the trends of the eight factors in any one profile, or else the trend of one specific factor throughout the ten profiles, depending whether we inspect the rows horizontally or the columns vertically.

Next comes the adding up of the symptomatic factors, first the "objective symptom factors" (open reactions) and then the "subjective symptom factors" (plus-minus reactions). This adding up is done for both the individual profiles and the individual factors throughout the ten profiles. On the scoring sheet, the two columns headed by $\Sigma \bigcirc$, and $\Sigma \pm$, after the factorial columns, serve to add up the daily amount of open and plus-minus reactions separately, and the last column in the whole scheme serves for adding up both kinds of symptomatic reactions.

The two horizontal rows below the row indicated by Roman numeral X for the last profile, serve for adding up first the open reactions, then the plus-minus reactions, then the two together, for the eight factors individually. $\Sigma \bigcirc$ again indicates the summing up of the open reactions in the particular factor, $\Sigma \pm$ indicates the sums of the plus-minus reactions and the initials T.sp.G. indicate the summing up of the two previous categories. (T.sp.G. stands for the German terms "Tendenzspannung Grad." For explanation and justification of the use of this concept see Szondi: *Experimentelle Triebdiagnostik*, pp. 57-59.) Szondi himself originated this concept, and the term to express a certain quality of tenseness of the symptomatic factors, which he derives from his genetic theory of drives. Since the genetic origin of drives is not included as a basic assumption in this book, we will not make use of the above concept, except in the sense of the sum of symptomatic reactions. Thus on the basis of this row where the sum of all the open and the sum of all the plus-minus reactions were added up in each factor separately, we can arrange a rank order of the factors according-ing to their tendency for symptomatic reactions. The largest number in this row will pertain to the most "symptomatic" factor, while the smallest number will denote the factor with the greatest dynamic effect, underlying the symptomatic behavior: this is the factor (or factors) Szondi calls "root-factors," indicating by this term their position in the "deepest" layers of the personality.

In our example there are five factors equally "sympto-matic"—in case we add up the "objective" and "subjective" symptomatic reactions. These are: e, hy, p, d and m (8 each). The least "symptomatic," in other words the deepest "root" factor, is the s (1), and between these two extremes we find the h with a total of 4, in symptomatic reactions.

A formalized expression of the relative proportion of symptomatic reactions in each factor is what Szondi indi-cates on the scoring-sheet as "Triebformel" ("Formula of drives"). The relationship between the symptomatic and root factors is symbolized in the form of a fraction with the *most* symptomatic factors in the place of the enumerator and the *least* symptomatic ("root") factors in the place of the denomi-nator. The initials of the factors with "middle" values of symptomatic reactions are put down in the middle row of the "formula." This symbolization gives a quick overview of the relative dynamic effectiveness of the eight factors. Actual symptoms have to be looked for in the psychologic areas corresponding to the factors in the upper line, while underlying causal factors have to be looked for in areas

corresponding to the factor in the lowest line. The diagnostic significance of the factors in the middle row is not
quite clear yet. There is no exact rule in regard to the exact
number of factors to be set down in each of the three lines
of the "formula," nor is there an exact rule about the absolute number of the index of "symptomatic" reactions on the
basis of which it may be decided whether a given factor
should be set down in the first, middle, or lowest row. The
placing of the factors in the "formula" has to be done solely
on the basis of the *relative* value of their index of symptomatic reactions. Accordingly, there might be cases with a
much greater number of "causal" or "root" factors than
channels for open symptom formation, as well as the reverse.
An example of the latter configuration is our present case,
with six "symptomatic" and only one real "root" factor.
Naturally, these various proportions of "causal" as against
"symptomatic" reactions are most important considerations
in interpretation. (Interpretation of the illustrative case
will be given in a later part of this chapter.) Diagnostic
tables for interpreting the specific meaning of the various
configurations of the "drive-formulas" are given in the
Appendix of Szondi's *Experimentelle Triebdiagnostik*
(Tables XI–XX).

While the "drive-formula" indicates the quantitative and
qualitative distribution of *all* the symptomatic factors versus
the "root" factors, the ratio on the right side of the scoring
sheet marked with Arabic numeral 1 *(Tendenzspannungsquotient)*, serves to express the quantitative relationship
between all the "objective" as against all the "subjective"
symptomatic reactions. The interpretation of this ratio as
an indicator of the degree of self-control in the subject's
behavior, has been discussed in connection with the open
and plus-minus reactions (pp. 37–38).

Now we arrive at the last computation which has to be
done on the basis of the sum of all the symptomatic reactions

in each of the eight factors. After adding the sum of all the open to the sum of all the plus-minus reactions in each factor, we obtain one value in each factor, which is referred to above as the "index of symptomatic reactions" and which Szondi symbolized on the scoring sheet with the initials: T.sp.G. *(Tendenzspannungsgrad)*. The next step consists of obtaining the difference of these two index values for each vector separately. This is done by subtracting the smaller from the larger index number in each vector; the difference thus obtained is entered in the last horizontal row of the scheme, which has four boxes for the respective differences in the four vectors, indicated by the initials of the vectors *(S, P, Sch, C)*. This last row is indicated on the scoring sheet with the German term, *Latenzgrosse* (degree of latency). Szondi originated this term in order to express the dynamic significance of this difference. What this differential value expresses is the degree of discrepancy within the four pairs of "twin" factors in regard to their proneness of exhibiting symptomatic reactions. The greater this value, the greater the difference in the two factors of the same vector in regard to the frequency of symptomatic reactions. The psychodynamic significance of the degree of similarity or discrepancy in the way the two factors of a given vector are handled, has been discussed in the previous chapter (pp. 38–44). There is only one difference in the foregoing psychodynamic considerations and the present one, in which we attempt to clarify the rationale underlying this concept of "degree of latency," which takes such a prominent place in Szondi's book, where practically his whole reasoning of interpretation is centered in this one concept.

In our previous considerations we always referred to the relative loading of two factors, the measure of loading being the absolute number of squares within one factor. When we mentioned the lack of self-regulatory balance in connection with the disproportionately charged vectors, it was meant in this sense. However, in Szondi's concept of "degree of latency," the criterion for the similarity or discrepancy in two factors is not based solely on the absolute number of squares within one factor, since plus-minus reactions (which according to the number of choices are always loaded reactions) and open reactions are thrown together into one category under the heading of "symptomatic reactions." Accordingly a vectorial configuration of the type $\begin{smallmatrix} 2 & 0 \\ 2 & 4 \end{smallmatrix}$ (where the absolute number of choices is identical) is evaluated in the formalized scoring as the same degree of discrepancy as if the configuration in another vector is $\begin{smallmatrix} 0 & 0 \\ 0 & 4 \end{smallmatrix}$.

The reasoning is that in spite of the relatively great number of choices, the plus-minus reactions have little underlying dynamic effectiveness as compared with what Szondi calls "root" factors (factors which are steadily plus, or steadily minus, or change from plus to minus or vice versa); because the ambivalence in a factor implies the subjective (many times conscious or close to conscious) experience of the conflict which in turn implies that the respective need is not acting from the deepest (unconscious) layers of the personality. Actually I do not know whether Szondi himself would quite agree with this psychodynamic explanation and justification of the process of how one arrives at the "degree of latency" in each factor, since in the *Experimentelle Triebdiagnostik,* he justifies the throwing together of ambivalent and open reactions in the same dynamic category on the basis of some innate ambitendency of needs.

After having gone this far into discussing the underlying rationale of the process of obtaining the "degree of latency" in each vector, we shall discuss its further use in interpretation. First, one more aspect of its scoring. It has been said that in each vector the smaller index of the frequency of symptomatic reactions (T.sp.G.) has to be subtracted from the larger index and the difference—indicating the "degree of latency" of the particular vector—is entered in the respective box of the last row. Now we have to add to the printed initial of each vector the initial of that particular factor which had the *smaller* index of symptomatic reactions. In other words, we specify the four main categories of the four vectors by attaching the initial of the factor *which has been subtracted* from the one with the larger frequency of symptomatic reactions, as a small "foot-index" to the capital initial of the vector.

For example, in Figure 5 the frequency of symptomatic reactions in the h factor was 4, of the s factor, 1; the difference (4–1) is 3, which denotes the "degree of latency" of the S vector and is entered after the initial S in the last row. Now we added as a qualifying index a small s to the capital S, in order to signify that in this case the s factor was the one with less frequency of symptomatic reactions, or in the case of our dynamic theory, the index of small s signifies that in this case the s was the *dynamically* more effective factor than the h, the s acting from deeper layers of the personality than the more symptomatic h.

This deeper dynamic effectiveness of the factor with the smaller frequency of symptomatic reactions was exactly the reason that made Szondi decide to qualify the vectorial "degree of latency" on the basis of the factor which originally had the smaller index of symptomatic reactions. The psychodynamic importance of a vector—from the point of view of its effect on the total personality—is determined more by the factor which is more latent, and therefore exerts its influence through unconscious mechanisms, than by the factor which serves as a channel for symptom-formation, or one which is consciously experienced as conflict. A further specification of each "degree of latency" can be done by attaching not only the small initial of the more "latent" factor to the symbol of the vector, but also by indicating whether the characteristic direction of this more latent factor is plus or minus. (It never can be plus-

minus or open, since those reactions are excluded by definition from the "latent" factors.) Thus each vector can have
four possible types of "degree of latency" depending upon
which one of the two factors is more "latent" (less symptomatic) and further, upon the characteristic plus or minus
direction of this more latent factor.

There are two more blank spaces on the scoring sheet,
indicated by Arabic numerals _3_ and _4_ on the lower right
side of the sheet, which have to be explained. _3_ is called
Latenzproportionen which can be translated into English as
proportions of latencies. All it means is, that the four values
of the "degrees of latency" for the four vectors should be
entered in order of their magnitude in the four pre-marked
spaces under _3_. In each space we write the vectorial initial
and the specifying index of the factor and direction above
the line, and the corresponding numerical value below the
line. Recording the "degrees of latency" this way, in order
of their magnitude, serves the purpose of helping us to get
a quick overview about the relative dynamic strength of
the four vectors, indicating simultaneously the specific needs
which act as "latent," unconscious driving forces.

Under _4_ on the scoring sheet, one has to enter the symbol
of that particular "degree of latency" which was the strongest
one, in other words the first one in the order of "proportions
of latency"—_s_ under _3_. Szondi believes that this vector and
factor, which was singled out on the basis of its relative
strongest degree of latency, represents the individually most
characteristic aspect of the subject's personality. He considers this particular factor, which represents the most
dynamic unconscious driving force, to function as a "key"
to the understanding of the total personality. That is the
reason why _4_ on the scoring sheet is indicated as _"Triebklasse,"_ ("Drive-class" or "category of drive"), meaning that
the subject can be described as belonging to that particular
"class" of individuals for whom the dynamic power of the

particular need which is indicated in the symbol, is the strongest determining factor in their personality. Szondi assumes that individuals can be classified on the basis of their strongest latent need and that individuals belonging to the same "class" have essentially similar personality patterns. A great part of his *Experimentelle Triebdiagnostik* is taken up by the descriptions of the personality types corresponding to the various "drive classes." (See pp. 73–83 and 224–250). Since there are eight factors, and further on each factor can be "latent" in either plus or minus direction, there are 16 basic variations of such classes (S_{h+}; S_{h-}; S_{s+}; S_{s-}, etc.). Szondi, however, goes further in subdividing these 16 basic "drive classes" on the basis of whether two or three of the remaining vectors show similar magnitude of their "grade of latency." On this basis he arrives at the classification of bi-, tri-, and quadri-equal "classes" which results finally in a total of 144 possible variations of subclasses. His book contains personality descriptions corresponding to the 16 basic classes and then brief, rather generalized characterizations of the individuals belonging to the so-called "tri-equal" and "quadri-equal" classes. This last category refers to individuals for whom no one specific factor has more dynamic significance than the other, and who therefore form a rather pathologic group in themselves, just because of the lack of any definite "vertical" structurization in their personalities.

Further on the "drive formulas" serve to differentiate between the various possible interpretations of one main "drive category."

For example, all individuals belonging to the class S_{s-} (that is, the "drive class" of the case illustrated in Figure 5) are characterized by the fact that repressed aggression is their most dynamic latent "causal" factor, forming the underlying dynamics for whatever character or symptom formations they develop. Whether or not this repressed aggression will result simply in a "passive" character, or in a masochistic character, or in some definite form of neurosis or psychosis, can be decided on the basis of its particular "drive formula" which indicates the possible channel or channels through which this repressed aggression can somehow be discharged (naturally in this particular "drive class" we can only mean roundabout, indirect ways of discharge of aggression, otherwise the "s" would not be the "root" factor, but a "symptom" factor).

The above-mentioned diagnostic tables (XI–XX) in Szondi's book can be used for differential diagnosis in the various "drive classes" on the basis of the "drive formulas." The use of those tables should be restricted for cases who are known to have some sort of pathologic symptoms, and the problem is to differentiate between the various symptoms of pathology, since the respective tables only furnish such diagnostic categories or one-word personality characterizations.

As was said in the introduction, my intention was that the content of this book not overlap with Szondi's *Experimentelle Triebdiagnostik*. Therefore there will not be any further discussion of various "drive classes" and "drive formulas" which really represent the core of Szondi's interpretation in his book. Because he centers his interpretation around these rather recently developed formal categories, and constructed the scoring sheet for ten profiles accordingly, I thought it necessary to discuss that much of the psychologic reasoning underlying the construction of these categories, so that psychologists using the test and the accompanying pads of scoring sheets would be able to follow at least the way of thinking involved in the construction of the various symbols and categories which are indicated on the scheme. For further details on the use of this method, however, I have to refer to Szondi's book, since this whole method is not so much the core of my usual way of thinking when interpreting a series of profiles, as it is in Szondi's

presentation. Yet it is essential to fill out completely all
the categories of the scoring sheet whenever we are dealing
with a series of profiles. In this way we have a sure safeguard that none of the important aspects of interpretation
have been neglected, which can be the case when we rely
solely on the interpretation of the graphic profiles. On the
other hand, I would never advise a reliance on the interpretation of the "drive-classes" and "formulas" alone, without careful qualitative analysis of the test profiles themselves. The interpretation of the eight factors, the description of the psychodynamic mechanisms represented by the
eight diagnostic categories of the test material, will be the
content of the next chapter. This kind of interpretative
reasoning is emphasized specifically in this book, since
Szondi's book contains rather the methods of interpretation
on the basis of his diagnostic tables.

Now that the formal scoring categories have been discussed, one can illustrate their use on the concrete example
of case F.T., whose series of ten profiles is completely scored
in Figure 5. Here we will interpret only on the basis of
the formal scoring categories. However, the same case will
be discussed again on the basis of the specific meaning of the
eight factors and correlations of the factors, at the end of
the next chapter.

First let us see the ratio of all his open reactions to all
his plus-minus reactions. The corresponding value of 1.08
falls within the range which has relatively little diagnostic
significance, still one can say that in this man there is the
same amount of forces functioning in the direction of self-
control as he has channels for the purpose of discharging
certain need-tensions. This constellation would exclude the
possibility of an uninhibited, "acting-out" type of a person.
He might or might not have pathologic symptoms, but even
if he does, he certainly still resorts to the use of mechanisms
of control.

From *3* and *4* on the right side of the scoring sheet we can see that this man belongs to the "tri-equal S_{s-} class. S_{s-} because the S vector is the one with the largest value of the "degree of latency" *(3)*, the h factor giving four times as many symptomatic reactions as the s factor (two plus-minus and two open h reactions); and the index of $_{s-}$ is attached to the S because the direction of the "latent" (nonsymptomatic) s factor is minus. Furthermore, the qualification "tri-equal" was added to denote his "drive class" because the "degree of latency" in the remaining three vectors is approximately equal (Sch:1, P:○, C:○). According to Szondi, the interpretation of the "tri-equal" classes has to be done on the basis of the one remaining vector in which the "degree of latency" is different from that of the three other vectors. Yet, he believes there are some characteristic features in common to all the members of the "tri-equal class," determined by the common dynamic characteristic that all these individuals have equal possibilities for discharging the *one* most dynamic latent need through the *three* remaining vectors.

On page 80 of the *Experimentelle Triebdiagnostik,* the following characteristics common to the members of the "tri-equal class" are listed:

1. Fixation regression to the stage of bisexual orientation.

2. Tendency for inverted forms of sexuality, either in respect to the object choice or to the goal of the activity in connection with the love-object.

3. Frequently found in manifest homosexuals, or

4. In juvenile types of megalomania.

5. Typical for individuals who find themselves in a crisis in regard to their most important object-attachment (critical forms of libido-cathexis),

6. Mechanisms of compulsion neurosis, or

7. Paranoid traits. (As *8,* Szondi adds that individuals

of this class are mostly offsprings of paranoid or manic-depressive ancestors.)

The general description of the class S_{s-} is given in two places of the book, a short description on page 74, and a detailed characterization on pp. 225–228. (This is one of the "drive classes" which Szondi worked out most in details.) The most characteristic features mentioned are: tendency for intensive but sado-masochistic type of object-cathexis. Individuals find themselves in the above described "crisis of object relationship"; they cannot rid themselves from the love object they hate and love at the same time. They cling to this object in a sado-masochistic way. Depending on the specific constellation of the "drive-formula" there are various possible "solutions" to "solve" this basic sado-masochistic conflict. ("Solution" in this context is not meant as a necessarily healthy solution, but only as a final resultant of the basic conflict plus the other forces operating at the same time.)

The drive formula which is most similar to that of our present case is found in the second vertical column under I on table XII in the appendix of Szondi's book. Here we see that for individuals who belong to class S_{s-}, and have a "drive-formula" of the type: $\frac{c;\ (m,\ p,\ d,\ hy)}{s}$ (in the tables only the symptomatic and the root factors are indicated without the in-between factors) the following symptoms are characteristic: obsessive and compulsive ideas and neurosis; inability to work; paranoid schizophrenia. This drive formula is not exactly identical with the one in Figure 5 but quite similar to it. Since our case belongs to the "tri-equal" class, the chances for pathologic symptoms are enhanced.

The coincidence between the interpretation based solely on the tables and the actual case-history is practically one hundred per cent. The man is a most serious case of compulsion neurosis. He is a man with equivalent of college education, who, at the time the profiles were taken, was unable to continue his usual office work because his compulsive ceremonies and rituals took up practically his whole day. His symptoms, mostly ceremonies in connection with cleanliness, started years ago with certain bathroom rituals and set ways of dressing himself which handicapped him considerably in the performance of his daily routine in the office where he was working. At the time of the testing, he came for psychiatric help of his own accord, because by then he was completely the victim of his obsessive ideas. In a way which is characteristic for compulsive neurotics, he knew intellectually all about his sickness and wrote lengthy dissertations, in the form of an autobiography, about compulsion neurosis and schizoid personality. Yet, all this intellectual knowledge did not alter his magic belief that unless he performed all his rituals, something terrible would happen to his mother, whom he "adored." The subject, who was 32 years old at the time, was never married, and lived with his mother with whom, due to his inability to go out of the house, he spent practically twenty-four hours of the day. The father died when the subject was a child. Thus with the help of his symptoms he succeeded in completely narrowing down his actual "life-space" until nothing but the mother and his bathroom ceremonies were included, and also his frequent visits to the outpatient clinic where he indulged in verbose descriptions and complaints about his symptoms. He and his mother irritated each other, still they were unable to live without each other.

A dramatic change took place after the tenth test profile had been taken. The subject suddenly gave up his compulsive defense mechanisms and a real paranoid schizophrenia broke out. Without any previously detectable symptoms (except the symptoms of compulsive neurosis) he suddenly became violent and attempted to injure his mother physically. At this stage he had to be institutionalized. His profile in this stage is shown in Figure 6.

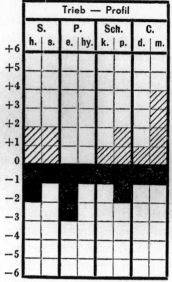

FIG. 6. T. F., 32 YEAR OLD MALE

The changes in the structure of the whole profile are obvious. The characteristic minus *s* changed into plus *s*, the *e* which was always plus-minus became completely minus, and most significant: the *Sch* vector shows the typical vectorial "mirror reversal" * (described in the chapter on changes under *f*, pp. 43–44). As can be seen, the use of the tables, at least in·this case, resulted in a perfect diagnosis of the symptoms as well as of the underlying dynamics. Even the latent paranoid schizophrenia which developed overtly only after the series of ten profiles had been finished, could be diagnosed on the basis of the "drive formula." I selected the above case for illustration at random from my own material and actually did not know whether or not the description on the basis of the tables would fit the clinical picture until I finished writing the previous pages, where

* Plus-minus "k" and open "p" changing into open "k" and plus-minus "p."

the respective characterizations of this particular "drive class" and "drive formula" were translated word by word from the German edition of Szondi's book. Yet, I would never advise a basis of interpretation solely or even primarily on this method. I think too much emphasis on the use of "tables" in interpreting the results of a projective technic has always the danger of mechanizing the process of interpretation. Relying completely on diagnostic tables * would mean that the interpreter arrives at certain conclusions without having gone through the actual psychologic experience of interpreting. This experience of interpreting consists of mobilizing the interpreter's own ability to project himself into somebody else's reactions and then have the ability to build up an integrated picture of the personality on the basis of having really understood, not only intellectually, but also emotionally, the psychologic mechanisms which are the component elements of the total personality as a functioning whole. All that implies a most complex psychologic process on the part of the interpreter, involving a fusion of certain intellectual and emotional processes, which probably can never be taught completely. All one can do in teaching is to explain as clearly as possible the "component" mechanisms and the final outcome of some of their most usual combinations; but much of the interpretation of *all* the possible combinations of the constituent elements (in our case that means the possible combinations of eight factors in four possible directions, or in other words, four vectors with sixteen possible intravectorial constellations, in all possible combinations) has to be left to the understanding of the individual interpreter. How much he will be able to utilize the elements of knowledge for the interpretation of practically never identical personality patterns, will depend partly on his general psychiatric experience with real people (and not

* I do not mean the proper use of statistical tables, but of qualitative diagnostic tables.

with textbooks), partly on his own personality, particularly on his ability to project himself emotionally into somebody else, and at the same time perceive and organize intellectually the material to be interpreted. The psychologic processes involved in interpreting projective technics are practically identical with those of the psychoanalyst's listening to and interpreting simultaneously the patient's verbal material.

After long personal experience of interpreting, everybody arrives at certain "shortcuts" in interpretation which he will use if the case warrants. However, it is dangerous to attempt to teach these shortcuts without detailed explanation of the way of thinking which was involved in the original arrival at those "shortcut" interpretations. Readymade formulas can be of great help to those who know the qualitative and dynamic interpretations of the mechanisms on which the formulas were based, for whom, therefore, the formulas have real meaning. But for those who do not have the broad background of basic knowledge, the immediate offering of shortcuts can have a stifling effect, because they might prevent the acquirement of more basic understandings of the dynamic processes involved.

In accordance with these considerations, now that we have illustrated the use of shortcuts and formulas on one case, we will proceed to the discussion of the "component elements," which in our case are the eight factors of the test. The ten profiles of subject F.T. (Figure 5) again will be interpreted on the basis of specific constellations and changes in the four vectors.

CHAPTER VI

Interpretation of the Eight Factors

IT IS known by now that the test contains *eight factors*, corresponding to eight different but interdependent psychologic need-systems or drives. The *eight factors* are divided into *four vectors,* each vector consisting of two factors. The two factors of any given vector are always "closely related" in the sense of referring to the same main area of the personality but at the same time representing opposite aspects of that same area.

The following is a schematic presentation, for the purpose only of offering a quick orientation, of the psychologic areas corresponding to the four main vectors and the eight factors.

I. The *sexual vector (S)* consisting of the

a. *h* factor (represented by pictures of homosexuals) which corresponds to the need for "passive" tenderness and yielding; and the

b. *s* factor (represented by pictures of sadists) which corresponds to the need for physical activity and aggressive manipulation of objects.

II. The *Paroxysmal vector (P)* describes the psychologic area of emotional control in general. Its two component factors are:

a. *e* (pictures of epileptics) factor describing the subject's way of dealing with aggressive, hostile, emotions; and

b. *hy* (pictures of hysterics) factor indicating the way the person deals with his more tender emotions.

III. The *Schizophrenic (Sch) vector* which is usually referred to as the *ego vector* because it reflects the structure and degree of rigidity or fluidity of the ego. It consists of the

a. *k* factor (pictures of catatonics), representing the need to keep up the ego's narcissistic integrity and separateness from the environmental objects; and

b. the *p* factor (pictures of paranoid schizophrenics) representing the expansive needs of the ego, the tendency to fuse into the objects of environment.

IV. The *Circular vector,* or rather *Contact vector,* as it will be referred to from now on. This vector indicates the general area of the subject's object relationships or in other words his contact with reality. The two component factors are:

a. the *d* factor (pictures of depressed patients) reflecting the possessive, "anal" type of object relationship; and the

b. *m* factor (pictures of manic patients), indicating the clinging "oral" type of object relationship.

In the following we are going to discuss the meaning of the eight factors individually. In describing a factor I shall try first to give a general psychodynamic interpretation of the corresponding disease category which, of course, at the same time will be the most general interpretation of the factor itself. Without the assumption that these eight types of mental disturbances imply well definable extreme manifestations of generally known psychologic mechanisms, the functioning of the test would be inconceivable. We also have to assume that the presence of these extreme and exaggerated psychologic drives are somehow expressed through the corresponding photographs, and further, that the subject's liking or rejection of the pictures is based on an unconscious identification or counteridentification with the processes depicted. Following a description of the general meaning of the factors there will be always a short description of the interpretations respective to the plus, minus, plus-minus or open positions of the same factor.

CHAPTER VII

The Sexual Vector

The h *Factor*

AS HAS been said the *h* factor represents the tender, more yielding part of sexuality, in general those manifestations of love which are usually in our culture referred to as "feminine." It contains little or no motoric energy. It is related to the deep needs of the organism for sensual contact through the sense of touch. It represents that aspect of love where grabbing and actively manipulating the object is absent. Instead there is a feeling of passively and submissively wanting to have contact with the love-object.

To derive all these psychologic characteristics from the actual stimulus material of pictures of passive male homosexuals, is not quite easy. However, on the basis of psychoanalytic experience with passive homosexual male patients, one knows, that exactly those above features are the most characteristic for the kind of sexual contact these patients are craving for. (There are a number of psychoanalytic case histories dealing with the above aspects of homosexuality. To mention the most outstanding one, there is Freud's study on Leonardo da Vinci. Also Schilder discusses homosexuality in the above sense. Healy, Bronner and Bowers' *Structure and Meaning of Psychoanalysis* can serve as a useful reference book for all the psychoanalytic concepts which will be used in interpretation.)

What has to be emphasized from the point of view of the interpretation of the *h* factor is that we believe that most characteristic of passive male homosexuals is not their need to have actual sexual intercourse with persons of their own sex, but more this general need for tender love. What these patients really want is to be loved by somebody the way they were loved by their mother. This is the need which has not been satiated (either because of the original "constitutional" extreme strength of this need, or because of environmental frustrations) and therefore its dynamic strength is determining the whole sexual orientation of even the adult personality. Individuals fixed at this level of development are not able to make the necessary transition toward a more active "masculine" type of sexuality, because this latter would imply a certain activity in regard to finding and manipulating a love-object which is incompatible with their childish need of wanting to be, rather, at the passive, recipient end of such relationship.

This concept of homosexuality coincides more or less with the concept of "Platonic" love, the classic Greek idea of homosexuality (see Plato: Phaedros) which can be characterized as the prototype of passive longing for an object without any release of tension because the motor activity necessary to secure the object is lacking. As can be seen from the general description of this factor, the basic need expressed by the h is a longing for tender love, which by itself is not only not pathologic but a necessary component factor of every mature sexual drive, in male or female equally. It becomes pathologic only when the total sexuality becomes dominated by this one drive, in which case it can lead to various symptom formations; among others it can lead to homosexuality.

A quotation from Schilder (quoted on the basis of Healy, Bronner and Bowers' *Structure and Meaning of Psycho-analysis,* page 401) is here in place: "It is one of the principles of psychoanalysis that we never find mechanisms in the neurosis which cannot also be found in the normal person. The differences are merely quantitative. There is nothing new in homosexuality, only something which exaggerates only what can also be found in the sex life of the normal male and female. Activity and passivity are characteristic of every human but . . . we can therefore say that we may understand the psychology of sex only if we consider it under the double aspect of the desire to intrude and the desire to be given to the body into which we intrude. Intruding and being within, being strong and being weak, these are the two poles of every sexual activity."

This quotation from Schilder expresses not only the basic meaning of the h factor but also that of the s, which will be discussed later.

As to plus h, one can say that it implies an identification with the needs described above. It means that the individual accepts and contains these sensual longings, unrelated to active moves toward satisfaction. Thus it indicates need to be the recipient of love, which is more characteristic for women than for men. Wherever it occurs it refers to a feminine identification as a dynamic element of the psychic structure. It refers specifically to nongenital need for love and caressing in an infantile sense.

If this need is not too strong (not *4* or more choices in plus *h*) and is well balanced by the choices in the other factors, then there is no reason that it should cause some pathology. If, however, the plus *h* is very strong (plus *5*, or plus *6*), then these characteristics of passive yearning are so marked as to constitute real immaturity. In what way this immaturity affects the total personality has to be decided on the basis of the constellation of the other factors. In case there are signs indicating that this strong craving for being loved as a child is frustrated, then we can expect serious pathologic symptoms, even to the degree of actual antisocial behavior. (This latter implies a plus or open *s*, a minus *e*, and a minus *m*, in conjunction with the strong plus *h*.) Because plus *h* also has the meaning of feminine identification, it is more likely to cause neurotic symptoms in men than in women. As far as the developmental stages are con-cerned, plus *h* is characteristic for children, under the age of puberty. The *h* starts to become negative during and after puberty, for those individuals who give minus *h* at all, because according to our data plus *h* is more frequent for the general population than any other *h* constellation.

From the point of view of pathology, some aspects have been mentioned already. Because of the frequency of the plus *h* in the average population one cannot say that it is "characteristic" for various psychoses as well as for anti-social behavior, but this statement is valid the other way around; namely, psychotics and antisocial individuals give plus *h* more frequently than any other *h* constellation.

Another characteristic trend of the plus *h* is that it is given more frequently by individuals whose work or occupation does not involve "sublimation" in the psychoanalytic sense of the word. However, this statement is true only if one compares large groups of subjects from various occupational levels. In studying individual cases, one comes across indi-viduals many times who do have some sort of "highly cul-tured" occupation, and give plus *h* nevertheless (especially with minus *s*). These are individuals who choose some form of work which involves the above described features of plus *h*, namely work which involves *personal* care of others which in turn implies getting personal affection from others in return.

The constellation of minus h can be interpreted as the counteridentification with whatever the *h* expresses in gen-eral. It means that the individual *does not want to accept* this need for personal tender affection but that does not mean that actually such needs are lacking altogether. This is particularly true if the minus *h* is strongly loaded.

As a general principle it has to be said here, while dis-cussing the first minus constellation that denial of a certain need does *not* mean lack of the need. On the contrary, it might mean a reaction formation, just because, under its original intensity, the person had to resort to this particular defense mechanism in order to save himself from otherwise unavoidable frustrations.

Keeping this mechanism in mind, we can say that individuals with minus *h* deny their need for passivity, or "femininity." Instead of personalized affection, these individuals are likely to identify themselves with more abstract forms of affection and love, such as: humanitarian love for all mankind, or other "conceptual" forms of tenderness. Many times minus *h* is obtained in people who on the surface are cool in interpersonal contact but show warm social or artistic attitudes.

Minus *h* is practically never found in children below puberty and would be an undesirable symptom of precociousness in such cases. It can be found with relatively highest frequency in a rather narrowly circumscribed group of "intellectual" adults who tend to sublimate their need for tender love into various forms of humanistic ideals and culturally desirable activities.

Minus *h* is a counterindication for *serious* forms of pathology such as psychoses or crime, but does not exclude various forms of neuroses. The probability of neurosis depends upon the intensity of the minus *h*. The stronger it is, the more likely that it has to be interpreted as active repression of its opposite, the plus *h*. It is a sign of masculine identification in women, and therefore in women it is more likely to cause neurotic symptoms, especially directly in the sphere of sexuality. Sexual frigidity in women is often indicated by strong minus *h*. The lack of even one balancing square in the other direction, which has been discussed in a previous chapter, has particular significance in those cases.

Plus-minus h indicates ambivalence in regard to this need of "feminine" passive type of love. It is usually the expression of ambivalent sexual identification and is subjectively experienced as conflict. Genetically, it refers often to an unresolved Oedipal conflict and is associated with unsatisfactory masculine or feminine identification. It can be expected in children before the resolution of the Oedipal conflict and then it appears again with relatively high frequency around puberty and in young adolescents. It is a symptomatic reaction for people with bisexual orientation and is given frequently by compulsion neurotics.

Open h is a sign that the need for being the passive recipient of love is "lived out" at the time being. This state of lack of tension in this area is seen either in small children whose need for tender love can be lived out in actuality, or else in infantile adults who succeeded in creating a situation where they are loved and pampered as a child. It can be obtained from impotent men or overt passive male homosexuals. In case of female homosexuals it still refers to the passive type. It can be given by women who have an extremely strong attachment to their mother, and who consequently easily attach themselves in a submissive, dependent manner to various "mother images." Whenever it is given consistently in a series it is an indication of low sexual energy. Open *h* can appear temporarily after sexual intercourse or after masturbation. In certain configurations, determined by the rest of the factors, open *h* can appear in individuals who are well able to sublimate intellectually, without being disturbed by sexual tension.

On the basis of what has been said about the meaning of changes in Chapter V, it follows that the fewer the changes in the direction of the *h* factor within a series of ten profiles, the more the probability that there are no really pathologic symptoms in this area. On the other hand, frequent changes of direction indicate the presence of a pathologic process in the sphere of sexuality. Frequent changes in the *h,* involving occasional "open" reactions, are characteristic for manifest homosexuals.

This is a statement which holds actually for each factor. The most characteristic reaction for patients with identical diagnosis with the particular stimulus pictures of the given factor is that the greatest variability of reactions is found in the factor corresponding to their own diagnosis.

The s Factor

The *s* factor has to be interpreted as corresponding to the psychological dimension active-passive. The *s* strongly refers to muscular energy and motoric tension and in this way relates to the action of the organism on its environment. As this tension becomes stronger, the possibility of destructive or sadistic behavior becomes increasingly likely. That is the reason why photographs of actual sadists can be used as "measuring unit" to indicate activity level in general. Experience with the Szondi test has shown the correctness of the assumption of linking the concept of motor activity with that of aggression. Similar conclusions concerning the relationship between aggression and general motor drive were reached by Bender and Schilder (Schilder, P. and Bender, L.: *Aggressiveness in Children II. Genet. Psychol. Monog.* 1936, 18, No. 5, 6, 410–525) and Caille (Caille, R. K.: *Resistant Behavior of Preschool Children. Child Dev. Monog.,* 1933, No. 11, pp. 142). In the sphere of sex, *s* represents the opposite pole to *h* in the same sense as indicated by the quotation by Schilder (pp. 68–69), *s* corresponding to the need to "intrude" and to be strong, while *h* corresponds to the need to be "weak." In other words *s* refers to the more active "masculine" aspect of sexuality, while *h* refers to the "feminine" one.

The *plus s* means that the person identifies himself with this outwardly directed tension in the activity area. The plus *s,* depending on its intensity (loading), and the constellations of the other factors, indicates a generally high degree of physical activity level, or else a tendency for uninhibited aggressive manifestations. Because plus *s* is related to active manipulation of *environmental objects,* one can also relate it to the concept, usually loosely used, of extroversion, although I prefer rather to draw the parallel between plus *s,* and what Goldstein calls "concrete behavior." Again, because of its relatedness to physical activity, it can be called a predominantly "masculine" reaction. From the point of view of sexuality it means an active going after the love object and the need to be the initiator in respect to every interpersonal relationship. Generally for individuals with a constant plus *s* it is characteristic to face and fight reality, rather than to withdraw into themselves; or in psychoanalytic terms: they are more inclined to make *alloplastic* than autoplastic adaptation. (Terms originated by Ferenczi.) It is also known that the excess of the latter type of "adaptation" is characteristic for neurotics, while the former one is characteristic for impulsive characters and criminals. (Naturally both types of adaptation have their wide range of normal variations; it is easier to characterize a tendency by its extreme forms of manifestation.)

Plus *s* is the characteristic reaction of children. However, similarly to the plus *h,* the plus *s* is the most frequent *s* constellation in the general population at large. It is the usual reaction of people with little intellectual interest, which, however, does not mean that plus *s* reaction is never obtained from highly cultured intellectuals. Yet, even in those cases the general interpretation of plus *s* is valid, and an intellectual activity or profession, if associated with plus *s,* has a different meaning from the point of view of the total personality than it does, for instance, in a person with minus *s.* In case of plus *s* it is more likely that intellectual interest is based on interest of "real" things; in other words, it will involve more empirical experimentation and actual physical activity, than purely speculative or contemplative type of intellectual interest. Taking an example from the field of art, it has been found that plus *s* is much more common among sculptors and next to sculptors in painters than among musicians (composers or performers) and writers, in the last group pure plus *s* being practically nonexistent. (Deri, Susan K.: The Szondi test applied to the study of various groups of artists and musicians. Unpublished study.) The relation of plus *s* to the tendency to manipulate actual objects of the environment (sculpting) as against manipulating purely symbolic material (tones or word symbols) came out nicely in the above study.

The general frequency of plus *s* decreases in adults and appears again in high frequency in old age, where it refers to "concrete behavior" in general.

The pathologic significance of plus *s* (as of any other factor's) depends partly upon its loading, partly upon the configuration of the whole profile into which the plus *s* is embedded.

Its most direct pathologic significance relates to antisocial behavior. This can be the case if plus *s* has a loading of five or six and is associated with a minus *e* and minus *m* and, most of the time, plus or open *d*.

Psychotics also give plus *s* frequently, especially if they have symptoms of hallucination.

In regard to neurosis, plus *s* has special diagnostic significance if encountered in women, because it is always a sign for masculine identification. This "masculine" trend in women can be either sublimated in work or be the source of difficulties in the sphere of sexuality (or both); in extreme cases it can lead to active homosexuality in women.

Minus s constellation means tension in the area of aggression but not accepted by the person. The consequence is that in such cases the primarily outward directed motor energy will be transformed into more intellectual energy, aiming at the *manipulation of concepts* rather than manipulating concrete objects of the environment. To use Goldstein's term again, minus s can be related to "abstract behavior."

Minus s is indication of a low lovel of physical activity but is often associated with intellectual activity; for example, in scientific work as a certain "civilizing" drive to conquer nature and control remote and abstract forces. Depending on its intensity it might mean simply a nonaggressive behavior (for instance in a constellation of $\frac{1}{2}$ or $\frac{1}{3}$); or if minus s is strongly loaded ($\frac{0}{5}$, $\frac{0}{6}$, etc.) we have to think of a moral masochistic character and feelings of inefficiency. Minus s therefore gives us some information about the superego structure of an individual without, however, trying to equate minus s with the psychoanalytic concept of superego. We will see that there will be other factors which in some constellations are related to the strength of the superego. In comparing minus s with plus s one can say that individuals with stable minus s, in case of conflict, have rather the tendency for withdrawing, than fighting reality. They are more inclined for *autoplastic* than for alloplastic adaptation (in contrast to plus s), which also implies that they are more likely to have neurotic symptoms than to develop antisocial behavior. As a matter of fact, minus s is one of the few "single" signs which by itself can be taken as a counterindication against serious antisocial activity.

Minus s is practically never encountered in children below the age of ten, but in the few cases when this constellation is found in young children, it is a sign for a precocious development of the superego, with ensuing guilt feelings. These are the children who are "too" good and try too hard to please the grown-ups.

Around puberty the appearance of minus s is more frequent, but actually it is a typically "adult" reaction (which by no means should be understood as meaning that minus s is characteristic for the "typical" adult). Actually, even in adults minus *s* is not very frequent because it implies certain ability to sublimate aggression which is not common in the so-called "average" man. Generally speaking, minus *s* is more common in women than in men, and in case we see it in men it has to be interpreted as some lack of identification with the "masculine" role, which in our culture implies more acceptance of physical activity and aggression. However, minus *s* is rather common in so-called "intellectual" men, whose work involves dealing with concepts and other symbolic forms rather than working with material objects. The occurrence of minus *s* in groups of unskilled workers, or even in skilled labor, is negligible. However, it is not infrequent in certain "nonintellectual" occupations; namely, in those which involve the serving or "waiting on" other people (i.e., department store salesmen, waiters, male beauty shop operators, etc.).

The pathologic significance of minus *s*, as has been mentioned already, is mostly in regard to neurosis, which depends on the intensity of minus *s* and other factorial correlations in the profile. Minus *s* can be obtained in any form of neurosis which is described in Freud's *"Civilization and Its Discontents,"* since the basic source of neurosis in such cases is the repressed aggression. Accordingly, neurotic traits corresponding to minus *s* can be pathologic inefficiency, difficulties in work, masochistic traits, irritability because of being oversensitive to real or imagined "insults." Because of this paranoid trend, minus *s* in some cases can result in ideas of reference or other forms of paranoid delusions. (In case of real paranoids, minus *s* is associated with plus *h* and a changing *p*.) Minus *s* is also a characteristic sign of depression, again because of the special significance of repressed aggression in this particular form of neurosis or psychosis. If encountered in men, minus *s* can be the source of difficulties in heterosexual adjustment. It can—but does not necessarily—mean, homosexuality. In many cases the sex of the love object is not inverted but only the act which is needed for sexual satisfaction shows signs of inversion; i.e., the man wants to be the passive and submissive partner in the sex act as well as in other aspects of the marriage. The probable solution is that a man with minus s will be attracted to a woman with tendency for plus s, in which case "marital adjustment" is well conceivable. Whether or not such cases can be called "latent homosexuals," depends on the definition of "latent homosexuality," which concept—at present—is far from being unequivocally defined.

Plus-minus s refers to an ambivalent way of handling aggression. Similarly to the plus-minus h, it also means ambivalence in regard to masculine or feminine identification, and—as in the case of any factorial ambivalence—both components are actually experienced as such. However, in the case of the s factor, satisfactory synthesis, or sublimation of the two opposing tendencies seems to be more feasible than in the case of h, probably because the basic meaning of the s is activity as such, which—almost by definition—lends itself easily to a number of various discharge possibilities. The manifold possibilities for "concrete" as well as "abstract" behavior in any one person's life, offers enough favorable solutions for plus-minus s, without the necessity of pathologic symptoms.

Certain types of scientific as well as artistic sublimation seems to be appropriate discharge of the "double" tension caused by the plus-minus s. Even in those cases where the main field of sublimation is not art, the type of work or hobby of individuals with plus-minus s, is likely to have a tinge of exhibitionism. In general they are attracted by "unusual" fields of activity.

The appearance of plus-minus s starts about the age of puberty and becomes more frequent during adolescence, when it refers to the usual vacillation in regard to controlling aggression and identifying oneself with a masculine role. It also coincides with the period of almost "physiologic" homosexual crushes in both sexes.

As mentioned before, plus-minus *s* can also occur in adults —although it is an infrequent *s* constellation—and even adults with ambivalent *s* have something of an adolescent quality in their personality.

In respect to pathologic symptoms, it can occur in people with sado-masochistic tendencies, which in turn can be the source of a number of neurotic symptoms. It can occur in cases of homosexuality or other forms of sexual perversions, if besides the plus-minus direction the *s* factor also shows a tendency for changing several times within a series of ten profiles.

Among neurotic symptoms, hypochondriac anxiety and compulsive symptoms are most common with ambivalent *s*. It is unusual to find this constellation in manifest psychotics; it can be rather interpreted as a counterindication for real psychosis in case the differentiation between prepsychosis and psychosis is doubtful.

Open s is an indication for continuous discharge in the area of activity or aggression. By all means it is an *active* picture, the quality of which depends on other factors. It can be seen in efficient behavior, in "busy" people, in people who sublimate their aggression in scientific work successfully (minus *h,* open *s*); or else in actively antisocial individuals (plus *h,* open *s,* minus *m*). Many times the interpretation from the point of view of observable behavior is similar to that of plus *s*. It differs from plus *s* primarily, in the lack of tension which results from continuous discharge, but which is hard to differentiate from active behavior *with* residual tension.

It is found in very young children (three and four years old) as well as in any other age group, since discharge of activity as such is not particularly characteristic for any age.

However, the combination of other factors in conjunction with open *s* varies with age.

Open *s* is a frequent constellation in many forms of psychopathology. It is a characteristic sign for compulsion neurotics (in conjunction with open *d*) who are able to release their tension in respect to aggression, through their compulsive symptoms. It is also common in motorically excited and excitable psychotics (in conjunction with plus *h*). Open *s*, besides strong plus *s*, is the most frequent *s* picture of active criminals (in which case it goes with minus *m*).

Thus we finish the discussion of the *h* and *s* factor separately, in all the four directions. The next step would be the discussion of the various combinations of these two factors. Since each vector is composed of two factors and each factor can occur in either of the four basic directions (plus, minus, plus-minus and open) the number of possible *vectorial variations* of the combination of both factors, is *sixteen*. Discussion of all the sixteen variations for the four vectors, would be beyond the scope of this introductory book. For respective tables which indicate the main characteristic features and percentile distribution of the sixteen variations of the four vectors in the various diagnostic and age groups, I refer to Szondi's *Experimentelle Triebdiagnostik*, Psychodiagnostik Tables II, III, IV and V, in the appendix.

In the following, I shall give a brief description of the most important combinations of the *h* and *s* factors.

Open h *with open* s

There is little or no sexual tension. It might indicate: (a) that sexual tension has been discharged recently (for example through sexual intercourse, or masturbation, or homosexual activity); (b) it might indicate fixation on an infantile level of sexuality, or (c) it might indicate organic or "constitutional" (endocrinological) reasons for lack of sexual tension.

It is often found in heterosexually immature adults, who were never really "weaned" from their parents and who construct their lives in a way that they can either stay living in the parents' house or find another "parent" group whom they can join and with whom they can live (priests, nuns).

Plus h *with plus* s

This is the most frequent of all the *vectorial* constellations in the S vector (30%). It represents a fusion and an acceptance of the two opposing needs corresponding to h and s. Thus in many cases it is a healthy picture of unrepressed sexuality. It is the usual sexual constellation of the so-called "average" adult, by which is meant a person with a relatively simple ego structure and no particular needs for sublimation. It is a common S vectorial picture in lower occupational levels. The sex act in such cases is usually more important than the careful search for a specific love-object. It is more common in men than in women.

It is characteristic for people who are interested in the realistic and materialistic aspects of life. From this it follows that it is a usual picture of childhood.

If either factor is more than four plus, then that implies so much activity ready to be discharged and outwardly directed, that antisocial behavior may result. Accordingly plus h, plus s is also common among criminals (with minus e and minus m).

In case there are other signs of an effective superego, or else of repressive tendencies within the ego, then the sexual tension caused by plus h, plus s might be the cause for "drive-anxiety" (plus h, plus s, minus e, minus hy, minus k). Otherwise it is rather a counterindication in regard to neurosis.

Among psychoses it is most frequently found in mania, hypomanic excitement, or in epilepsy, all of these diseases being characterized by strong need for motor discharge.

Another pathologic group for which a high plus h and

a high plus *s* (at least plus 5 in each) is characteristic, are feeble minded children who—we know from other investigations— (Goldstein, Werner) live one "concrete" level to a pathologic extent.

Minus h *with minus* s

This is the only other *s* vectorial constellation which represents fusion between the two basic component needs (feminine tenderness and masculine aggression) of sexuality. However, in spite of this successful amalgamation, neither of the two basic drives is accepted in an unmodified form. The amalgamation usually indicates an individual who is inclined rather to sublimate his sexual energy than to discharge it easily on a primarily sexual level. Szondi found that in his "general population," which consisted of 4117 individuals, only 5.5 per cent yielded minus *h* and minus *s* in the *S* vector. The percentage of minus *h*, minus *s*, increases consistently if we follow occupational levels from unskilled labor (where this .constellation is nonexistent) to professions involving highly conceptual operations. Minus *h*, minus *s* is relatively most common in writers, musicians, psychologists, literary and art critics, etc., or in those devoted to intellectual or artistic creations or productions. This *S* vectorial constellation appears usually in conjunction with complex ego structures, which will be discussed in connection with the *Sch* vector. In such combinations, the minus *h*, minus *s* usually indicates successful sublimation so that— although it always implies a tendency to intellectualize needs which are basically of sexual origin—it does not necessarily indicate neurotic repression. The sexuality of such individuals can be characterized as displaying a high frustration tolerance, the specific love-object being more important than the act.

If, however, minus *h,* minus *s* are strongly loaded (at least one of the two factors being minus five) neurotic repression of sexual needs is indicated. Thus, this *S* vectorial constellation is found in cases of sexual frigidity in women, or of lowered potency, or impotence, in men. This constellation also can be associated with hysteroid symptoms in both sexes.

The possibility of *overt* psychoses or antisocial acts, however, is practically ruled out by this one *S* vectorial picture.

The constellation is one of the rare "signs" in the Szondi Test which determines the general personality structure to such a high degree that certain statements about the basic *"humanistic"* and *socially positive attitude* of the subject do not have to be modified, whatever constellations are found in the remaining six factors. Thus, in discussion of the remaining factors, whenever it is mentioned that a given factorial constellation is highly correlated to psychoses or anti-social behavior, it should be understood with the qualification: unless it occurs with minus *h,* minus *s* in the *S* vector.

From the characterization described above, it follows that minus *h,* minus *s* is a typically adult configuration, rarely obtained in childhood or senility. Apparently, the psychic energy of young adults (late adolescence) or adults is needed to keep up the complex mechanisms implied in this constellation.

Plus h *with minus* s

Characteristic of plus *h,* minus *s*—as well as of the reverse (minus *h,* plus *s)*—*S* vectorial constellation is a dissociation of the two above discussed component needs of sexuality. That such a dissociation of the two related drives in one main area is less desirable from the point of view of psychologic balance in that area than a fusion of the two drives has been discussed in Chapter V. However, there are possible solutions within the range of "normal" manifestations for these drive constellations, although the probability for

disturbances in the primarily sexual sphere is greater in
the "dissociated" constellations, than it is in the previously
discussed "amalgamated" sexual pictures of the plus *h*, plus *s*
and the minus *h*, minus *s* type.

The plus *h*, minus *s* configuration points to acceptance
of the need for tenderness, with simultaneous rejection of
the need for uninhibited motor discharge, or aggressive
manipulation of concrete objects. Thus, it is the picture
of a basically dependent, submissive individual of low need
for physical activity. It suggests sensitivity, and the tendency
to detach oneself from the material, physically tangible
aspects of reality, with proportionately increased interest
in the conceptual, symbolic representation of outside as well
as inside reality.

In conjunction with constellations in other factors indicating good possibility for sublimation, the above described
characteristics of plus *h*, minus *s*, can appear in a variety
of socially positive or sublimated manifestations. In men,
this is achieved mainly by choice of intellectual or artistic
professions of the type described previously under minus *s*,
which combine intellectual activity and aggression with
"serving" humanity. The less intellectual "serving" occupations also go frequently with plus *h*, minus *s*.

From the point of view of pathology, plus *h*, minus *s* is
more significant in men than in women. Because of the
basically submissive, sensitive character of this constellation,
it frequently indicates latent passive homosexual tendencies
in men. As mentioned before, this does not necessarily take
the form of choosing a love object of the same sex, but often
manifests itself, in spite of heterosexual object choice, in
the choice of a domineering, aggressive partner with whom
the man can play the submissive role. In case the plus
direction of the *h* changes within a series of ten profiles,
with an occasional "draining" (open) of the *h*, but with

the *s* remaining minus, one can think of manifest homosexualitv

If the minus *s* is strongly loaded (four choices or more), especially if it shows the tendency of becoming increasingly loaded in the minus direction during a series of ten profiles, then the normal "sensitivity" might have increased to paranoic symptoms, particularly if there are simultaneously changes in the *p* factor.

Plus *h,* minus *s* is also found in cases of neurotic or psychotic depression, with the exception of the form of agitated depression. Similarly, it can occur in compulsion neurosis, since all these disease entities are dynamically characterized by the repression of overt aggressiveness. As a counterpart, it can be mentioned that plus *h,* minus *s* is counterindication for real epilepsy (great motoric seizures) and manic psychosis.

In regard to age distribution, one can say that this *S* vector constellation is rare in childhood, is relatively frequent in adolescents and in adults, and most frequent in old age.

Minus h *with plus* s

This is the other typical *S* vectorial constellation in which the "feminine" and "masculine" components of sexuality are not integrated.

It is given by people who repress their need for tenderness, and identify themselves with physically active or aggressive behavior. Thus, it is a typically "masculine" pattern, given by physically active men or masculine women.

These tendencies can be sublimated in professions involving active manipulation of the environment, and because of the minus *h,* it is likely that this drive for activity will take a cultured form. Occupations involving physical activity (for example surgery, electrical engineering, etc.) or organizational work (examples: personnel work, group work, social work, etc.) are usual and good forms of sublimation for individuals with minus *h,* plus *s.*

This constellation has special pathodiagnostic significance in women because of the masculine identification implied. Actual female homosexuality of the aggressive type is a possibility, but again not a necessary consequence of this S vectorial configuration. The statement, however, that women with minus h, plus s always tend to "take charge of situations" in marriage as well as in other interpersonal relationships, is true in every case. The positive channelizations for this tendency have been mentioned above.

In other instances, when the presence of minus h, plus s indicates the existence of domineering and aggressive drives but at the same time other factors (minus k) indicate the presence of repressive tendencies in the ego, the outcome of the conflicting forces is likely to result in symptoms of conversion hysteria.

This S vectorial constellation is most frequent in adolescent boys, where it corresponds to the exaggerated emphasis of "masculinity." Incidentally, this interpretation is often valid for minus h, plus s in cases of adult men, too.

In adults it is less frequent than in adolescents and it practically disappears in old age.

Some children give it near the final stage of the Oedipal phase, when identification with the "strong" father sets in. This developmental stage is naturally desirable for boys, but when it occurs in girls, it leads to the above described masculine identification with all its consequences in women.

Now that we have discussed those five constellations of the h and s factors which correspond to the five most clear-cut personality characterizations which can be interpreted on the basis of the S vector, we will turn to the interpretation of the factors in the P vector.

It is hoped that the remaining eleven S vectorial configurations can be more or less understood on the basis of the foregoing analysis. The five "classes" of the S vector discussed above can be considered as "basic" constellations, from which the interpretation of the other eleven "classes" can be derived by means of appropriate combination of the respective parts of "basic" interpretations. For example, the constellation of plus-minus h with plus s, can be interpreted on the basis of combining the characterization of plus h, plus s with that of minus h, plus s. In a similar manner, one can derive the rest of the S vectorial constellations. The complete discussion of all the sixteen variations of the four vectors, sixty-four vectorial pictures altogether, would be beyond the scope of a manual, which bears in the title the word "introduction."

CHAPTER VIII

The Paroxysmal Vector

The concept of paroxysmality is less known and less used generally in psychology and in psychoanalysis than that of sexuality. In medical science, the adjective "paroxysmal" is used to describe certain emotional or physiologic processes which follow a specific pattern. This is a pattern of periodically recurring accumulation of energy which reaches a climax, then suddenly discharges. Graphically, there is a repeated, wave-like rise in tension to a culminating point, followed by a plunge to a point nearly zero. Prototypical of paroxysmal discharge is the gradual approach and sudden outbreak of an epileptic seizure.

The e Factor

The interpretation of the *e* factor is centered in this paroxysmal storing up and sudden release of energy. In the Szondi test, epilepsy is interpreted psychologically as the purest manifestation of aggressive outburst. This conception of epilepsy coincides with that of Freud as it is expressed in his "Beyond the Pleasure Principle." *

The epileptic's mounting aggressiveness, accompanying the approach of seizure, is well known to all clinicians dealing with epileptic patients. There is an increasing irritability and motor restlessness which sometimes reaches a point at which epileptics feel a compulsion to injure people in their environment. This period of aggressiveness is terminated by the actual attack, which is followed by coma. The next stage comprises the so-called inter-paroxysmal period, characterized by the epileptic's strict emotional control of

* Freud, Sigmund: Beyond the Pleasure Principle. London, Int. Psa. Press, 1922.

his aggressive tendencies. The "e" photographs in the test are portraits of epileptic patients, in this controlled inter-paroxysmal period. In this stage, the epileptic patients are overly-good, religious, and helpful. The term "morbus sacer," denoting epilepsy in the old European textbooks of psy-chiatry, intends to express just this aspect of the epileptic character. Again, clinicians who have had experience with epileptic patients know very well that the kindness and help-fulness of epileptics has something of a "sticky" and forced quality. One can almost sense the degree of energy spent on retention of this strict emotional control which probably serves the same dynamic purpose as a reaction formation. The Rorschach records of epileptics in the seizure-free period show, usually, all the characteristics described above. Rorschach himself mentions that epileptic subjects imply value judgments in their answers and in their preoccupation with details and symmetry of the blots.* The predominance of stereotypy and perseveration has been observed by prac-tically all Rorschach workers studying the records of epilep-tic subjects.†

All these details need mention because interpretation of the *e* factor is based completely on the assumption that the *e* factor relates to the control and discharge of aggressive energy and, therefore, reflects those aspects of the personality which are closely bound to the development of the superego.

Plus e

The plus *e* constellation results from the subject's identi-fication of himself with portraits supposedly expressing strict control over the discharge of rough, aggressive feelings. Thus, plus *e* is in some ways the counterpart of minus *s* as indication of a dynamically active superego, which implies that it is associated with people who are concerned with questions

* Rorschach, Hermann: Psychodiagnostik. Bern, Hans Huber, 1937.
† Klopfer, Bruno and Kelley, Douglas: The Rorschach Technique. Yonkers, World Book Co., 1942.

about "good" and "bad" in general. In other words, plus *e* is a sign of ethical control. More than three plus *e* choices suggest a reactive, compulsive control which is likely to accompany temporary inconsistencies in behavior. Individuals with strong and consistent plus *e* are often moralistic, critical, and are likely to suffer guilt feelings resulting from aggressive urges which never found their way to being carried out in reality. The control of plus *e* seems to insure that whatever antisocial urges the subject experiences will not be transmitted into motor activity. Even though both minus *s* and plus *e* reactions are indications of control over aggression, they seem to function in slightly different layers of the personality. In the case of minus *s,* the word "control" is not even quite appropriate; rather, one may discuss a transformation of outward-directed aggression into physically passive behavior, with simultaneous manifestations of sublimated or introverted aggression. In topological terms one could say that the minus *s* reaction indicates that a transformation has taken place within the inner-personal region corresponding to aggression, while in the case of the plus *e* reaction, the control function can be localized rather on the *boundary* of the motoric region surrounding the personality. From the psychoanalytic point of view, both can be considered as different aspects of the superego function. When the plus *e* is loaded, or when there are other components in the profile indicating repression, it can be regarded as a sign of compulsion neurosis. In the Szondi test, the plus *e* constellation is, again, one of the few constellations which by itself can be interpreted as a counterindication of antisocial, criminal activity.

The plus *e* constellation is rarely obtained in children. Its frequency increases gradually from puberty on, and reaches its maximum (about forty per cent of the population) in adulthood, between the ages of twenty and forty. The frequency of the plus *e* constellation decreases again with old age.

In clinically symptomless adults, the plus *e* is usually correlated with a rather high cultural level, and is found most frequently in occupations and professions which are concerned primarily with helping others. In pathology, the plus *e* is characteristic of compulsion neurosis and conversion hysteria. The theory described above, which regards the plus *e* as a restrictive control on the boundary of the motoric region, is supported by these data (Szondi: *Experimentelle Triebdiagnostik* Psychodiagnostic Table XXIV). The plus *e* is also associated relatively frequently with schizophrenics, an empirical finding for which the psychodynamic rationale cannot easily be stated. It might be attributed to the fact that such a *par excellence* ego-disturbance as schizophrenia is correlated with inhibition in regard to discharging emotions freely through the motoric system. One could even hypothesize a causal relationship between the two phenomena. The fact that the plus *e* constellation is most uncommon in manic-depressive manic psychosis, which is prototypical, among psychotic disturbances, of motorically active object-directed symptomatology, is in line with the "motor" hypothesis in the interpretation of the *e* factor.

In addition to throwing light on the meaning of a specific factor, the above considerations illustrate how careful study of various data of the test can contribute to the understanding of psychodynamics underlying various neuroses and psychoses. Because the Szondi test can be compared to an octagonal gauge which permits the psychologist to measure, through eight planes, the reactions of clinically symptomless, neurotic, psychotic, and antisocial subjects alike, it is probably the instrument most suited to make visible the deep psychodynamic mechanisms which form the basis of such common diagnostic labels as schizophrenia, mania, etc. Following discoveries of workers in psychoanalysis, the use of a tangible testing instrument is of the greatest importance for further research. And, of course, progress would involve the setting up of experiments which finally can prove or disprove the hypotheses reached on the basis of the Szondi test.

I have inserted these observations for the following reason. Ever since I made my first study on schizophrenics in 1939, the frequency of the plus *e* constellation in this group has been puzzling to me, since I could not see the dynamic connection between the two. If there were really truth in the hypothesis that the plus *e* constellation in schizophrenia expresses the disability of discharging violent emotions, goals for further research, as well as some hints for therapy, could be developed.

Before going on to the discussion of the minus *e* constellation, I am going to quote a legend from the Talmud which I found in Werner Wolff's *The Expression of Personality* * in the chapter in which he discussed difficulties in judging personality from the physiognomy. The quotation gives a perfect description of the dynamic meaning of the plus *e* constellation.

The King of Arabistan, who had heard of the miracles of Moses, wanted a portrait of Moses, and for this purpose sent his best painter to him. When the King got the painting he gathered together his physiognomists and asked them to tell him the character of this man and to explain to him the source of Moses' magic power. "Your Majesty," answered the sages, "this portrait shows a man who has all the vices existing in the world; he is brutal, proud, greedy, and ambitious."

"That must be wrong," shouted the King. "This cannot be the character of that man who performed the greatest miracles in the world; either the painter made a false portrait or the physiognomists are worthless men."

There began a violent dispute between the painter and the sages. Finally the King decided to seek his information from Moses himself and he set off to visit him. When the King stood before Moses he became convinced that the painter had made a faultless portrait. He

---

* Wolff, Werner: The Expression of Personality. Harper Bros. New York, London, 1943.

told Moses of the dispute and added: "Now I am convinced that there
is no such thing as a science of physiognomy."

"There is such a science," answered Moses. "Both the painter and
the sages are right. I was marked by nature with all the vices the
physiognomists spoke of. But I struggled with all these evil forces
until I suppressed them in myself, and all forces opposite to them
became my second nature. This battle gave me my power."

Minus e

The interpretation of the minus *e* constellation already
has been implied to a great extent. It signifies rejection of
stimulus material supposedly expressing strong control over
emotional outbursts. Therefore the minus *e* constellation
is obtained from people who are likely to have aggressive
outbursts. The correlation of negative *e* with plus *s* is obvious. The plus *s* constellation gives information about the
state of tension resulting from the need for aggression felt
by a subject, while the minus *e* constellation shows how
this need is handled. The "minus *e* state" is experienced
by the subject as strong emotional tension with no positive
mechanisms of control. Such a tense state is likely to result
in some kind of sudden emotional release, since the minus *e*
constellation represents a state of unstable emotional equilib-
rium, in which people usually do not remain for long
periods of time. These changes are indicated on the test
by the frequency with which minus *e* changes into open *e*.
Individuals for whom minus *e* is characteristic are usually
impulsive; ethical problems are not of primary importance
to them, and generally they are characterized by a lax superego. (As will be seen later, this statement needs some qualification, depending on the constellation of the *hy*.) Invariably,
a constant minus *e* results in a general restlessness and a
tendency to act out id impulses spontaneously.

The age distribution associated with the minus *e* follows
logically from the general character of this constellation.
It is most frequently given by small children, and gradually
decreases through puberty to the fifty year age group, from

which it increases again until, near the seventy year age group, it reaches the frequency with which it is found in the young children (about forty-two per cent). This curve represents the well known fact that emotional control is a characteristic of adulthood.

The pathodiagnostic significance of the minus *e* consists mostly in indication of the potential danger of a violent emotional outburst. Depending on the loadedness of the minus *e,* and on its relation to the total configuration, emotional outbursts may or may not result in antisocial acts. In children, the minus *e* constellation is often an indication of an approaching temper tantrum. Similarly, the approach of a real epileptic seizure is also often indicated by an increasingly loaded minus *e* within the series of ten profiles, which drains suddenly immediately after seizure.

The minus *e* constellation is a counterindication of compulsion neurosis. More frequently than it can be found in any other pathologic groups, minus *e* is found in antisocial individuals of all kinds, from vagabonds to murderers. The minus *e* constellation is one of the three basic constituents of the typically antisocial syndrome, the other two being plus *s* and minus *m.* Of course, if the syndrome is not complete, one has no right to predict antisocial behavior. In the clinically healthy population the minus *e* is usually found in lower occupational levels involving physical labor. In cases in which it occurs in individuals of higher professional level, it still indicates a certain aggressiveness in the character.

Plus-minus e

Similarly to the plus-minus *s,* the plus-minus *e* constellation indicates ambivalence in the subject's way of handling aggression. This ambivalence is experienced subjectively as an emotional conflict and is likely to lead to periodic outbursts, though not usually to the antisocial outbursts associated with minus *e*. Individuals with plus-minus *e* do have a strongly functioning superego, but their superego is not well integrated into the total personality. Rather, it is experienced as an independent foreign agent which tries to exert power over the actions of the organism. It corresponds somewhat to the pseudo superego referred to by some psychoanalysts. The behavior of such subjects might be over-righteous and at times inconsistent, leading to guilt feelings.

The fact that the most characteristic pathologic symptoms accompanying the plus-minus *e* constellation are compulsion neurosis and stuttering is in accordance with the above dynamic consideration. This *e* constellation is rarely found in cases of manifest psychoses of any kind. It appears that the subjectively experienced emotional ambivalence implied in this constellation is not compatible with actual psychotic states.

The plus-minus *e* constellation is not characteristic for any one age group. From young childhood to the twenty year age group, the frequency of the plus-minus *e* does not show much variability, ranging from fifteen to seventeen per cent. Then there is a drop to about nine to ten per cent between the twenty and forty year age groups, followed by a gradual increase to fourteen per cent. There is a second, sharp drop in old age.

Open e

The open *e* constellation indicates that there is no tension in this area of emotional control, which means simply that emotions can be discharged readily. As in all other open factors, there is an important difference between its occurrence as a constant pattern and its occurrence as the result of a periodic, sudden draining of the factor.

If open *e* is constant, steady mechanisms of discharge are available. Open *e* by itself does not indicate, of course, whether this steady discharge is the result of healthy or neurotic mechanisms; that is, whether it indicates that small amounts of aggression are discharged readily before accumulation induces strong emotional tension, or whether a steady symptom, for example, a psychosomatic symptom formation, achieves the constant discharge. Which one of these two possibilities is responsible for the open *e* cannot be decided without consideration of the complete test profile, or preferably, consideration of the complete test series. A hint aiding differentiation between healthy and neurotic discharge lies in the formation of the open *e;* i.e., whether it is made up of one positive and one negative choice, one choice only, or no choice. No choice may well result from a symptom formation, since discharge so complete that there remains not even the slightest residual tension is unusual.

If the open *e* constellation occurs as part of a changing pattern, i.e., loaded minus *e* constellations alternating with open constellations, some kind of paroxysmal outburst was most probably taking place between the two states. This pattern is also characteristic for real epilepsy, although the change in the *e* factor alone is not enough for diagnosis. Real epilepsy is associated with plus *s* and minus *m* constellations and a weak ego, in addition to its association with the changing *e* constellation.

The pathodiagnostic significance of the open *e* is implied in the general description of this constellation. In addition to the states mentioned above, open *e* is found with relatively high frequency in manic psychosis, a finding which can be understood dynamically on the basis of the motor significance of the *e* factor, discussed above.

The open *e* constellation is not characteristic for any particular age group. In all age groups it occurs in approximately thirty per cent of the subjects, except in old age (around seventy years) when it becomes more frequent. This most probably indicates the constant irritability without control characteristic of old people.

The hy Factor

The second factor within the paroxysmal vector, the *hy* factor, is closely linked to the function of the *e* factor because it also indicates the way in which the person handles his emotions. Nevertheless, the *hy* factor can be considered as an opposite to the *e* factor because the *e* factor expresses the way in which violent emotions, linked with the *s* factor, are handled, while the *hy* factor relates more to emotions corresponding to the *h* factor in the sexual vector. The relationship between epilepsy and hysteria is mentioned more and more in modern psychiatry. In psychopathic hospitals, the diagnosis "hysteroepilepsy" is made rather frequently to indicate that motor seizures resembling epilepsy are believed to be reactions to disturbing emotional experiences. The part emotional experience plays in inducing epileptic seizures is being recognized more and more by psychiatrists. Thus the differentiation between epilepsy and hysteria often becomes a matter of arbitrary decision. It was just this similarity of hysterics to epileptics, in regard to emotional explosiveness accompanied by motor discharge, which led Szondi to categorize hysteria as well as epilepsy in the paroxysmal vector. Since both diseases have in common a certain unpredictability of emotional manifestations, both may be formally characterized as disturbances in the sphere of emotional control.

Of course, the quantitative as well as qualitative difference between emotional explosiveness corresponding to the *hy* and explosiveness corresponding to the *e* factors must be kept in mind as corresponding to the difference in the quality of the emotions in the *h* and the *s* factors, respectively. The finer emotions, oriented toward a love object, find expression through the *hy* factor; and just because the content of the *hy* is this nonaggressive libido, its explosiveness takes place on a quantitatively much smaller scale than that of the *e*. The explosiveness of the *hy* consists of a frequent oscillation in the manner in which affection is displayed; thus, instead of violent paroxysmal outbursts, there is exhibitionistic discharge of smaller amounts of libido.

Within the framework of the theory of the Szondi test, we think of hysteria as depicting the following type of personality structure: either the functional barrier between the inner-personal regions, corresponding to tender emotions of love, and the region of motoric surrounding the personality, is too weak, or the emotions themselves are too strong. In either case, the result is that emotions break through to manifest themselves in visible motor symptoms too easily.

This Lewinian topological representation * is given in figure 7. This topological representation of the person was first developed by Dembo.†

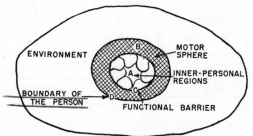

FIG. 7. TOPOLOGICAL REPRESENTATION AFTER LEWIN

Although for purposes of finer analysis one should draw a more detailed topological representation, for our purpose it is adequate to view the personality macroscopically as consisting of two main parts: (a) The innerpersonal regions corresponding to the person's various emotional needs (indicated in figure 7 by the area divided into various smaller areas within the shaded sphere), and (b) The motor sphere which

* Lewin, K.: *Dynamic Theory of Personality,* New York and London, McGraw-Hill Book Company, Inc., 1935.

† Dembo, T.: Der Arger als dynamisches Problem, Psychol. Forsch., 15, 1931.

functions as the region through which the person expresses his needs in a visible form, or in any other form which can be perceived by a person in his environment (indicated in figure 7 by the shaded area). This region is represented as surrounding the person because it functions as the means of communication between the person and his environment. The extent to which needs and emotions can be expressed through the motoric sphere depends upon the strength of the functional barrier (indicated in figure 7 by the circle, c) which we assume to exist between the innerpersonal regions and the motoric sphere. Dynamically, we think of this barrier as built of restraining forces which act on the emotional drives in the direction opposite to overt motor manifestations. Thus the strength of these restraining forces—or in other words, the strength of this functional barrier—decides the extent to which and the way in which emotions are expressed. The interpretative meaning of the *hy* factor centers just on this boundary: on its strength as well as on the qualitative peculiarities of its functioning. Under normal circumstances it is expected that this boundary functions smoothly in a flexible way, permitting the necessary amount of motoric expression of emotions, speech, gestures, and facial expressions belonging to this group of phenomena.

In the case of hysterics, however, there are disturbances in the functioning of this boundary. Because of the weakness of the boundary, or because of the extreme intensity of the emotional drives, the motor expression of emotions takes an exaggerated or distorted form.

We have intended to present here the formal dynamic description of the visible symptomatology of hysteria, without considering, in this context, the genetic origin of these motor symptoms. The apparent overemotionality of hysterics, the unpredictability of their overt emotional reactions, the visible outbursts of positive affects as well as of anxiety and even conversion symptoms, can be described in the above sense as reflecting the erroneous functioning of the motoric-expressive region. In all these instances the motor apparatus is used to express emotions in such a way that it interferes with the rationally purposeful and integrated functioning of the total personality.

Further characteristic for all the hysteric phenomena mentioned above are their exhibitionistic manifestations of emotions. The term "exhibitionist" is used in this context in its broadest literal meaning; namely, to describe one who actually exhibits, i.e., displays, his emotional state to the persons in his environment. In this sense, hysteria is the prototype of an exhibitionistic disturbance. Accordingly—to return to the test interpretation—reactions to the portraits of hysteric patients are presumed to reflect the intensity and quality of the "drive for exhibitionism" as it exists in the subject reacting to these portraits.

Just as all other needs, (or drives) represented by the eight factors in the Szondi test, this "need for exhibitionism" is presumed to be present not only in the psychologically maladjusted, but in all individuals, since the ability to demonstrate one's feelings—at least to a certain extent—is necessary for psychologic adjustment.

Plus hy

Positive reactions to the pictures of hysteric patients indicate that the subject identifies himself with the need to exhibit emotions in a perceptible way. The extent to which this need is socialized depends on the intensity of the plus hy as well as on the constellation of the other factors. In every case a positive hy reaction does indicate that the subject is inclined to be demonstrative emotionally, which inclination should not be confused with the actual intensity and depth of the emotions. There is a negative correlation; namely, that superficial emotions are often those which lead more rapidly to emotional expression than do the more serious emotions. Dembo reaches the same conclusions in regard to the dynamics of discharging emotions in her study * of the experimental creation of anger.

In my experience with the Szondi test, I also found that definite and constant plus *hy* constellations are the reactions of those subjects who, in spite of easy expression of emotions, can still be characterized—in colloquial terms—as having a rather shallow emotional life. It is tempting to draw a parallel of plus "*hy*" with the proportion of C reactions in the Rorschach test, except that I have no quantitative data to support the actual existence of this correlation between plus *hy* constellations and the number of C's. Yet, it seems to me a promising correlation for which to look.

In terms of the scheme of personality represented by fig. 7, a plus *hy* constellation indicates the weakness of the functional barrier between the emotional and the motor regions. The threshold of translation of emotional tension into motor behavior is low. Plus *hy* individuals are able to structure their lives in ways that win them considerable amounts of attention. They enjoy playing roles, and have a definite need for audience, which need often drives them into occupations or professions particularly well suited to satisfy this exhibitionistic, narcissistic need. Professional actors, performing artists, politicians, certain types of organizers, teachers, or the followers of any profession which permits appearance "on stage," can be numbered among those who have found acceptable socialized channels to satisfy the needs implicit in plus *hy*.

For the purpose of clinical diagnosis, the plus *hy* constellation has twofold significance: it is as definite an indication of certain psychopathologic states as it is counterindication of others. Thus, immediately within the group of the various types of hysteria, the plus *hy* constellation can be used as a diagnostic sign in either of the two ways. It frequently

* Dembo, Tamara: *Ibid.*

occurs in conversion hysteria (in about thirty per cent) while
it is practically never found in cases of anxiety hysteria, nor
in hypochondriac anxiety. It is also found relatively frequently in cases of so-called hysteroepilepsy.

These findings support what has been said about the relation of the plus *hy* to the poorly functioning barrier between
the motor and emotional spheres. Any form of conversion
hysteria implies that the motoric (muscle) apparatus functions in an improper way, in which some parts of the muscle
system are used for innervations which have rationally (from
the point of view of conscious, logical thinking) no purpose
whatsoever. In conversion symptoms, such parts of the motor
system are used for the purpose of expressing unconscious
emotional drives which, under normal circumstances, are
used for completely different functions, such as locomotion,
intake of nourishment, breathing, etc. However, due to
improper innervations the organism is inhibited in the exe-
cution of these rational functions and is practically "forced"
by the dynamic strength of the emotions to use the respective organs to exhibit emotions in the form of a symptom
which is usually quite apparent for the outsider even though
its full meaning—what the symptom is expressing in a distorted way—can be understood only by the lengthy process
of psychoanalysis. In ahistoric dynamic terms, such exhibitionistic but irrational motor symptoms are due to the mal-
function of restraining forces on the boundary of the motor
region so that the emotions are expressed in the wrong area.
The frequency of the plus *hy* in conversion hysteria, as well
as in hystero-epileptic seizures, can be understood on the
basis of this dynamic theory.

The lack of plus *hy* in anxiety hysteria and in hypochondriac anxiety follows from the same considerations since
anxiety states are, from this ahistoric point of view, the outcome of the inability to demonstrate affects through the
means of motor discharge which leads to an inner accumula-

tion of affects and to a subjective feeling of tension and anxiety. These are the cases in which the threshold of translation of emotional tension into motor expression is pathologically high. More will be said about this mechanism in connection with the minus *hy* constellation.

From the point of view of development, the plus *hy* occurs most frequently in small children and decreases gradually around prepuberty. Its lowest frequency is reached in puberty and early adolescence. In old age there is again a sudden increase in the frequency of the plus *hy*, resulting in approximately the percentage (22–25 per cent) that occurs in very young children. This curve illustrates the well known fact that in early childhood and in advanced age, emotions are most readily exhibited, while in the long period between these two poles of development one is usually compelled by inner and outer urgings to exert more control in the display of personal feelings.

Minus hy

Negative choices in the *hy* factor indicate that the subject rejects the stimulus material representing exhibitionistic tendencies; thus, minus *hy* is characteristic of those individuals who are either unwilling or unable to demonstrate their feelings in an overtly perceptible way. People who give minus *hy* constellation have some quality of emotional shyness which, however, does not necessarily exclude an intensive emotional life. This correlation—that the serious emotions are less likely to be expressed readily—has been mentioned in connection with the plus *hy*. The functional boundary between the emotional regions and the motor sphere acts—in the case of the minus *hy* constellation—indeed as a barrier blocking emotions from visible manifestations. This emotional control, if it is not too rigid, can be the sign of a well-functioning superego, which has overcome the infantile need for narcissistic, exhibitionistic satisfaction and thus the person is able to live an intensive emotional life without the need to display feelings to an audience. From this description, one can already conclude that the minus *hy* constellation shows a strong correlation with plus *e*, which is actually the case. However, if emotional control is too rigid, there follows—in psychoanalytic terms—repression of the libido, which can lead to a number of neurotic symptoms.

Psychologic characteristics which accompany the minus *hy* constellation include a vivid phantasy life, a tendency for daydreaming, and an ability for playful, "prelogical" thinking. The dynamics of all these traits can be derived from the fact that emotions are not acted out, but rather are felt as an inner, subjective experience.

Here we should re-emphasize the general dynamic principle that denial of a need and indication of this denial by the minus reaction in any factor, does not mean the absolute lack of that need in the personality. On the contrary, it might mean that the need which is denied by the ego or superego is present as a potent unconscious dynamism, inhibited from overt manifestation by some censoring agent. Thus, the minus *hy* constellation does not mean that the person has no need to "exhibit" himself. All these exhibitionistic needs are implied in the minus *hy* as well as in the plus *hy;* however, whereas they are acted out in the plus constellation, they are kept latent by controlling forces in the minus constellation. As a matter of fact, the minus *hy,* more strongly than the plus, indicates that the above needs are of specific dynamic importance in the total structure of the personality just because overt discharge has been denied them.

These apparent paradoxes in the interpretation of single constellations in the Szondi test make interpretation of the test so complex a psychologic process. The interpreter must be familiar with the equally paradoxical dynamics of the unconscious, which ignores the rules of logical thinking in its use of the same symbol to signify one thing and its opposite simultaneously. The fact that the Szondi test reflects the subject's emotional reactions at this level of deeply unconscious ambivalence makes it an instrument unique among the various psycho-diagnostic procedures, but it limits the number of individuals who are able to make maximum use of the diagnostic possibilities of this instrument.

Returning to the interpretation of the minus *hy* constellation: if the constellation is loaded (four or more choices in minus direction), we interpret it as an indication that the person does have strong exhibitionistic drives which are frustrated. The more loaded the minus *hy* is, the more probable it is that exhibitionism is apparent in actual behavior in some distorted form, although the loaded minus constellation is a definite sign that whatever manifestations break through are inadequate to relieve frustration in the subject.

The minus *hy* constellation is generally more frequently obtained than the plus. The psychodiagnostic groups for which it is particularly characteristic are homosexuality (many times only latent, but felt as dynamically strong homosexual drives), anxiety hysteria, states of diffuse anxiety, phobia and hypochondriac anxiety. In children, it can occur in pseudologia phantastica. The lowest frequency of the minus *hy* constellation occurs in conversion hysteria.

The dynamic relation of the minus *hy* constellation to the various forms of anxiety has been mentioned in the discussion of the infrequency of these symptoms in cases of plus *hy*. This relation of repression of libido to anxiety was the core of Freud's first theory of anxiety, and fits in very well with the experimental findings in the Szondi test that the most common indication of anxiety is a strong minus *hy* reaction. The frequency of minus *hy* in homosexuals is not quite easy to understand. It most probably reflects the neurotic anxiety characteristic for homosexuals. It also might be due to the fact that homosexuals actually never dare really to "show" themselves. Primary guilt feelings because of the forbidden |

yet dynamic incestuous drives—the original cause of homo-sexuality—as well as secondary guilt feelings resulting from general social disapproval, might all be reflected in the minus *hy*.

The fact that the minus *hy* is rarely found in conversion hysteria can be understood on the basis of what has been said about the relation of conversion symptoms to plus *hy* constellations. The high threshold of expression of emotional tension through motor symptoms in minus *hy*—in contrast to the low threshold in plus *hy*—prevents the formation of excessive muscle innervations characteristic of conversion hysteria.

The frequency of minus *hy* is fairly constant in the various age groups, except that it occurs rather rarely in very young children (three to five years), and reaches its highest frequency in prepuberty and puberty.

Plus-minus hy

The interpretation of this *hy* constellation can be deduced by combining what has been said about the plus and the minus *hy* constellations. As in all ambi-equal reactions, the plus minus *hy* constellation reflects subjectively experienced conflict and tension in the individual. In this case it reflects conflict in those who cannot resolve to conceal or disclose their feelings. However, in the *hy* factor this subjective experiencing of the two opposite tendencies appears to be satisfactorily resolved more readily than it is, for example, in the *e* factor. In this respect the plus-minus *hy* can be compared to the plus-minus *s* pattern, even in its fields of sublimation. In both factors, various fields of artistic sublimation serve as adequate outlets for the tension implied in the ambivalent factorial reaction. And even in those plus-minus *hy* subjects for whom art is not the main field of work, one can often find a tendency for some sort of exhibitionistic extravagance (not in the pathological meaning of the word), in the form of hobbies, mannerisms in the general conduct of life, choice of clothing, etc.

The clinical implications of the plus-minus *hy* lie mainly in the realm of neuroses. Its relatively highest frequency occurs in compulsion neurosis, most probably as a result of the basic ambivalence characteristic for compulsive subjects, and as a reflection of the frequent mannerisms of compulsive characters.

The distribution of plus-minus *hy* throughout the various age groups is fairly even, showing some fluctuation, between the frequency values, of about fifteen to twenty per cent. Thus, the occurrence of this *hy* constellation is found to be generally about half the frequency of the minus *hy*. The one age group in which plus-minus *hy* is relatively least frequent (about ten per cent) is young adulthood, between the ages of twenty and thirty. The decrease in this age group is due to the increase in pure plus and pure minus *hy* patterns, indicating that subjects of this age take more definite stands in regard to the manner in which they direct their libido than do subjects in younger or older age groups.

Open hy

The draining of the *hy* factor means that the person's needs to give some perceptible manifestation of his libido is being lived out—at least for the time being. Since, more than are any of the other factors, the *hy* factor is particularly prone to show variations from one test administration to the next, usually in the form of draining under the influence of momentary experiences, generalizations about its "open" constellation are particularly hard to make. And even in those cases where the open *hy* constellation appears as a consistent feature of a series of test profiles, it is more difficult to characterize in general terms than are the same constellations in other factors because of the variety of ways exhibitionistic needs can appear in surface behavior. The one interpretation valid for all cases of open *hy* is that something is being acted out: whether this indicates the uninhibited acting out of libidinal feelings towards the actual love-object, or whether it indicates the acting out of compulsive ceremonies in an exhibitionistic way, cannot be decided from the *hy* factor alone. In any case, individuals giving constant open *hy* constellations do not exercise strong control over their emotions and are likely to show their emotional reactions to outside experiences quickly. Even within the range of "normality," they are usually what can be called "hysteroid" individuals.

From the foregoing it follows that the open *hy* constellation can be found in a variety of clinical groups. Its greatest percentual frequency is found in manic psychosis and in antisocial, emotionally unstable psychopathic personalities, including criminals. Freedom in acting out drives and lack of emotional control are characteristic of all these subjects.

Among neurotics, the open *hy* is found relatively most frequently—although to lesser degree than in the psychotic and psychopathic first mentioned groups—in compulsive neurotics. The hypothesis that in these cases it is the exhibitionistic acting out of compulsive rituals and ceremonies which drains the tension in the *hy* factor has been mentioned previously.

The open *hy* constellation is least frequent in anxiety hysteria. It is frequent in small children, up to the beginning of the latency period, when it becomes the rarest of all the four main *hy* constellations. It becomes again more frequent in adolescence and shows a slow increase throughout the years, reaching about the same frequency in old age as it has in young children.

P Vectorial Constellations

In the following the most important combinations of the constellations in the *e* and the *hy* factors will be characterized briefly. As in the case of the *S* vector, I shall have to limit myself to the presentation of those *P* vectorial constellations which correspond to the most clearly distinguishable types of personality. Thus it is hoped that on the basis of a few "basic" *P* vectorial constellations the remaining variations can be deduced. The order of presentation will follow the degree to which the constellations lend themselves to clear-cut personality characterizations.

Plus e *with minus* hy

Concurrence of the plus *e* with the minus *hy* forms the most controlled *P* vectorial constellation. The plus *e,* as well as the minus *hy,* indicates that emotions are controlled strictly, precluding any exhibitionistic display. Of the sixteen possible configurations in the *P* vector, that is, of all the possible combinations of the two factors in four directions, this configuration indicates the strongest superego, which is the same as saying that the plus *e* and minus *hy* vectorial pattern is characteristic for ethical individuals and is the most definite sign on the profile against any form of antisocial or criminal behavior. Plus *e* alone, as well as minus *hy* alone, is indication against criminality, but alone neither of them excludes it to the degree of certainty to which it is excluded when these two constellations appear as parts of the same *P* vectorial configuration. The plus *e,* minus *hy* configuration is given often by religious individuals, or by those who show particularly strong interest in problems of general social welfare. Emotions are felt strongly, but are not easily expressed by subjects in this category.

If this configuration shows inflexibility by remaining unchanged within a series of ten profiles, it is a sign of an emotional control too rigid and indicates a compulsive character.

Among the various psychoses, the plus *e,* minus *hy* configuration is found most frequently in catatonic schizophrenia. The psychodynamics underlying this empirical finding have been mentioned in connection with the plus *e* constellation. A conceivable causal connection was hypothesized between the extreme strength of the functional barrier between the emotional and the motor regions and the development of catatonic schizophrenia. Of all the *P* vectorial constellations, plus *e* and minus *hy* represent the greatest disability to discharge emotional tensions through the motor apparatus. Further findings that agitated forms of catatonic schizophrenia are not found in this *P* vectorial group support the theory.

The fact that this is the most frequent *P* vectorial configuration in conversion hysteria and in cases of well structured phobic anxiety (the expression "well structured" being here used as the opposite of "free-floating") can be understood also on the basis of the strict superego and the difficulty in regard to free motoric discharge of tension. The differential diagnostic signs between catatonic schizophrenics and the two forms of neuroses mentioned above can be found in the *Sch* vector. While the strict control over emotional manifestations result in a similar configuration in the *P* vector, the additional sign of plus *k* (autism) appears in conjunction with catatonic symptoms, whereas neurotic conversion or phobic symptoms go with minus *k* as indication of the basic repression in the ego.

The plus *e*, minus *hy* is a typically adult constellation and if found in children is a sign of precocious development of the superego. It is one of the most frequent *P* configurations in adolescents and adults up to the age of approximately sixty, after which there is a sudden drop in its frequency until, in old age, it is even less frequent (about six per cent) than it is in children.

Minus e *with plus* hy

The minus *e*, plus *hy* constellation opposes the plus *e*, minus *hy* constellation in visible configuration as well as in its psychodynamic meaning. The minus e component indicates the tendency to accumulate aggressive tension without any positive mechanism of control, and the plus hy component indicates the tendency for exhibitionistic discharge of emotions. In other words, portraits of epileptics are rejected with a simultaneous liking for portraits of hysterics by people who generally tend to direct their emotions in an antisocial way.

In the whole test there is not a single other vectorial configuration—in none of the four vectors, with all their sixteen constellations—in which I would feel as justified to reach conclusions containing so many ethical value-judgments as I do in the case of plus $e,$ minus hy configuration and its opposite.

Individuals with minus $e,$ plus hy configuration are little concerned with the way their actions affect others, and generally—even if within socialized limits—they belong to the type of "go-getter" whose main concern is his own egotistic advantage. These characteristics are particularly obvious if the minus $e,$ plus hy configuration appears concurrently with the plus s and plus d constellations on a profile in which there is no minus $k.$

The general occurrence of the minus $e,$ plus hy configuration is about half the frequency of the opposing plus $e,$ minus hy configuration. Its pathodiagnostic significance lies in the realm of antisocial forms of behavior, whether in the form of criminality or in other forms of psychopathology. In its highest frequency it is found in murderers and other types of overtly aggressive criminals, in manic psychotics, in epileptics near seizure, and in agitated cases of general paresis. Antisocial and impulsive motor excitability is the common dynamic characteristic of all these groups.

The minus $e,$ plus hy configuration is rare in neurotics, since the strength of the superego—even though unwanted in part by the neurotic person—is usually a dynamic precondition for the symptom formation of various neuroses. It might be found in asocial, hysteroid characters.

In its relatively greatest frequency this *P* vectorial constellation is found in old age. The only other age group in which this constellation figures as one of the four most frequent *P* vector configurations is early childhood, under the age of six.

This parallel in the frequencies of certain constellations in young children and in old age, must have been obvious throughout our discussion. To a certain extent it can be considered as validating interpretations associated with the various factor and vector constellations because of the psychodynamic consistency implied in these symmetrical distribution curves. This distribution most probably is due to the fact that each factor of the test can express the presence or the lack of a controlling mechanism, either self-regulating or of some other type, depending on the specific direction of the factors. Further, we know from other studies of genetic psychology, as well as from clinical observations, that early childhood and old age are dynamically similar in their relative lack of such controls in behavior.

Minus e *with minus* hy

Unlike the *S* vector, in which both factors forming constellations in the same direction represent fusion between two related but opposite drives, constellations in the same direction in the *P* vector express just the opposite; namely, simultaneous existence of emotional control indicated in one factor with the lack of control indicated in the other factor. The reason for this discrepancy in the interpretation of the *S* and *P* vectorial configurations lies in the fact that while the primary interpretations of the two factors in the *S* vector —the basic drives represented by the *h* and *s* photographs— are the basic id-drives themselves, in the *P* vector the stimulus material of one of the two factors, the *e*, represents not the basic id-drive in its original form, but in a form representing the superego's control over the particular drive. Accordingly, in the P vector the previous vectorial configurations represent unified ways of handling emotions, whether in a socially positive or negative way, while constellations in which both factors are in minus or both in plus directions represent self-contradictory, conflicting ways of handling emotional drives.

In the case of the minus e, minus hy configuration, violent emotions accumulate in potential readiness for an outburst (minus e). However, the actual discharge of these emotions is barred, or at least delayed, by the controlling function of the minus hy, which acts as a barrier against any exhibitionistic display of emotions. As a consequence of these conflicting tendencies the whole emotional sphere is tense and is experienced subjectively as free-floating, diffuse anxiety. The more constant this P vectorial configuration proves to be within a series of ten profiles, the more is this subjectively experienced discomfort. Actually, more frequently than not, the tension implied in the minus e, minus hy configuration does find some outlet during the course of administration of a series of ten profiles which then is indicated by the draining, or at least relative draining, of the whole vector.

Clinically, this constellation is a well-known sign for all those diagnostic groups which imply the presence of diffuse anxiety. Characteristic of such diffuse anxiety is the individual's inability to project his anxiety on one specific object or one specific exigency he fears; rather, he talks vaguely about fears of death, or insanity, or other disintegrative catastrophes. Since the minus e, minus hy configuration in the P vector appears most frequently with the plus h, plus s configuration in the S vector, the fear most probably is concerned many times with the danger of a socially undesirable break-through of sexual and aggressive impulses. Or it might indicate the "drive anxiety" as described by Anna Freud,* which means that the person feels uncomfortable

* Freud, Anna: The Ego and the Mechanisms of Defense. London, Hogarth Press, 1937.

and anxious from experiencing his own impulses, which does not necessarily imply that discharge of the drive would result in antisocial behavior. In such cases the patient is afraid of nothing but his own id.

In children the constellation in the *S* and the *P* vectors described above is often indicative of masturbation anxiety and ensuing guilt-feelings. The minus *e*, minus *hy* configuration is the most frequent *P* vectorial configuration of adult stutterers, another group for whom unresolved emotional tension is characteristic.

This constellation occurs often in many kinds of delinquencies, and even in severe crimes. However, in the latter there is a tendency for periodical draining in the *P* vector. Thus the criminal act itself could be considered as a dynamic consequence of the extreme panic-stricken tension implied in the loaded minus *e*, minus *hy* configuration. In other instances one might wonder whether the psychodynamic significance of committing an antisocial act is release of an existing emotional tension, or rather the creation of a situation which realistically justifies the previously existing but apparently irrational fears. According to my own experience with children referred to me from the juvenile court, the latter is often the case.

The minus *e*, minus *hy* configuration occurs most frequently in childhood up to adolescence. It decreases in frequency until it reaches approximately the sixty year age group, then increases again. However, it does not again reach the frequency with which it appears in childhood (about twenty per cent.)

Plus e *with plus* hy

The plus *e*, plus *hy* configuration is generally a rarely occurring *P* configuration, its frequency of occurrence in an average population being about one-fourth of the frequency of the minus *e*, minus *hy* constellation. However, the distinct emotional peculiarities corresponding to this configuration justify its separate characterization.

It resembles the minus e, minus hy P vectorial constellation in the concurrence of emotional control in one component and lack of control in the other. However, it differs in the quality of the emotional tension resulting from these contradictory tendencies in regard to the way emotions are directed, since there is a more genuine control of aggression indicated by the presence of the plus e component. Thus in this configuration there is the tendency for emotional exhibitionism implied in the plus hy component, the antisocial use of which is prevented by the superego (plus e). The outcome of this constellation of forces is experienced as emotional inflation, exhibitionistic drives are let through but only in the service of socially acceptable goals. Individuals giving this P vectorial configuration are usually overly kind and charming in an exhibitionistic way. They spend much of their time expressing and taking interest in emotions. They like to be good and helpful, and they are careful that other people notice their goodness.

The plus e, plus hy configuration is not characteristic of any particular clinical group. It is a complex emotional pattern yielded by "hysteroid" individuals usually, however, without any definite symptom formation. It appears that the ability to act out emotional drives prevents these formations. Further, antisocial behavior seems to be prevented by the control of the plus e component.

The distribution of the plus e, plus hy configuration throughout the various age groups shows exactly a curve opposite to that of the minus e, minus hy configuration. It is most frequent in adulthood and in late adolescence, less frequent in old age, and least frequent in children.

Plus-minus e *with plus-minus* hy

The plus-minus e, plus-minus hy constellation contains as components all the configurations discussed above. One could call this the most ambivalent of all emotional patterns, since it contains all the components indicative of emotional control (plus *e* with minus *hy*) as well as those indicative of readiness for an aggressive and exhibitionistic emotional outburst (minus *e* with plus *hy*). This unresolved tension is subjectively experienced as an extremely uncomfortable situation. Yet, because of the existence of the controlling mechanisms in this configuration, discharge of tension through explosive outbursts is less likely to occur than it is in the case of minus *e* with minus *hy*. Consequently, the present *P* configuration is not characteristic for delinquents or criminals, or for antisocial psychotic behavior. Generally it is among the rarest *P* configurations; it occurs even less frequently throughout the general population than does the plus *e,* plus *hy* vectorial patterns. Its highest frequency occurs in adult stutterers; its second highest frequency, in compulsive neurotics.

There is only one age group in which the plus-minus *e*, plus-minus *hy* vectorial pattern figures as one of the four most frequent *P* patterns; and that is in seventeen to eighteen year old adolescents. In this group it most probably reflects the emotional conflict resulting from the adolescent's search for the limits to which drives should be expressed or inhibited, a characteristic problem of this age.

Open e *with* Open hy

The draining of both factors in the *P* vector indicates momentary lack of tension in the area of emotional control. It is even more difficult than it is in cases of other constellations to describe an open *e,* open *hy* configuration alone, since usually it occurs within a series as the result of a sudden emotional outburst. However, in those cases in which the open *e,* open *hy* is a consistent constellation within a series of ten profiles, it has to be interpreted as a sign that emotions are lived out without difficulty. The boundary illustrated in figure 7 as functioning on the edge of the emotional sphere does not function as a barrier in subjects yielding a steady open e, open hy vectorial pattern, but permits emotions to drift through easily. Subjects in this P vectorial category are likely to react to everyday experiences in an "emotional" way, expressing emotional reactions through gestures, intonation of voice, etc., quickly. They may be easily irritated without, however, letting anger accumulate to a high pitch. Their lack of ability to control emotions, even in situations in which control is required, they often experience subjectively as a feeling of helplessness. Moreover, the flood of emotions resulting from the laxity of the boundary around emotional regions may handicap sustained intellectual concentration.

The open e, open hy configuration is frequent in both extremes of manic-depressive psychoses, but it is most frequent in the manic stage. It also has been found rather frequently in early childhood stuttering. Among criminals, this constellation appears twice as frequently as it does throughout the average population, of whom five per cent yield open e with open hy.

This P vectorial constellation is distributed fairly evenly throughout the age groups, occurring with relatively highest frequency in old age.

In the following chapter I shall digress in the order of presentation of the single factors from the order as indicated on the test profile. Instead of discussing the Sch vector, which on the profile follows the P vector, we will consider the interpretation of the two factors of the C vector and leave the discussion of the Sch vector for later. The reason for this order of presentation is that the Sch vector reflects the structure of the ego, which in some way represents the resultant of all the partial drives corresponding to the other six factors. The way this elaboration of drives through the ego is taking place will be discussed in connection with the Sch vector.

CHAPTER IX

The Contact Vector

Originally the *C* designation of the Contact vector was intended to indicate the group of circular psychoses which in the terminology of European psychiatry comprises the manic-depressive manic and manic-depressive depressive forms of psychoses, and includes what is known as melancholia.

However, the more was learned about the interpretation of this vector, the more Szondi was inclined to call it contact vector, since choice-reactions to pictures of manic-depressive patients represent psychologically the subject's attitudes toward the objects (in the psychoanalytic sense of object of libido) of the environment or, in other words, the subject's contact with reality.

In interpreting the two factors of this vector, the *d* and the *m,* we make more use of psychoanalytic concepts—mainly those in regard to pregenital "component" impulses of anal and oral drives—than we did in interpreting any of the other vectors. The reader is referred to those works of Freud * and Abraham † which contain their theories concerning the significance of the pregenital phases of sexuality in regard to the later character formation of the individual.

* Freud, Sigmund: Three Contributions to the Theory of Sex. New York, Nerv. and Ment. Dis. Pub. Co., 1910. Character and Anal Erotism. Collected Papers, Vol. II, 1929. The Predisposition to Obsessional Neuroses. Collected Papers, Vol. II.

† Abraham, Karl: Selected Papers. Hogarth Press, Inst. Psychoanalytic Library Series, No. 13, 1927.

The d *Factor*

Reactions to pictures of depressive patients are assumed to be related to those features of the personality which can be traced back to the specific way in which the subject has passed through the anal phase of psychosexual development. Thus, in interpreting the *d* factor, personality traits which are known in psychoanalytic literature as "anal characteristics" primarily will be mentioned. Anal characteristics refer mostly to certain types of the individual's object-relationships: that is, to his attitudes toward the objects of his environment. Possessiveness, orderliness, pedantry, and parsimony are among the most frequently listed anal character traits. The typically anal aspect of object relationship centers in the problem of retention or surrender of objects, and in the person's reaction to the loss of a libidinously cathected object.

To establish a psychologic relationship between character traits like those listed above to the child's early anal functions is difficult enough, yet it is an easier task than to establish an acceptable hypothesis which relates this whole group of traits to the reaction of liking or disliking photographic portraits of depressive patients.

The relationship between certain aspects of the personality and various stages of the psychosexual development was first observed and described by Freud, and was later supported and elaborated by Ferenczi, Abraham, and others. Freud found in his patients that those who in their childhood have particularly strong and long-lasting interest in their excretory processes develop later into the so-called "anal characters." The link between the two phases is established through the assumption that the child cathects his own feces positively, considering it as part of himself, as something he owns, and over which he can exert will and power. This hypothesis is supported by published case histories as well as by case histories of individuals whom I have observed.

The stage of frustration, or feeling of deprivation, which interferes with the primitive narcissistic enjoyment of being the sole master of one's own excretory processes begins with the sphincter training imposed upon the child by adults of his environment. This is the period in the child's maturation in which, depending on the force or persuasion through which he becomes aware of sphincter control, basic attitudes towards handling possessions and towards discipline in general develop.

On the basis of psychoanalytic experience one can assume that the narcissistic, emotional overestimation of the feces in childhood is transferred, through unconscious mechanisms of symbolization and displacement, to other objects of the environment representing real values. For later character formation, the unconscious identifying of feces with money, gifts, and valuables in general is of great importance. Those for whom the learning of sphincter control in childhood was a psychologically traumatic experience are most likely to develop in their later life irrational feelings in regard to anything they possess, either in overestimating or in underestimating the significance of tangible objects. The specific experience which acts traumatically on these individuals is the compulsion under which they *had* to give up something which belonged to them—their feces—at the request of others. This traumatic experience may result in personality characteristic of being unable to give up objects, or trying to compensate for the loss of the primary, libidinously cathected object by hoarding or avidly accumulating possessions.

In interpreting the Szondi test we assume that symptoms of depression are likely to develop in those individuals who are characteristically "anal." The psychologic link between depression and anal characteristics is the constant anxiety of depressive patients in regard to remote possibilities of losing money or of running out of whatever supplies are of particular importance to them. This anxiety is well-known to any clinician who ever worked with depressive patients who must have more than they need, and who fear loss even in the case of overabundance.

According to our interpretation, the *d* portraits in the Szondi test reflect this tight, worrying attachment to objects, a reaction formation to the trauma of the loss of the "primary" object of libido. The psychodynamics of depression as a reaction to the loss of an object is described in detail in Freud's *Mourning and Melancholia.** There he differentiates between the psychologically normal process of mourning and the pathologic symptoms of depression (melancholia), which—on the surface—differ mainly in the length of time the symptoms of depression can be observed. The additional premise needed to fill out the gap still existing between the interpretation of anal characteristics and the reactions to portraits of depressive patients is that pathologically long-lasting symptoms of depression following loss of a love-object occur in individuals who have shown typically anal characteristics prior to their manifest illness. A particularly strong, "sticky," attachment to the love object whose loss elicited the depressive symptoms is assumed. Furthermore this typically anal tenacity of the libido is presumed to have developed genetically from early childhood experiences constituting the foundation of the development of anal character traits.

Another possibility—which takes the constitutional elements of the personality more into consideration—is that, irrespective of any specific traumas which occur during training of sphincter control, and irrespective of the type of discipline experienced, certain individuals will develop anal characteristics. In these individuals one assumes a constitutionally determined inclination to develop just these and no other characteristics, so that incidents in sphincter training

* Freud, Sigmund: Mourning and Melancholia. Collected Papers, Vol. IV, 1925.

merely strengthen constitutionally predetermined, or heredi-
tary, patterns of reaction. Such persons, presumed to be
"traumatophyl" by constitution, would have abstracted characteristic traumatic experiences for themselves no matter
what treatment they received from their environment. The
same idea is expressed in Freud's theory concerning the
significance of what he called complimentary series, which
assigns to heredity a role more important in the formation
of various neuroses than one would assume from reading
some of the more recent psychoanalytic literature.

Plus d

A positive reaction in the *d* factor is indication that the
subject identifies himself with anal characteristics. Thus the
following features of the individual's object-relationships can
be interpreted on the basis of a plus *d* reaction: there is a
strong need for concrete objects which implies that real
objects are highly estimated, and there is a general interest
in outside reality as the source of all material things. This
realistic, extrovert interest which results from the high value
attached to real objects, necessarily accompanies a tendency
actively to manipulate and pursue objects, which reveals
the close link between the plus *s* and plus *d* characteristics.
This relationship can be anticipated by what is known about
the usual coexistence of anal and sadistic character traits.
The basis for this close association is not quite clear, although
several hypotheses can be made. From the point of view of
the correlation between the plus *s* and the plus *d* reactions in
the test, it is enough to point out that both the sadistic
impulses (the physically active, manipulative drive implied
in the plus *s*) and the anal type of object relationship (implied
in the plus *d*) have in common the tendency to control
objects. Actually these traits are quite typical for subjects
with a steady plus *d* reaction. Of course this basic tendency
to control objects can have a variety of manifestations,

depending on other factors. It might take the form of antisocial aggression in some individuals (in conjunction with
plus or open *s,* minus *e,* and minus *m* patterns) as well as
pedantry, orderliness, or scientific attempts to force things
into a system (in conjunction with a minus *h* plus *k* or plus
p and plus *m,* associated with the plus *d.*) In other instances,
the anal tendencies of plus *d* find expression in such sublimated interests as collections (stamps, books, coins, etc.) or
professions systematizing and criticizing works of others.
The author's unpublished study on various groups of creative and performing artists (cited previously in connection
with the *s* factor) showed that plus *d* was by far most common
among sculptors, next among painters, and least common
among musicians. These data bear out the earlier findings
of psychoanalysts who concluded that interest in molding and
sculpting can be traced to the infantile anal pleasure of
smearing.

Other character traits which can be deduced from the specific "adhesive" quality of the libido in anal personalities,
and are characteristic of the plus *d* constellation, are general
possessiveness, tendency for rivalry, and a persistence in
reaching a goal which might even lead to obstinacy. Dispo-
sition for depressive mood is indicated by the plus *d,* probably because the loss of possessions is experienced as a constant potential danger.

Accordingly, the plus *d* constellation is found with greatest
frequency, among diagnostic groups, in depression. As has
been said, it also frequently occurs in antisocial individuals.
The plus *d* and the open *d* are the two most frequent *d*
factorial constellations in the general population. The frequency of plus "d" constellation reaches its peak in the
seven to eight year old group and in extremely advanced
age. Its frequency in seven or eight year old children
coincides with the period when collecting various objects
becomes generally important to them. A deeper interpre-

tation of this phenomenon suggests that this is the age when children start to lose their strong attachment to their mother, for which emotional loss the accumulation of various concrete objects might serve as a substitute. Incidentally, this dynamic interpretation of the searching, collecting quality of the plus *d* in children is presumed to hold for plus *d* in general.

Minus d

It has been found that portraits of depressive patients are disliked by subjects who refuse to identify themselves with the anal type of possessive and aggressive object relationship described in connection with the plus *d* reaction. The adhesive quality of the libido cathexis, which is a typically anal characteristic, holds for any loaded *d* reaction, plus as well as minus, or plus-minus. However, there is a great difference between the evaluation of material objects in plus *d* and in minus *d* individuals. Minus *d* reaction indicates that the attachment to the primary object has not been surrendered, hence the individual depreciates the other concrete, material objects. Subjects in this *d* category are likely to be extremely loyal to the object once cathected with libido. They stick to their love object disregarding the realistic possibilities of whether or not they can reach their goal. This attitude makes them generally more idealistic and less practical than individuals with plus *d*. In this sense, minus *d* subjects are the real "conservatives" who shrink from innovations and changes because they are not able or willing to invest their libido in new objects. They could also be characterized as generally passive in their object relationship, since somehow cathecting the object, without motor efforts to secure the object, is all they seem to care for. The correlation between minus *d* and minus *s* is indicated by this common feature of physical passivity, as well as by the finding that both minus *s* and minus *d* patterns are reactions

more common in women than in men. Reverse correlation
of these two factors on the profile, for example plus s with
minus d, are interesting problems for interpretation since
they indicate a contradiction inherent in the subject's personality in regard to aggressively (or only actively) goal-
directed behavior. Such persons usually impress others as
being "aggressive," while they conceal an underlying passive
fixation on a love-object by this surface activity.

At this point in our discussion, more complex combinations or factorial constellations can be inserted briefly to
illustrate the reasoning implied in interpretation. The
most difficult question associated with the minus d constellation is the nature of the "primary" object of libido. In
its deepest meaning, the term probably refers to the mother;
however, for the purpose of interpreting the minus d reaction in the Szondi test, this basic interpretation is not
inclusive enough. Even though this interpretation may
always be at the bottom of every minus d reaction, on the
behavior level individuals with minus d often display
extreme adhesiveness to objects or ideas which—at least on
the surface—do not seem to relate to the mother or to any
obvious mother image. From the point of view of test
interpretation it is not necessary to trace the links which,
through various processes of symbolization and displacement, finally might reveal the connection between the
original mother fixation and objects cathected with almost
the same intensity in the individual's later life. All that
need be remembered in interpreting the minus d reaction
is that it indicates strong attachment to one particular object
or one idea, in contrast to the desire to possess many objects,
characteristic of individuals associated with plus d reaction.

Since anal characteristics have been mentioned throughout our discussion of the d factor, and since the symbolic
role of money for anal characters is so widely recognized in
psychoanalysis, something ought to be said about the signifi-

cance of money in individuals associated with plus d and minus d reactions respectively. Superficially, stinginess or overestimation of money as such appears to be characteristic of individuals associated with the plus d reaction. However, clinging to money, paradoxically, is more characteristic of those giving minus d. Plus d subjects are active in seeking ways to earn money primarily as a means to secure other objects, and may even resort to ruthlessness in the search. However, since the pursuit of money is not the interest of individuals associated with minus d, it is all the more difficult for them to part with the money they have on hand. (The possibility that the minus d subject cathects money itself, with all the adhesiveness of his libido, is not excluded).

There are other apparent paradoxes, in minus d subject's relationship to material objects. For example, even though he is indifferent to the accumulation of wealth he may feel a personal deprivation amounting to trauma if he is forced to separate from an object, even more so than a typically plus "d" person. In spite of characteristic hoarding, a plus d subject probably is aware of his ability to replace materials. On the other hand, sentimental attachment to an object may make the minus d subject inconsolable at its loss.

I have discussed this one specific problem because of the apparent inconsistency which is at first impression inherent in it. The relationship of the minus d to the subject's attitude toward money was one of those most puzzling problems in the Szondi test in which pragmatic knowledge preceded by far a theoretical understanding of the phenomenon, and only recently have I been able even to this extent to formulate a theory which helps to reconcile results which formerly seemed contradictory.

Among the various diagnostic groups, the minus d occurs most frequently in hypochondria and in paranoid schizophrenia. This constellation seldom occurs in psychotic depression. In its relation to social behavior, minus d

can be taken as an attribute to ethical behavior because of the idealism and nonaggressive behavior implied in its dynamics.

Among the various age groups, the minus *d* constellation occurs most frequently in adults between twenty and forty. It is most uncommon in children between seven and nine, when the plus *d* reaction prevails.

Plus-minus d

Since plus-minus reactions are by definition always loaded reactions, they reflect tension in the particular area in which they occur. The plus-minus *d* constellation indicates strong and subjectively experienced tension in the area of object relationship. There is ambivalence in regard to looking for more and new objects or to clinging to the old ones. Under all circumstances object relationship as such is an important problem for individuals yielding a plus-minus *d* constellation, and the observable signs through which this problem becomes noticeable to others in their environment is that much of their conversation is centered in their present and past relationship to various persons. In spite of their great need for intensive attachment and loyalty to one person (minus *d*), they have a tendency constantly to get involved in new relationships which might thwart the continuation of relationships they have established (plus *d*). The result is that most of the time they feel insecure in regard to the permanence of any of their object-relations, which in turn is the cause for a general feeling of indecision.

The tension indicated by the loading of the plus-minus *d* reaction explains why all these subjects can be described as anal characters, while the ambivalent attitude implied in the plus-minus direction accounts for the existence of apparently contradictory anal personality characteristics. The subject reveals this general ambivalence by such fluctuating traits as generosity with money in some matters and stinginess in others; exaggeration in self-esteem coupled to feelings of inferiority; inconsistent idealism and materialism; self will and defiance coupled to compliance and conformity, and concurrent desires for privacy and association with large groups. A number of other inconsistencies in the overt behavior of subjects with plus-minus *d* reaction could be listed. Quite characteristic of them are constant plans to start something new: to move to a new place, to seek a new career, etc. These steps may or may not be carried out, but even when they are, the surrender of the previous status is slow and is experienced as a painful process. Thus the plus-minus *d* constellation gives a certain heaviness to the personality which handicaps easy locomotion in the life-space. Yet, from the point of view of any serious pathology, the plus-minus *d* seems to be rather a favorable constellation, most probably because of the self-regulatory function inherent in the plus-minus reaction. The extent to which an ambivalent reaction indicates conflict in the negative sense of the term, and to which it indicates a balance between opposing forces, is a problem common to all the plus-minus reactions. In the case of the plus-minus *d* constellation, these two possibilities seem to resolve into a rather difficult type of personality structure which counteracts, nevertheless, the development of serious forms of pathology.

Accordingly the plus-minus *d* pattern is not particularly characteristic for any of the usual diagnostic categories. It is found relatively most frequently in epileptics, which may account for the general slowness and "stickiness" of the epileptic character. Among the various groups of criminals and delinquents, this constellation occurs most frequently in petty thieves. The fact that even though they are antisocial, these persons refrain from committing more serious forms of crimes (robbery for instance) may be due to the moderating effect of the minus *d*.

Plus-minus d is the least frequent d factorial constellation in the general population. Its maximum frequency, fifteen per cent, is found in the youngest group of children who can be tested, the three to four year olds. This is the age in which occurs the first real crisis in object relationship, the period when the ambivalence towards the parents due to the Oedipus situation reaches its maximum. After this period the occurrence of plus-minus d decreases and does not reach a frequency even of ten per cent until the 70–80 year age group, in which it occurs in about twelve to thirteen per cent of the cases.

Open d

The open d reaction indicates lack of tension in the area of object-relationship; in other words, the problem of whether to hold on to old objects or to search for new is not particularly important to subjects yielding open d. However, the fact that "anal" aspects of object relationship are not important to these individuals does not deny the importance of the object from the point of view of an "oral" type of object relationship. Oral object relationship will be discussed in connection with the m factor.

In common with all other open reactions, open d is the most difficult d factorial constellation to characterize in terms of behavior because of the variety of ways in which discharge of actual tension can be achieved. It suggests a generally loose kind of object relationship, in which one object can be substituted for another rather easily. The subject himself usually does not make any particular effort to secure a certain object, but is inclined, rather, to cathect those objects which are easily available. In contrast to the "heaviness" of the plus-minus d reaction, open d has something of an easy-going quality because the person does not feel the need to accumulate objects or to exert much effort to keep the object under control. In certain cases this type of object relationship can be characterized as apathetic rather than easy-going. It might be found after the actual loss of a real object, in which case it reflects a lack of concern and an indifference in regard to objects in general. Thus, if the rest of the test profile shows certain configuration open *d* can even mean an actual state of depression; however, only in the apathetic sense described above, which is quite different from the tense and anxious worrying depression characteristic for the plus *d*. This apathetic loss of interest in outside objects occurs more frequently in incipient catatonic states than in real psychotic depression. In other instances, if the general configuration of the test profile shows signs of good adjustment, open *d* can indicate good possibilities for intellectual or artistic sublimation since the person is not tied down through his concern with material objects, but can freely devote himself to nonmaterialistic interests. A possible relationship between tendency for depression and artistic creativity can be mentioned in this context; although exploration of the theoretical implications of the relationship lies beyond the framework of this manual.* A series of articles by Dr. Harry B. Lee, dealing with the problem of artistic creativity, elaborates in detail the above hypothesis.†

In some cases, complete lack of tension in the psychologic area corresponding to the *d* factor is caused by the fact that important components of the early childhood analerotism have not been absorbed, by various processes of transformation, into personality characteristics, but still

---

* The data of the author's unpublished study, mentioned above, in which the Szondi test was administered to a group of fifty artists, support this theory.

† Lee, Harry B.: A Theory Concerning Free Creation in the Inventive Arts. Psychiatry, Vol. 3, Number 2, May, 1940. On the Esthetic States of the Mind. Psychiatry, Vol. 10, Number 3, August 1947. The Cultural Lag in Aesthetics. The Journal of Aesthetics and Art Criticism. Vol. VI, No. 2, December, 1947. Art as a Form of Projection. Presented at the 1948 Annual Meeting of the American Orthopsychiatric Association.

retain their significance at the primary anal level. In such individuals, the actual excretory processes are still cathected libidinously and serve as a source of pleasure, sometimes being connected with definite bathroom ceremonies. Since data in this area about any subject are difficult, if not impossible, to secure—unless one can obtain psychoanalytic material regarding the subject—the frequency of the above characteristics in connection with the occurrence of open d cannot readily be established. However, I have studied psychotherapeutic patients who yield open d, through whom I have learned much about this meaning of the open d reaction.

The open d is pathodiagnostically significant chiefly in regard to catatonic schizophrenia, already mentioned in connection with a loss of interest in outside objects, and a general apathy. We will see that it is not an unusual constellation in certain types of criminals, excluding the most severe criminals. (In reflecting antisocial behavior, open d appears with minus m and plus or open s).

Open d is the most frequent d factorial constellation appearing between the ages of ten and sixty. (In ages less than ten, plus d is most frequent.) The highest frequency of open d is reached in young adults between the ages of eighteen and thirty. This seems to be the age range when outside objects are evaluated more from the "oral," pleasure-giving point of view than from the more aggressive and possessive anal type of object-relationship.

The m Factor

In interpreting the m factor, we will deal with those personality characteristics which can be derived from the early oral phase of psychosexual development. This stage is characterized by the fact that libidinal satisfaction is obtained mainly through the mouth zone by the act of sucking on the mother's breast. Among psychoanalysts it was Abraham * who did most to develop the concept of the "oral character," beginning with the sucking impulse, following up the vicissitudes of the oral drive, and describing how the satisfaction or frustration of this drive will influence the social attitudes of the adult. According to Abraham, the most important step the individual makes towards acquiring a satisfactory attitude in his social relationships is to deal successfully with his early oral-erotism. If the infant's sucking-pleasure is undisturbed his whole later attitude toward life will be optimistic, and he will have a friendly attitude toward his environment. In case there is overindulgence of the infant's oral needs, he might develop later a carefree, indifferent personality, assuming that somebody will take care of him as his mother did. If, however, the infant is frustrated in the gratification of his oral needs, his later personality might reflect either aggressively demanding social attitudes, or erratic and exaggerated attempts to cling to others.

The information we get about the subject on the basis of his reactions to portraits of manic patients lies exactly in the dimension of those personality traits which Abraham described as having their origin in the oral drive. Thus the task is again to formulate an acceptable hypothesis which can account for the fact that portraits of manic patients can be used as a measuring stick for oral character traits. In linking the psychodynamics underlying mania with strivings originating in the oral phase of psychosexual development, we must rely, of course, on concepts known from psychoanalysis without, however, suggesting that the following theory has been stated *per se* in psychoanalytic literature as an interpretation of the psychologic dynamisms underlying mania.†

* Abraham, Karl: Selected papers on psychoanalysis.
† This qualification might well have been stated in the discussion of the theory of depression from the point of view of the Szondi test interpretation.

In considering the types of interpretation we derive from the various *m* factorial constellations, we have to assume that the symptoms of manic psychosis can be traced to the frustration of the early oral sucking drive. The first manifestation of the oral drive is the infant's sucking on and clinging to the mother's breast. In the course of development, the oral drive undergoes a number of changes in its manifestation, and in its place and function within the total personality. One form of later manifestation is the need for social contact, the "clinging to society" instead of clinging to the mother's breast. In our hypothesis, we assume that the symptoms of mania, starting with the typical hypomanic state, develop in those individuals who, in infancy or early childhood, failed to obtain a satisfactory amount of pleasure from the original sucking situation. Whether this frustration was caused primarily by realistic environmental factors such as the mother's attitude toward feeding, or by the constitutional strength of the infant's oral drive which necessarily entailed frustration despite the attitude of the mother, is a question that can be put aside for the moment. In actuality, these two sets of factors most probably interact in the way Freud described as the functioning of the complementary series.

Important from our present point of view are the later consequences of this early oral frustration. In connection with the *m* factor, we assume that the restless behavior of the hypomanic or manic patient (in the state of hyper-elation and hyperactivity, but not in the state of agitated aggressive and offensive behavior) represents pathologically distorted attempts to make up for the oral pleasures he failed to obtain from the feeding breast in his early childhood. The hyperactivity characterizing the incipient stage of mania is to be understood in this light as a succession of attempts to extract the maximum amount of pleasure from the world in general. In the hypomanic state these attempts take the form of increased interest in the objects of the environment; the hypomanic person is—so to speak—overcathecting the outside objects which, temporarily, might make him feel happy, since the feeling of attachment to many objects is accompanied by a certain feeling of security, with the hope that these outside objects will at some time return the libido invested in them.   Thus, the hypomanic patient is still optimistic because he hopes to draw pleasure and love he missed in his childhood from object relationships established in his later life.   Hence, the characteristic attitude of expectation in hypomanic persons, or in oral characters in general.   For this reason such individuals are likely to join many organizations, to make great and manifold plans, to start new undertakings in their field of work.   The turning point in the apparent behavior of the manic patient occurs at the time of realization of his false premises: when he recognizes that new objects of his libido will not live up to his exaggerated expectations and will not furnish the necessary amount of gratification to compensate for pleasure and love missed in childhood. This new disappointment breaks down the friendly and optimistic attitude of the patient and brings about his outbursts of manic rage and aggressive attempts to destroy the objects which have "betrayed" him again.

On the basis of what is known about the interpretation of the *m* factor, we must assume that the stimulus portraits reflect the first phase of the above described "manic" process.   We must assume, that is, that the subject reacts to the need to cling to objects for the sake of obtaining pleasure and support, as expressed through the portraits of the *m* factor.

The various forms this oral clinging can take, from, literally, oral gratifications such as drinking, eating, smoking, and talking, to all the sublimated forms of the oral type of object relationship including social and artistic gratifications, will be discussed in connection with the various *m* factorial constellations.

However, before going into the interpretation of the single constellations, I want to summarize the characteristics of the *m* factorial or oral type of object relationship by contrasting the oral type briefly, with the *d* factorial, or anal, type of object relationship.

m *Factorial* *(Oral) Object Relation*	d *Factorial* *(Anal) Object Relation*
Objects wanted for the pleasure to be derived from them; for the support they can give, for clinging to them.	Objects wanted for the sake of owning them; to accumulate them and to control them.
Essentially passive relation to the object. Related to the *h* factorial object relationship.	Active, manipulative relation to the object. Related to the *s* factorial object relationship.
Impatience and restlessness in regard to reaching a goal object.	Perserverance and persistence in regard to reaching a goal.
Ability to give love and emotional support to the love object (through identification with the giving mother and through identification with the person who needs love and support).	Tendency to overwhelm love-object with material gifts.
More possibility for sublimation without resorting to the defense-mechanism of reaction formation (no exaggerated anticathexis needed in sublimating oral impulses).	More need for resorting to reaction-formation in order to overcome the originally aggressive attitude toward objects; hence, the compulsive quality of "anal" type of love.

Plus m

The plus *m* reaction indicates identification with the need for external objects for the sake of "oral" gratification. Plus *m* alone gives no reference for the primitivity or sublimitation of this need: the constellation of the remaining seven factors determines whether this oral need to cling to objects for the sake of enjoyment and support will manifest itself in primary oral activities, such as talking, eating, drinking, smoking, or in sublimated form, such as a drive to cling to objects for either artistic or intellectual pleasure. In actuality, these various levels of manifesting the basic oral need often appear concurrently in the same person; for example, in the person who likes to eat and smoke while pursuing intellectual work. Subjects for whom the plus m is a characteristic reaction may be described as oral characters, and the typical pattern of their object-relationship may be described in terms of all those characteristics which were listed in the lefthand column of the summary of the oral versus the anal type of object relation. Thus plus m implies a basically passive attitude towards the love object, the purpose being to enjoy the object and to lean on it for support. There is a need for dependence which, if not too strong, is an asset in establishing social relations. However, if this need reaches more than optimal intensity (four or more choices in plus m), then this clinging to objects acquires the quality of anxiousness about the possibility of losing the object. It should be remembered that the anxiousness of plus m is different from the worrying about the possible loss of the object mentioned in connection with plus d. In the latter case, the person is worried about the possibility of a material loss, while a plus m person is afraid to lose the emotional support inherent in the object-relationship. Plus m generally indicates a warm social attitude and is given by subjects who not only are in need of positive emotions from others, but who also are able to give love and affection to others. Although this constellation, particularly if strongly loaded, is a sign of an unsatisfied oral need, it still implies the essentially optimistic attitude that the subject has not given up hope of obtaining gratification from external objects. As a matter of fact, it appears that a certain amount of tension in this area is desirable; or in other words, it appears that there exists an optimal amount of frustration in regard to the primary oral impulses which results in the sustaining of a need to establish new social contacts. This state is indicated on the test by two to three plus *m*'s. Accordingly, plus *m* is rather a counter-indication for antisocial behavior. This is probably the only constellation among all the eight factors in any position about which I dare to make such a categorical statement: well-adjusted adults who are able to form and maintain satisfactory social relations, are expected to give plus *m*. Well-adjusted, that is, in the sense that they themselves feel content and have found their place in society as well as within a smaller ingroup of people, such as family or close friends. This specification is needed because—as will be seen later—one does find highly sublimating and socially valuable individuals with other than plus *m* constellations; however, in those individuals the subjective feeling of contentedness and the ability to derive pleasure from close interpersonal relationships are missing.

Plus *m* is generally found in adults of the professional groups and is also the most usual *m* constellation in artistic sublimation achieved by writers, painters, sculptors, musicians, or those who form the appreciative public for any artistic production or creation. These findings bear out the psychoanalytic theory which considers artistic sublimation, creation as well as intensive enjoyment, a successful sublimation of the oral component drive of sexuality; successful, first of all, since it is a socially positive channelization, and successful from the subjective point of view since the clinging to artistic or intellectual values is safer than the clinging to particular individuals whom one can lose in reality. The latter interpretation of plus *m* is usually correlated with minus *h* and minus *s* and a general plus tendency in the *Sch* vector. Plus *m* is infrequent in serious forms of pathology. It can be found in neurotic disturbances more frequently than in psychotic disturbances or than in any form of antisocial behavior. The connection between strong

plus *m* and anxiety has been mentioned above. Its highest
frequency is found in hypochondriac anxiety and in adult
stuttering. It is also frequent in homosexuals, perhaps supporting the relationship of homosexuality to fixation at the
oral level of psychosexual development. It also points to
the inner correlation between the *h* and the *m* factors already
mentioned.

The frequency of plus *m* in the various age groups shows
great fluctuation. It is not very frequent in young children
although the earlier we are able to administer the test
to a child the greater is the probability of obtaining plus *m*
(still clinging to the mother in reality around the age of
three). Plus *m* is most unusual (not more than about 3
per cent) in children between six and nine years old. This
disappearance of plus *m* in children coincides with the great
increase in plus *d* reactions, pointing toward the two facts
that children of this age have given up (or were forced to
give up) the closest attachment to their mother, and that
they are more interested in collecting and manipulating
objects than in continuing to cling to the mother or to a
mother substitute. Plus *m* occurs again more frequently
around puberty, and becomes the most usual *m* factorial
constellation from the age of seventeen on. This distribution is most probably due to the fact that oral impulses
lend themselves relatively easily to sublimation through
everyday social contacts. The preponderance of plus *m* over
the other *m* factorial constellations is particularly marked
in advanced age between sixty and eighty, which indicates
the anxious clinging to objects for support characteristic of
older persons.

Minus m

Negative choices in the *m* factor represent a denial of
the need to lean on others. They indicate a frustration
of the early oral needs but, opposing the still optimistic

attitude characteristic of plus m, subjects yielding the minus m reaction are those who have given up hope of compensating for early frustration through new social contacts. Instead, there is withdrawal and a certain sadness and coldness in interpersonal relations. Minus m subjects are lonely even though they may feel a great need for dependence on and gratification from external objects.

In adults, minus m is always a sign of unhappiness, although in favorable configuration it might still accompany socially positive solutions of this basically negativistic attitude. Thus an individual might feel basically isolated in society, especially in regard to smaller ingroups, but still act in a highly ethical way even in regard to helping others to avoid the same fate he knows from experience. In these cases, minus m appears in conjunction with minus h and minus s and, usually, plus e. However, in these individuals the helping attitude has usually all the characteristics of a reaction formation, and the exaggerated and sometimes aggressive way in which it is carried out betrays the strong anticathexis which has to be invested in the assumption of the role of "helper" and "giver" by those who are themselves in greatest need of support and love. Thus one can see that in the case of plus m it is psychologically easier to sublimate the unsatisfied oral need than it is in the case of minus m. This difference might be due either to an original difference in the strength of the primary frustration, or to a different attitude toward this primary frustration. In the first case, there is an acknowledgment of this need, and the plus m subject shows positive attempts to make up for the original loss, while subjects with minus m deny to themselves the existence of the need to lean on others for the sake of obtaining pleasure and support. This attitude by itself implies a certain degree of anticathexis or, in popular words, a certain amount of self-deception. The second "dose" of anticathexis is needed when a minus m person not only denies his own need for support but tries to identify himself with the role of the "supporter" without acknowledging that what he really expects is love and affection in return (the latter is true for plus *m* individuals who are also able to identify themselves with the giving mother). The outcome of this whole complicated and unconscious process, which takes place when a minus *m* person succeeds in channelizing his basic frustration into a helping social attitude, is an ascetic quality of the character which might enable the person to achieve high humanistic goals. Such individuals have a high frustration tolerance for realistic disappointments in life, since they never allow themselves consciously to expect much from life in the first place. The frustration tolerance of plus *m* individuals is considerably less, just because of their optimistic expectations.

The socially positive solution of the minus *m* constellation has been discussed to this degree because it represents an extreme and a rare outcome of the oral frustration indicated by this reaction. Our discussion of the anticathexis and reaction formation needed in order to maintain the ascetic altruism of minus *m,* is borne out by the findings that actually minus *m* is the most frequent *m* factorial constellation for seriously antisocial (criminal) behavior. The logical implication of this finding is that in most cases destructively antisocial behavior has to be considered to be a reaction, or rather a revenge, on the external objects which fail to satisfy the person's intense need for oral gratification. Thus the frustrated need for dependence would be the dynamic force underlying the "need" for destruction. The same dynamic process was described in the beginning of this chapter in our discussion of the turning point in the apparently elated behavior of the manic patient, during which we offered as explanation for the sudden outbreak of manic rage that it occurs when the patient realizes the futility of his attempts to extract satisfactory amounts of oral gratification from libidinously cathected objects of his environment. The results of the test show that actually minus m is the most characteristic m factorial constellation for manic patients in their antisocial phase. The third pathodiagnostic group in which the minus m reaction is the most frequent is represented by epileptic patients approaching the outbreak of seizure. The similarity between the reactions of active criminals, manic psychotics, and epileptics before seizure is apparent in practically all the eight factors.

There is one group of neurotics in which minus m is a frequent reaction; that is in conversion hysteria. In these cases the total test pattern resembles that of those subjects who were described as ascetic and altruistic despite their strong oral frustration. Conversion symptoms are most probably related to the basic repression of oral needs in these individuals.

Minus m is most usual in children under puberty, particularly in the seven to eight year olds. The relinquishment of the strongest ties with the mother, which coincides with the highest frequency of the minus m, has been discussed in connection with the high frequency of plus d and the infrequency of plus m in this age group. Actually this is one group in which the usual interpretation of the minus m has to be somewhat modified since it does not imply the same kind of unhappiness and isolation as it does in adults, unless it is strongly loaded (four or more), in which case it does indicate that the child is unusually lonesome and unhappy. Otherwise it corresponds to the "physiologic" process of growing up which involves necessarily a gradual detachment from the mother, and it is not even desirable that the same clinging attitude should be transferred immediately towards new objects. In "normal" development there is an intermediate period (the latency period) when the child gets satisfaction from other than oral types of object attachment, such as curiosity in the construction of objects, exploration of their practical usefulness, etc. Then, in puberty and in adolescence when various social contacts and intellectual enjoyments can take the place of the original clinging to the mother, the frequency of minus m decreases with a simultaneous increase of the plus m. Least frequent is minus m in old age.

Plus-Minus m

The plus-minus m position of the m factor expresses the subject's ambivalence in regard to clinging or not clinging to objects of the environment. Because of this ambivalence, it reflects a critical state in the object-relationship. Subjectively, this state of attempting to derive enjoyment from the environment (plus m) while denying the possibility of this enjoyment (minus m), results in a feeling of dissatisfaction, even more so than in the case of completely minus m. In the latter, there is at least no more conflict and there is a solution, even though in the negative sense of resignation. In the case of plus-minus m, however, the indecision whether or not to give up unsuccessful attempts to obtain support and pleasure from objects of the environment, is more energy-consuming and depressing. Another explanation for the feeling of greater dissatisfaction and depression in plus-minus m subjects than there is in minus m subjects is that in the former instance the plus m component indicates that there is much less possibility of resorting to the defense mechanism of reaction-formation than there is in the case of a completely minus m. In other words, plus minus m subjects do not deceive themselves by denying their need to cling for support and love: they merely experience their disability to secure or maintain such satisfactory relationship. This is again one of the rare single factorial constellations which has definite diagnostic value in itself, in whatever configuration it occurs; namely, it always indicates an unsatisfactory object-relationship with subjectively experienced frustration in this sphere. The general characterization of plus-minus reactions (see Chapter IV) in regard to their implying an ambivalence at the conscious or at least close to the conscious level of thinking, is particularly true in case of plus-minus *m*. According to my experience with individuals giving plus-minus *m*, whose personality I know well from therapeutic work with them or otherwise, this frustrating object relationship could be traced back in practically all cases to a basically undecided sexual orientation. They were individuals who actually experienced their basic bisexuality, thus being unable to derive satisfaction from either hetero- or homosexual object cathexes.

Among the well-defined clinical groups, plus-minus *m* is most frequent in compulsion neurosis and in depression. Individuals entertaining suicidal phantasies frequently give this *m* factorial constellation. The psychodynamic explanation for all these outstanding frequencies has been implied in the foregoing.

Plus-minus *m* occurs most frequently in small children, 3 to 4 years of age, and again in old age, beyond eighty years. In all the age groups between these two extremes, plus-minus *m* is the least frequent of all the four possible positions in the *m* factor. The two outstanding frequencies refer most probably to the crises in regard to clinging to objects at the height of the Oedipal phase (3 to 4 years), as well as in senile regression.

Open m

The drained reaction in the *m* factor shows that oral tension is continuously discharged, indicating that oral character traits are a part of the manifest behavior rather than a dynamic source of energy in the unconscious layers of the personality. Just what form this discharging of oral need takes on the behavior level is hard to say—a statement I feel compelled to repeat in the case of almost every open reaction. Usually it implies the excessive indulgence in some form of actual oral activity, such as overeating, drinking, talking. From the point of view of psychosexual development, it means that the oral component drive of sexuality has not subsided in its importance in favor of the supremacy of genital sexuality. In other words, open *m*, in adults, is an indication that genital primacy has not been completely established, thus being a sign of sexual immaturity. In individuals with constant open *m*, the stimulability of the oral zone retains too much of its original strength and importance within the structure of the total personality. In the primarily sexual sense, in such individuals the oral excitability, instead of furnishing "forepleasure" which helps to bring about complete genital gratification, still remains and end in itself. This lack of mature sexual organization is usually associated with certain infantile characteristics of the personality, the sexual origin of which is not apparent unless it can be perceived by psychoanalysis. These infantile traits are reflected in the kind of object relationships the person is likely to establish. In case of open *m*, the person is likely to establish numerous such relationships which, on the surface, give the impression that the person is finding his place easily in any situation. However, on closer examination, one finds that none of these relationships is really intensive and there is an easy interchangeability of objects. The typically open *m* person can be characterized as trying to "eat up" the world, thereby attempting to establish quickly as many object relationships as possible to derive maximum amounts of enjoyment from the objects. This intense craving for objects, characteristic of open *m*, is different from the need to cling to an object, as described in connection with plus *m*. The latter is of a definitely more passive nature; in open *m* the original oralsadistic elements are more pronounced. The restless trying

out of one object after the other, due to an anxiousness
that something might otherwise be missed, can also be
derived from the basic ambivalence characteristic for the
original oral-sadistic phase of psychosexual development. It
is obvious that even though these subjects, at first glance,
might give the impression of being exuberant, "happy-go-
lucky" individuals, they are basically dissatisfied because of
the lack of mature, unambivalent relationship to one definite
love-object which can be reached only at the stage of genital
maturity. This genital immaturity is the root of the apparent contradiction in experimental findings that open m is
characteristic of the superficially charming, apparently most
sociable *bons vivants,* as well as of those who are weary of
all these exaggerated, yet basically unsatisfactory, attempts to
secure pleasure, and are ready to consider the possibility
of suicide as a way out of this turmoil.

In the socially positive forms of solutions, open m can
be found rather frequently in writers, actors, public speak-
ers. The pathologic significance of open m has been implied
in the characterization of this position. Thus, it is found
in cases of sexual immaturity and in those who have a
tendency for oral perversion, in certain types of unstable
"acting out" psychopaths, and frequently in those cases of
anxiety hysteria in which anxiety manifests itself in fear
of disability to enjoy the world fully enough. Belonging to
this group are the gamblers, avid nightclub goers or, in general, all those individuals who feel uncomfortable unless
every free minute is filled with plans promising enjoyment.

Among the various age groups, the highest frequency of
open m is found in puberty and between forty and sixty
years of age. (Theoretically, it ought to be a typical reaction of the youngest children; however, the corresponding
age group is below the age limit at which the test can be
administered.) The two highest points in frequency might
be indicative of the greediness of children in puberty in

regard to enjoying the world, and also of the reinforcement of this hedonistic tendency in the later years of middle-age.

C VECTORIAL CONSTELLATIONS

There are nine patterns of the d and m constellations which have to be described briefly, because each of them refers to a characteristic way the subject relates himself to objects of his environment. More variations are discussed separately here than in the case of the P vector because of the special importance of anal and oral character traits in determining the person's social attitudes and his general type of contact with reality. Again, the meaning of the remaining seven C vectorial configurations can be derived from the interpretations of the nine individually described C vector patterns.

As in the previous vectors, the presentation will follow the degree of clarity of the personality characteristics corresponding to the various d and m patterns.

Minus d with plus m

The situation in the C vector is similar to that in the P vector, in that those constellations in which the two factors point into opposite directions actually indicate that the two respective drives operate in the same direction. In the case of minus d with plus m, both factors express the need to hold on and cling to an object strongly cathected with libido. One could call this the most "faithful" constellation, since the minus d indicates that the person is attached to one specific object and is not in constant search for new ones (which would be indicated by plus d), while the plus m shows that the need to cling for love and support is accepted. It also shows that there is still a basically optimistic attitude, and the environment is considered in an emotionally positive way as offering possibilities for "oral" gratification. Individuals with minus d and plus m are fixated to the "primary" object in the sense discussed in connection with minus d. Thus it does not necessarily imply an obvious attachment to either of the parents but means that something (a person, an idea, or a thing) is cathected with the same intensity as was the first main object of libido (always the mother or the person who takes the place of the mother). At the same time, when minus d indicates this strong attachment to a person or idea, the plus m shows that, whatever the object of this strong libido cathexis is, it is certainly something which can be actually enjoyed and to which it is possible to "cling." Enjoying and clinging in case of this particular C vectorial configuration, has always a non-aggressive and sometimes—depending on the loadedness of minus d—a definitely passive character. Individuals who give this pattern do not exert physical effort to assure themselves of the possession of the highly cathected object. In most cases, it is not even a material object but rather a person or an idea, and not infrequently the mere idea of a person, to which they are faithfully attached. Thus holding on to such "objects" of libido does not necessitate physical action or grabbing but rather an ability to sublimate and to derive enjoyment from nontangible values. This statement is supported by the findings that minus d with plus m is discovered rarely in the lower occupational levels and practically never in criminals, nor in asocial psychotics. It occurs frequently in fairly well-functioning adults, mostly in professional groups to whom the kind of work they do is more important than the financial gains of the work. In other words these are the persons we usually call "idealistic." They might experience difficulties in regard to outward success, because of the passivity inherent in this configuration, particularly if associated with minus s. They are conservative in the sense of disliking change, and being forced to leave a situation to which they are accustomed is experienced as painful. These reactions

follow from the adhesive quality of libido-cathexis characteristic for minus *d*-plus *m* individuals. Once an object
is really cathected it is practically never given up. Even
though there might be no outward signs of adherence
between the subject and his object of libido, on closer examination one finds that the attachment is still there and not
even in a diminished form. And the particularly interesting
characteristic of these subjects is that such unrealistic attachments are not experienced as serious frustrations, since they
are able to derive satisfaction from intangible ideas. To
them, the thought of the object has nearly the same emotional value as its possession. This is another illustration
of the exaggerated loyalty and high sublimating ability so
characteristic of subjects associated with this *C* vector pattern.

This pattern, as we have said, is rarely found in psychoses.
It may be associated with various forms of neuroses because
of the basically incestuous fixation implied in its deepest
interpretation. However, even in those cases it may be
interpreted as indicating a socially positive attitude and
satisfactory ethical control. (Minus *d* with plus *m* is frequently associated with plus *e* and minus *hy* in the *P*
vector.)

The pattern is typically adult; most unusual if it occurs
in children. Its frequency is fairly stable from adolescence
to old age. It occurs rarely in childhood, probably because
it indicates a sublimated (or transposed) form of attachment to an original "primary" object (the mother or
mother-substitute) which the child still possesses. And a
need for attachment so intensive as indicated by minus *d*
with plus *m* can rarely be satisfied in the most realistic
normal contact with actual parents.

Plus d *with Minus* m

The plus *d*, minus *m* pattern in the *C* vector is in every
way the opposite of minus *d*, plus *m*. It means that there

is no intensive attachment to one specific object of libido:
rather, the person who yields this pattern eagerly pur-
sues many objects. This aggressive search is assumed, on
the basis of clinical observations, to be the reaction from
forced relinquishment of attachment to the most important
"primary" object (the parents). To these subjects, the
specificity of the objects is not nearly so important as the
quantity. This configuration indicates definitely activity,
and frequently aggression, in contrast to the physical passivity characteristic of the minus d, plus m. Individuals
giving plus d, minus m are anxious to manipulate and master
the objects in their environment; however, the minus m
component indicates that, actually, there is no pleasure
derived from all this activity. (This interpretation needs
modification when this C vector pattern is found in children between the ages of six and eight.) Plus d, minus m
indicates a generally realistic attitude toward the world
insofar as real objects are considered important, but this
materialistic viewpoint is associated with a certain pessimism
toward the world as a potential source of enjoyment. The
individual, that is, is able to secure a number of real objects,
but is unable to enjoy them. There is little possibility
for sublimated forms of enjoyment in subjects yielding this
constellation in the C vector. In the clinically symptomless
population, this pattern is obtained mostly in the lower
occupational levels, frequently by unskilled laborers who
work hard and without enjoyment, with little opportunity
or ability to derive pleasure from things in general except
on the most concrete level. Among individuals belonging
to higher occupational or professional groups, the pattern
is more an indication of depressed mood, and generally,
of a tendency actively to accumulate and master objects.
When the pattern is associated with plus s, these individuals can be ruthless in pursuit of their goals. Because
of the lack of intensive attachment to any one object, person,

or idea, these subjects move through their environment more easily, and change more flexibly from one situation to another, than do those who yield the opposite pattern (minus *d* with plus *m*) in the *C* vector.

The pathologic significance of the configuration refers first of all to antisocial behavior. In any form of crime, this is one of the most frequent *C* vectorial patterns, usually associated with plus *s* and minus *e* to yield the typical picture of an anal-sadistic individual. Moreover, similarity between the test reactions of criminals and epileptics has been found in this *C* vector configuration.

In certain configurations of the total test pattern, when there are reactions indicative of repression (primarily minus *hy* and minus *k*), plus *d*, minus *m* can occur in conjunction with hysteric symptoms. The psychodynamics underlying this experimental finding refer most probably to the basic asocial attitude of hysterics, and to their inability to form pleasurable object relationships.

The curve of age distribution of plus *d*, minus *m*, points to a trend exactly opposite to the curve of minus *d*, plus *m*, although the absolute frequency in the population of the former is about three times the frequency of the latter. Plus *d* with minus *m* is the most frequent *C* vectorial configuration given by children from approximately four to nine years of age. From prepuberty on it gradually decreases in frequency, becoming one of the rarest patterns in those beyond the age of sixty. Possible reasons for the high frequency of this pattern in childhood have been discussed, in connection with the age distributions of the two component elements of this configuration, in the section concerning plus *d* and in the section concerning minus *m*. To recapitulate briefly: this is the age at which, due to external and inner reasons, children are forced to loosen their attachment to the mother and to "stand on their own feet." It is the period at which they explore the possible use of a number of environmental objects, and acquire skills to manipulate these objects. The well-known childhood habit of collecting various objects is yet another phenomenon understandable from the attitude implied in plus d with minus m. Although in this age group the plus d, minus m pattern does not indicate a socially negative attitude nor a tendency for depression in the sense indicated for adults, it nevertheless most probably reflects the fact that children of this age do feel lonesome and to a certain extent frustrated "orally" as a part of the physiologic process of growing up. The beginnings of "gang" formation, around the age of seven, which usually has a slight antisocial tinge, though still in a playful way, may also be regarded as a reaction against the world of frustrating adults, which fits well into the interpretation of the corresponding plus d and minus m.

Minus d with Minus m

The minus d, minus m pattern in the C vector occurs rather infrequently in the general population. Nevertheless it demands discussion because it corresponds to a type of personality so clearly definable. It indicates fixation on a certain object (minus d) with simultaneous negation of the need to cling to this object (minus m). The result of this inner contradiction is a restless tension and a general feeling of detachment from reality. This detachment does not necessarily result in pathologic lack of contact with reality, although minus d, minus m is a relatively frequent configuration in acute psychoses.

If the rest of the test pattern reveals a good balance between the factors, minus d, minus m can mean that the person, subjectively detached from everyday reality, is able to live on a "higher" plane of humanistic idealism. However, this interpretation is valid only when this pattern of the C vector appears in conjunction with minus h and minus s, and there is a plus tendency in both factors of the

Sch vector. Individuals yielding this unusual combination of reactions are deeply unrealistic, but rational, in that intellectually and practically they act in accordance with the expected laws of reality, while emotionally they reject these laws together with the conventional scale of values. Thus, within the limits of reality, they are basically nonconforming and autistic. The unconscious psychodynamics behind this attitude concern a reconciliation to a frustrating situation in which there is realization of the fact that the love-object which is still all-important is not available, while there is no attempt to search for a substitute. Subjects in this group have an ascetic quality of self-denial and a high tolerance for frustration. In contrast to the optimistic attitude corresponding to minus *d*, plus *m*, whereby the individual also basically fixated on a love-object not attainable is nevertheless able to transpose this love to an abstract level and derive enjoyment from this sublimation, subjects with the minus *d*, minus *m* configuration deny the importance of enjoyment altogether. Under unusual circumstances, this disinterest in pleasure might give these individuals unusual strength in regard to self-sacrifice, bearing out the well-known signs of exaggeration characteristic of all behavior resulting from reaction formation.

As we have mentioned, this configuration in the *C* vector is found frequently in psychoses, particularly in the beginning stages, indicating immediate loss of contact with reality. Minus *d*, minus *m* forms the greater part of an important syndrome on the test, which usually is referred to as the "block of irreality" and consists of minus *p* (unconscious projection), minus *d*, and minus *m*. Among the neurotic symptoms, diffuse anxiety occurs most frequently with this pattern in the *C* vector.

The curve of age distribution of this configuration shows two peaks: the first, which is the lower of the two, occurs in young children; the second, in adulthood. This pattern is least frequent in adolescence and in old age. In young children, the pattern usually appears as part of the "block of irreality," corresponding to the age of infantile autism, which is an expected phase of development.* In adults, it is a sign of irrealistic resignation. The rareness of this C vectorial pattern in adolescents is understandable, since adolescents definitely have outgrown the stage at which autistic withdrawal from frustrating reality is permissible under normal circumstances, but have not reached the age at which they need to resort to arbitrary self-denial. The psychic energy needed in order to maintain the anticathexes necessary for the latter attitude explains the observation that elderly people do not reveal this energy-consuming mechanism.

Plus d with Plus m

In contrast to the irrealistic social attitude characteristic of the minus d, minus m configuration in the C vector, the plus d, plus m configuration could be called the "block of reality," plus d and plus m being the two most important component factors. This pattern indicates that the material objects of the world, as well as interpersonal relationships, are valued highly. The behavior of these subjects is apparently most sociable, yet subjectively they experience difficulties because too many objects (in the sense of material objects as well as person or ideas) of the environment seem equally desirable. Expressed in Lewinian terms: there is a conflict situation in which the person has to choose between two or more objects representing equally positive valence, so that frustration is unavoidable since in actuality only one of these objects can be chosen. This multiorientation of the libido explains the greediness of these subjects in regard to securing more and more objects, and establishing more and more relationships, since anal and oral needs

* Piaget, Jean: The Child's Conception of the World. New York, Harcourt, Brace and Co., 1929.

equally are accepted.   Objects are wanted so that they may be mastered (plus *d*) as well as enjoyed (plus *m*).   This pattern in the *C* vector accompanies a definite tendency for competitiveness, since the possessions of others are desired as fully as possessions attained.   Yet this tendency for envy and insatiability does not have antisocial manifestations of the kind described in connection with plus *d* and minus *m,* since in the configuration under discussion the plus *m* is a kind of safeguard against harmful, overtly aggressive behavior.   Rather, subjects associated with this configuration are over-eager and anxious not to miss anything in life; although they might experience the desire to step over others, the socially positive qualities implied in plus *m,* which psychologically consist of needs to be loved and to win support, keep this desire within socially acceptable limits.   Even the term "greediness" in these individuals must often be understood as primarily nonmaterialistic, since it is often manifested in attempts to accumulate a great quantity of knowledge in diverse fields.   Tendency to acquire the skills of several occupations or to change professions frequently, is characteristic of subjects in this group.

The pathologic significance of this *C* vector pattern refers mostly to the feeling of insufficiency inherent in the mechanism which is the consequence of the tendency to undertake more tasks than can be carried out in reality.   This can result in various neurotic symptoms which have the common characteristics of hyper-activity and difficulty in concentrating, rather than the withdrawal associated with minus *d,* minus *m.*   In primarily sexual disturbances, this *C* pattern is found frequently in bisexual individuals, in whom multiorientation of the libido implies that persons of either sex are cathected with equal intensity.   The result of this bisexual orientation is, also, the feeling that no object can yield gratification by itself, while simultaneous attachment to several objects necessarily implies frustrations of another sort.

Plus *d*, plus *m* is found most frequently in old age, and least frequently in children. In old age, it might reflect the regressive disintegration of sexuality into its pregenital component drives of anal and oral needs. It also corresponds to the concern in elderly individuals about their relationship to objects (including persons) in their environment rather than the structuring of their own egos. (Experimental results supporting this statement will be discussed in connection with the configurations in the *Sch* vector and their frequencies in the various age groups.)

Open d with Plus m

The open *d*, plus *m* constellation can be understood on the basis of the configuration just discussed if—to use a mathematical metaphor—from the previous configuration we subtract the interpretation corresponding to the plus *d* component. The remainder, the open *d*, plus *m* pattern contains the elements of the sublimated oral needs (plus *m*) without being accompanied by a tension in the area corresponding to the need for a possessive, anal type object relationship (open *d*). This lack of any tension, in the plus as well as in the minus direction, in the area corresponding to anal needs accounts for the characteristic passivity of subjects with open *d* and plus *m* toward objects in their environment. (It should be remembered that in the case of any open reaction "no tension" refers to lack of tension indicated on the test profile as compared to other test factors in which tension is indicated by the number of choices, and not to an absolute lack of tension in the particular area of the personality.) The open *d* indicates that there is no search for new objects, nor is the person attached strongly to the primary object or to any other object which might have taken its place during the course of development. The lack of strong attachment to any object, indicated by the draining of the *d* factor, refers only to the lack of the anal type of interest in objects; in other words, there is no drive in regard to actively manipulating and controlling objects, but this does not imply the lack of the "oral" need for objects. Quite the contrary is true for persons who give open *d*, plus *m*; namely, there is a strong need to cling to objects for love, support, and enjoyment (tension in plus *m*). These are individuals who can be described in psychoanalytic terms as "oral characters." Depending on the intensity (loadedness) of the plus *m*, this oral need to cling to objects can manifest itself in socially most desirable forms of optimistic and nonaggressive attitudes, or—in cases in which the plus *m* is strongly loaded—the clinging to an object might acquire a quality of anxiousness, a fear about the possibility of losing the object. This anxiousness is different from the worrying about the possibility of losing an object as described in connection with the plus *d*, in which it referred to an anxiety about losing a possession, or losing control over a part of the environment; in other words, to anxiety about inability to assert one's strength and power. In anxiety associated with high plus *m*, there is no question of power involved; the person is simply anxious about losing the psychologic support which the object of his libido has meant to him. These subjects are frustrated in their oral needs, but instead of reconciling themselves to this frustration, they constantly try to find ways to gratify this need, and the fact that they give plus *m*, and not minus *m*, shows that they are able to derive enjoyment from oral types of object relationship even though they might feel that the amount is insufficient. In social contact, these subjects are pleasant and, because of the realization and acceptance of their own need for love and support, they are also able to identify themselves with the role of the donor of such emotions. Because they lack energy to secure specific objects (open *d*), individuals with this *C* vector pattern are rather inclined to cathect those objects in their environment which are easily available, and once cathected, they cling to them. Once an object-relationship has been established, they experience a certain inertia against any change in the situation; however, if the change is unavoidable, new relationships similar to the previous relationship, are established rather easily, owing to the inherent need of these individuals to find objects ("object" always implying persons) to cling to, and their basically hedonistic attitude in that they want to enjoy the world. The frustration tolerance of subjects with open d, plus m, is low. They do not want to suffer and usually they are able to structure their lives in a way that actually they do not need to. Their usually good capacity for sublimation is one of the main reasons that even under apparently unfavorable circumstances, they are still able to derive some enjoyment, since enjoyment on this sublimated level does not depend on the possession of material objects or on realistic attachments to persons, but rather on the possession of abstract ideals or values which can not be lost by changing external circumstances. Whether or not such abstract values were cathected originally because of an underlying fear of exposure to frustrations if the libido were to be invested in more tangible objects which could be easily lost is an open question, but by all means a conceivable possibility. The genetic development of these subjects usually shows that they did get much love in childhood, which might account not only for their basically optimistic attitude in later life, but also for their sometimes inordinate need for supportive love even as adults.

This pattern in the C vector is frequently found in so-called well-functioning and fairly happy individuals who, besides a general positive attitude to society, feel themselves also a part of a more closely knit ingroup, such as family or group of close friends. Tracing through occupational levels from hard physical labor to the professions requiring greatest degrees of artistic or scientific sublimation, we find a steady increase in the frequency of the open *d*, plus *m* configuration. In my study of various groups of artists, musicians, and writers, this has been by far the most frequent pattern in the *C* vector.

The most important pathologic significance of this constellation lies in the proneness for anxious clinging, mentioned above, which, in the event that there are other signs for anxiety on the profile (plus *h*, strong minus *hy*, minus *k*), can result in obviously neurotic symptoms. Agoraphobia—although a rare symptom in its most clearcut form—is characteristically associated with the above pattern. The combination of a strong plus *h* with plus *m* is always a sign indicating the subject's intense need of dependence. If this correlation of reactions is found in adults, it can be interpreted as genital immaturity and a fixation on the original parent-child relationship pattern. Another group in which this constellation is frequent is represented by adult stutterers, the underlying dynamics of this finding being most probably identical with the dynamics described.

The open *d*, plus *m* is one of the three most frequent *C* vectorial configurations in the general population (in all the sixteen possible variations in which the two factors of the vector can be combined.) Most frequently it is found in old age, although it is frequent in adults, and not infrequent in adolescents. It becomes increasingly rare in the younger age groups, until its occurrence in young children is most unusual. The rarity of this configuration in childhood can be understood if one thinks of the children's strong need to attach themselves to the mother in reality, which need can not be gratified by substituting another object, particularly not an abstract concept, in the place of the mother. This insistence on a particular object is indicated by the lack of the open *d*, plus *m* constellation in childhood; instead, we find *C* vector patterns in this age,

which indicates actual frustration in regard to oral gratification. On the other hand, the high frequency of this
constellation in old age (between the ages of sixty and
eighty, open d with plus m is by far the most frequent pattern in the C vector) reflects most probably the generalized
need to cling to practically any object in the immediate
environment, which is a characteristic trait of old people.

Open d with Minus m

In contrast to the open d, plus m configuration, which
implied socially positive and optimistic characteristics in
the main, and was the most usual C vectorial reaction in
socially well-adjusted adults, the open d, minus m reaction
is given by those subjects who have the most negativistic
attitude toward society and are socially least adjusted. If
encountered in adults, this constellation in the C vector
indicates social maladjustment, no matter what the configuration of the rest of the test profile is. The lack of
concern in respect to choosing specific objects (open d)
coupled with the denial of the need to lean on others
(minus m), results in a socially desperate attitude of indifference. This negativistic social attitude occurs usually in
individuals who originally felt frustrated in regard to gratifying oral needs in their childhood and have also reached
the conclusion in later life that the objects available for
libido-cathexis will not furnish the gratification needed to
make up for what they have missed in childhood. Thus,
subjects with open d, minus m are essentially disappointed
in life, and this disappointment is easily turned into aggression against the frustrating environment. The transition
from disappointment into manifest aggressive behavior is
usually brought about by way of the mechanism of unconscious projection (minus p), which enables the person to
attach the blame for his basic frustration on specific persons
or objects in his environment. The high frequency of this

constellation in the *C* vector among criminals is most probably due to the sequence of mechanisms outlined above.
Open *d* and minus *m* in these cases appears in conjunction
with plus *h*, open or plus *s*, open or minus *e*, and minus *p*.

The other pathologic group for which this pattern in the
C vector is characteristic, are the hypomanic patients, or
cases of incipient mania. It is assumed that the indiscriminate grabbing attitude of these patients is also based on
strong frustration of the oral need to cling to and enjoy
the objects of the world. Again, the minus *m* indicates
that the subject has given up more constructive and optimistic attempts in regard to satisfying this need; instead,
he is trying to derive some sort of pleasure from any object
he comes across (open *d*), many times in an asocial or antisocial way (minus *m*). However, these indiscriminate
attempts do not furnish any real satisfaction, which accounts
for the quick discarding of objects and the general instability
and unpredictability of the behavior of these subjects.

Besides these two pathologic groups, open *d*, minus *m* is
frequent in any form of psychosis in the stage at which
the patients are ready to be institutionalized because their
behavior has become antisocial.

Comparing the pathologic significance of this *C* vector
pattern with its opposite, the open *d*, plus *m*, it is obvious
that while the open *d*, plus *m* could be generally interpreted
as a sign against any serious form of pathology—anxiety
neurosis representing the worst cases in which it was found—
the present constellation is one of those essential determinants in the test which give an unfavorable interpretation
to the whole profile, no matter what the reaction in the
other six factors are. With this constellation, neurotic
symptoms are much less frequent than are psychotic symptoms or antisocial behavior.

The distribution curve throughout the various age groups
shows trends exactly opposite to the previous configuration

in this vector. Open d, minus m is most frequent in children, and shows rapid decrease in frequency with increasing age. In adults, it occurs less than half as frequently as it does in children (about 10 per cent in adults) and is most unusual in old age. As in the case of the plus, d, minus m configuration, the interpretation of the open d, minus m, if encountered in children, is not nearly so unfavorable as it is if encountered in adults. The underlying psychodynamics for the relatively high frequency of both of these C vectorial configurations in childhood are most probably also practically identical. Both reflect the children's actual frustration because of the necessity to give up their most intimate attachment to their mother, and both reflect their attempts to find substitutes for the mother figure by cathecting numerous objects of the environment, without, however, being able to "cling" to these new objects the way they did to the mother. It seems that substitute satisfaction in this area is linked to the ability to sublimate the original oral need, and thus can not be achieved before maturity, which coincides with the age when open d, plus m, becomes frequent. According to my experience, it is not even favorable for later personality development to skip this stage of oral frustration—as indicated by the minus m reaction in children—or the adult personality will show too strong a need for dependence, and too low a tolerance of unavoidable frustrations.

The rarity of open d, minus m in old age is most probably owing to the intensive clinging of old persons to everybody in their immediate environment, and to their effort to keep up contact with life. (Cf. high frequency of open d, plus m in this age group.)

Open d *with Open* m

Only the most concise characterization will be given of this and the following two constellations in the C vector, since the four basic forms of reactions of the two component factors have been discussed in detail, first as single factorial .reactions, and later in relation to the six most characteristic configurations in the whole vector. Nevertheless, at least a very brief separate characterization of the following two constellations is warranted because of the distinct types of object relationships corresponding to them.

Open d, open m is yielded by subjects for whom object-relationship as such is not an area of concern. They can be characterized as easy-going individuals who experience no particular difficulty in changing from one situation to another. Their attitude is more or less the same toward all objects and persons with whom they come in contact; namely, a childish curiosity concerning ways the object, person, or situation may be most enjoyed. They are hedonists, as a spoiled child is a hedonist in assuming that the duty of the mother is to take care of his well-being. Thus, the carefree attitude of these subjects hinges on the expectation that somebody will take care of them as their mothers did. That the d factor, as well as the m, is drained is an indication that, actually, these subjects are able to bring about such situations; otherwise tension would be indicated in at least one of the two factors. On the other hand, the fact that there is no tension in regard to either the anal type or the oral type of object-relationship is in itself and indication of a genitally immature sexual organization, since some degree of tension in at least one of these pregenital component drives is expected following successful establishment of genital supremacy.

Accordingly, this configuration is found frequently in cases of neuroses in which sexual immaturity is among the obvious symptoms. So-called anal and oral perversions appear frequently in conjunction with this pattern in the C vector.

Although personality types corresponding to this configuration have been characterized as "infantile" in their relationship and expectancy toward environment, it has been found infrequently in children. This may be due to the simple fact that the test can not be administered to children less than approximately three and a half years old, at which age they have outgrown the developmental stage corresponding to this C vectorial pattern. This constellation occurs with relatively highest frequency in adolescents, and with next highest frequency in adults, being given in both groups by those individuals who are inclined to be indiscriminate hedonists.

Plus d with Plus-Minus m

This configuration occurs in no more than approximately 5 per cent of the general population, yet whenever it does occur it has great diagnostic value. Subjectively, this constellation is experienced as unhappiness to a greater degree than any other constellation in the C vector. Subjects yielding plus d and plus-minus m feel depressed, and are conscious of their conflicts in regard to their relationships to objects in their environment. In this sense, the present configuration corresponds psychologically to an attitude diametrically opposite to that described in connection with the open d, open m constellation. The plus d with plus-minus m shows that objects of the environment are needed and highly valued (plus d), but that they cannot be enjoyed (plus-minus m). The fact that the plus-minus direction of the m indicates attempts to derive enjoyment from the environment (plus m) concurrent to denials of the possibility of attaining the enjoyment, accounts for the experience of an acute and hopeless conflict which, in behavior, appears as a depressed mood. In other words, the individual needs anal possession of objects as well as oral adherence to them, and feels unhappy if either of these two aspects of object-relationship can not be materialized. On the other hand, the plus-minus m reaction indicates that the oral clinging can not be gratified. In any other configuration in which one of these needs represents a less salient component of the motivational structure of the personality—either because there is less tension or because the individual is more resigned to unavoidable frustrations—the mood is not as acutely depressed as it is in the pattern under discussion.

Subjects yielding plus d, plus-minus m are often able to verbalize the exact nature of their problem. They feel that they would be inclined to be greedy and hedonistic, but are not able to satisfy these needs. They may appear to be successful because the plus d gives them enough "anal" persistence to reach concrete goals, but they have too much "oral" need to feel gratified by mere ownership of objects. Despite their possession of many objects they feel lonesome (minus m). On the other hand, they are "anal" enough to drive themselves constantly in the search for new objects.

It has been implied in the general characterization that this pattern is characteristic for pathologic forms of depression. It also occurs frequently in certain types of hysteric patients for whom a restless search for constantly new objects is characteristic.

There is no specific age group for which this constellation is characteristic. It occurs least frequently in middle-aged adults.

Plus-Minus d with Plus-Minus m

A cursory glance at the plus-minus d, plus-minus m pattern might lead to the conclusion that there is more tension and subjectively experienced conflict here than there is in plus d, plus-minus m. This, however, is not the case. Restless tension and moodiness are, undoubtedly, characteristic of subjects with plus-minus d, plus-minus m, yet they do not feel so acutely depressed as those individuals yielding plus d, plus-minus m. This can be understood if one realizes that plus minus d, plus-minus m contains in itself the main factors of the "block of irreality": the minus d, minus m. Characteristics discussed in connection with the latter configuration account for the paradoxical finding that individuals who give this pattern of "double" conflict have more ways to solution at their disposal than those who show conflict in only one of the two factors, in the m. The minus d, minus m components of this double conflict make it possible for the individual to withdraw to find some satisfaction on an abstract level of irreality in lieu of frustrating fights in reality (plus d, plus-minus m). (For a detailed topological representation of the personality from the point of view of various levels of reality and irreality on which behavior can take place, see Lewin's *Topological Psychology*, op. cit.) Thus, whether we call it sublimation or escape, these subjects are able at times to avoid realistic frustrations by turning to mechanisms of depreciating realistic, conventional scales of values and retreating into their own autistic world. On the other hand, the plus d, plus m components of the present configuration in the C vector, show that the same subject at other times is eager to secure a multitude of material objects in order to master as well as to enjoy them.

Thus, according to my experience, the ambivalence toward reality of individuals yielding plus-minus d, plus-minus m manifests itself more in the succession of small time units than in the unbroken experience of hopeless conflicts, associated with those who reflect the C vectorial configuration in which the definite plus d shows that, in spite of actual frustrations, the individual is consistently attached to material reality beyond a willingness to deny its importance.

Plus-minus d, plus-minus m is generally the pattern occurring least frequently among all the sixteen possible variations in the C vector. It occurs with relatively greatest frequency in compulsion neurosis, in manic-depressive psychoses, and in early stages of paranoid schizophrenia. In the first group it corresponds to the basic ambivalence underlying all the object-relationships of compulsion neurotics. In manic-depressive psychotics, it reflects the moodiness, and in the early stages of paranoid schizophrenia, it most probably corresponds to the tenuous contact with reality which, in actual frustration, is given up easily in favor of an autistic irrealism.

This pattern in the C vector is virtually never found in children, and very rarely in puberty or adolescence. In other words, it appears most frequently in adulthood and old age.

CHAPTER X

The Sch Vector and the Stages of Ego Development

WE HAVE delayed discussion of the *Sch* vector because the constellation of its two component factors reflect the structure of the ego which can be considered the resultant— the elaboration on a more abstract level—of the partial drives corresponding to the other six factors; primarily, those contained in the *S* and *C* vectors.

A definition of the term *ego* as it is used generally in psychology would be in place here to facilitate discussion of the concept of the ego as conceived in the Szondi test. Unfortunately, a generally accepted definition of the ego does not exist. Widely used with more or less varying connotation, depending on the personal views of the author using it, the variety of meaning of the term is also evident within the so-called strictly Freudian psychoanalytic literature. Our definition is based primarily on concepts developed by Freud,* Nunberg,† and Schilder.‡ We will also refer to the concept of *self* as developed by Jung.§

Freud, in *The Ego and the Id*, describes topographically the personality as consisting of three main constituents: the id, the ego, and the superego. Of these constituents, the id is viewed as primary, representing the source of all instinc-

---

* Freud, Sigmund: The Ego and the Id. London, Hogarth Press, 1927.

† Nunberg, Herman: The Synthetic Function of the Ego. Internat. J. Psycho-Analysis, XII, 1931.

‡ Schilder, Paul: Introduction to a Psychoanalytic Theory of Psychiatry. Nerv. & Ment. Dis. Pub., 1927.

§ C. G. Jung: Psychological Types. New York and London, Harcourt, Brace & Co., 1923.

tive energy, and remaining practically unaltered during the course of the individual's life. This means that the id can be described as unaltered since the changes resulting from contact with the external world are conceived of as forming a separate organization within the psyche, the organization called the ego. Thus, basically the ego is a derivative of the genetically older psychic organization, the id. As a matter of fact, the word "organization" should hardly be applied to the id, since it is by definition disorganized, and since it is the tendency for organization and unity which differentiates the ego from the id.

The function of the ego is to mediate between the instinctual demands of the id and the requirements of the external reality. Topographically (visually) Freud represents the ego as being located on the surface of the id and taking notice of the external world through the perceptual system. The perceptual system also notices processes originating within the organism. By virtue of its relation to the motor system, the ego regulates the form of discharge of instinctual demands originating in the id. The primary striving of the ego is to establish a coherent organization of the personality by synthesizing conflicts of various origin into a resultant which will satisfy to some degree the original id-demands and avoid painful clashes with the limits determined by external reality or moralistic demands of the superego. There are various methods at the disposal of the ego to reach this goal of compromise; namely, the methods of identification or repression. We mean by identification that the original object of the libido is assimilated by the "synthetic" force inherent in the ego, so that the object which originally had been cathected in a libidinous way is incorporated in the ego, and thereby becomes not only desexualized but actually no longer needed as an external object.

Thus it is obvious that, through identification, drives originating in the id are drawn within the realm of the ego, thereby becoming more rational and easier to satisfy without clashing with limits set by reality or the superego. Yet it is also obvious that, as a result of this process, the original id-drives leave their imprints upon the structure of the ego, the ego being formed, to a great extent, by abandoned object-cathexes. This point should be stressed as a reminder that the dividing line between the id and ego is, to a great extent, arbitrary, and that these two concepts should not be regarded as two strictly separate entities, which is often the fallacy in superficial description of the psychoanalytic theory of personality structure by nonpsychoanalysts. This wariness should accompany delineation of all three constituents of the personality: the id, the ego, and the superego. All three are intimately related, and any separation can serve only the purpose of facilitating discussion of a specific aspect of the total personality.

From the point of view of the *Sch* vector, it is very important to keep in mind this arbitrariness in dividing the mental life into three constituents, since—as we shall see—on the one hand the interpretation of the *Sch* vector cuts across this division, and on the other hand the division is still useful in characterizing the psychologic functions of the k and p factors, respectively.

Thus, it might be more accurate to call the *Sch* vector the vector of the *self* than to call it the *ego* vector, since the *self*, according to Jung's definition, is a more inclusive concept than the ego.

The ego vector indicates the dynamic strength of the "instinctual" drives: the degree to which the urgency of these drives reaches consciousness, or the degree to which these drives appear in a symbolized form in consciousness (p factor) and the way in which they are integrated in the coherent organization of the mental life called the ego (the integration being the function of the k factor). Separate discussion of the two factors comprising the *Sch* vector is more forced and more difficult than separate discussion of any other vector, since the function of the *k* and *p* factors are more intimately bound together than are the functions of the two factors of any other vector. Yet delineation is necessary for purposes of discussion.

Our study of the *p* factor will preced that of the *k*, since the *k* factor reflects the manner in which the integrative part of the ego responds to drive-tensions indicated by the *p* factor.

The p *Factor*

In our study of the functions of the two factors within the *Sch* vector we are aided by the topological representation of the personality. This visual representation (fig. 8)

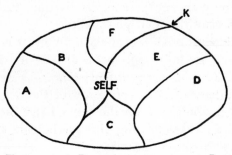

FIG. 8. TOPOLOGICAL REPRESENTATION OF THE PERSONALITY
A–F are various needs of the person. K is the boundary line between self and the environment.

is more adequate for our purposes than the visual representation given by Freud * in The Ego and the Id. As figure 8 indicates, we conceptualize the ego † as being formed of a number of areas corresponding to various needs, and

---

* An elaborated form of Freud's diagram is given in Healy, Bronner, and Bowers: The Structure and Meaning of Psychoanalysis, page 56.

† *Ego* will be used always in the wider sense outlined above, including, to a certain extent, psychic functions which according to psychoanalysis are located in the id. Closer examination of the similarities and differences between the functions of the *p* factor and those of the Freudian id will follow later in this chapter.

separated from each other by functional boundaries. The strength of the boundaries between the various need-systems determines the degree of ease or difficulty of communication between the corresponding needs. By "communication between need-systems," we refer to such psychologic processes as spreading of tension, the degree to which discharging one particular need has a concomitant releasing effect on another need, etc.*

The circular line surrounding the need-systems represents the boundary between the ego (personality) and the environment. The strength of this boundary determines the degree of separateness of the ego from the outer world.

The most general psychologic interpretation of the p factor refers to a need for communication between the own need-systems and the outer world. The function of the p factor is to dilate the ego by fusing into the objects of the environment. Thus, the dynamic goal of the drive inherent in the p is to break down the wall between subject and environment. The interpretation of the p factor is projection in the widest sense of the concept, not in the strictly psychoanalytic sense of the defense-mechanism of projection, whereby we mean the unconscious process of attributing something originating within the subject to an outside object because the specific content is unacceptable to the subject himself. This type of projection can be also implied in certain positions of the p factors, but what p indicates in every case is the need to project one's own needs on the environment, in the sense of finding appropriate objects in connection with which one can live out the specific need in question.

* The experimental work which furnishes more concrete, operational definitions for these topological dynamic concepts has been done by the psychologists of the Lewinian school. A condensed presentation of the most important original studies can be found in Lewin's *Dynamic Theory of Personality*, op. cit.

This is projection in the sense we use the term when we talk about "projective technics," by which we mean that the unstructured material offered in those technics makes it possible for the subject to *project* his personality on the material through manipulating it in the required way. The basic rationale of all projective technics is that by every action of ours we project our personality on the specific object we are dealing with; in other words, we continuously reveal our personality through a series of projections whether we are conscious of projection or not. In the Szondi test, it is the *p* factor which indicates this tendency of the organism for continuous self-expression through whatever action it performs. To express it in a grotesque form: projective technics would not work if we had no *p* factor.

Now that we have discussed all the other factors of the test with the exception of the *k,* we can compare the different types of object-relationships reflected by the different factors (*k* is the one factor representing the need *not* to have object-relationships). The plus *h* has indicated a strong need for an object for the sake of being loved tenderly by the object; the plus *s* showed the need of objects for the sake of manipulating them physically; the plus *hy,* in order to have an "audience"; the plus *d,* for the sake of possessing and controlling them, while the plus *m* shows the need of objects for the sake of deriving pleasure from and clinging to them. All of these various types of needs for object-relationships are more specific than the need to cathect objects as reflected in the *p* factor. This most general need to cathect objects is a need of different order from all the previous ones because it includes or refers to all of them. It is not a tautology to say that the *p* factor corresponds to the need to live out needs, whatever the specific content of these may be. Thus, the *p* corresponds to an expansive dynamic tendency of the organism to transgress its own boundaries and live out its needs in connection with environmental objects. In this sense, it widens the radius of the ego because, by driving the person to search for adequate objects which can be instrumental in the gratification of the various more specific needs, the ego fuses, at least temporarily, into those objects which were found adequate for this purpose. The factor p always refers to communication and contact with the outside. The more specific type of this contact has to be read from the quantitative distribution of choices within the other factors, and from their position. For example, a loaded plus m, with a strong p, indicates that the person is driven to live out his need to cling to others for support and to derive pleasure; while a strong p with a plus s, indicates that the person is driven to live out his need to manipulate objects aggressively. Of course, the basic tendency of any need is always in the direction of being lived out, which might give the impression that the p factor does not really add anything new to the interpretation based on the loadedness and position of the other factors. This, however, is not the case. Here we have hit a great difficulty in attempting to characterize the function of the p factor without opportunity to refer to its dynamic opposite, the k. The full meaning of either of these two factors can be understood only in relating their functions to each other.

The interpretation of the p factor, even if its specific content is reflected in factors of the other three vectors, does add something in particular to the interpretation of the total personality just because it corresponds to a need of a more inclusive order. It is because of its more general and more formal character that we refer to this factor as an ego need, in contrast to the other needs which are named according to their specific content. In explaining the character of this ego-need with the aid of figure 8, one could say that there is no particular inner-personal region corresponding to the p need, but that this is rather an overall need which can be referred only to the personality as a whole. It is a dynamic trend in the personality, additional to the specific dynamic trends characteristic for each single need. It is the need corresponding to the p factor which finally brings about object relationships. The more primary needs, which from the psychoanalytic point of view can be localized in the id, strive for satisfaction in a disorganized way without ability to discriminate between more or less adequate objects, since discrimination as a psychologic process is not considered as one of the functions of the id. Thus, in order to find an appropriate object to be cathected with the instinctual drives originating in the id, the function of the ego is also needed in order to find an appropriate love-object. According to this theory, object-love is always the result of the joint functioning of the id-drives and the guiding of these drives towards an appropriate love-object, which is the function of the ego. This guiding of the id-drives towards environmental objects is the function of the p factor. Therefore, we are justified in including this factor in the ego vector, since it corresponds to a drive more goal-directed than are those localized within the id. Yet the p factor reflects the strength of the id-drives, as they appear within the ego in the form of a rather coherent and organized drive to find objects adequate to be cathected with the id-drives. Thus, the strength of the p factor can serve to indicate the influence of the id-drives upon behavior.

The rationale underlying interpretation of this complex psychologic process on the basis of choice-reactions to portraits of paranoid patients is still to be clarified. Paranoia—in this context—is considered as the prototype, or as the pathologically exaggerated form, of that psychologic state in which the boundary around the ego has been broken down so that there is no more definite delineation between subject and environment. The paranoid patient pushes his thoughts and feelings into the outside world to the extent that he perceives processes originating within himself as having been originated in another individual, which could be the formal description of the pathologic forms of projection found in paranoics. Ideas of reference, ideas of persecution or delusions of grandeur, are the characteristic symptoms of paranoid patients and all of these symptoms have in common the tendency of dilating the ego in the sense of fusing irrationally into an outside object. The first symptoms of paranoia are typically disturbances in the sphere of perception and in the thought processes in the form of relating everything to oneself. The paranoid person connects everything around him with himself: he thinks people talk about him, he believes he can read the minds of others; he views even newspapers as dealing with his own most personal problems. This pathologic need to connect oneself with the environment explains why we are able to interpret the general need for communication and contact with the outside, from the subject's reactions to stimulus material representing paranoid patients. These characteristics of paranoids can be considered as the manifestations at one end, the pathologic end, of a continuum, at the beginning of which the corresponding manifestations are the normal need to establish contacts and to project one's needs in the environment by the very process of living.

Plus p

This p constellation means that the individual identifies himself with the above described need for emotional contact with the environment. It indicates a "fluid" ego, in the sense of readily allowing the libido to "flow out" and cathect outside objects. Subjects with plus p have always the tendency to "fuse" with something outside themselves. This might take the form of having the need to fall in love with a person, with an idea, or, in some cases, with humanity as a whole. The main characteristic is the need to transgress one's own boundaries, which need often results in personality traits one usually calls "idealistic."

Probably the most beautiful illustration of this need for communication is given in Schiller's ode, *An die Freude,* which has been set to music by Beethoven in the last movement of his Ninth Symphony:

> ". . . Alle Menschen werden Brüder
> Wo dein sanfter Flügel weilt.
> Seid umschlungen, Millionen!
> Diesen Kuss der ganzen Welt!
> Brüder, überm' Sternenzelt
> Muss ein lieber Vater wohnen.
>
> Wem der grosse Wurf gelungen
> Eines Freundes Freund zu sein,
> Wer ein holdes Weib errungen,
> Mische seinen Jubel ein!
> Ja—wer' auch nur eine Seele
> Sein nennt auf dem Erdenrund!
> Und wers nie gekonnt, der stehle
> Weinend sich aus diesem Bund."

A more adequate description of the need corresponding to plus p could not be given. There is the expression of the need to embrace the whole of humanity, the need to make friends, the need to love, and to express one's emotions. (The last two lines could be referred to the psychologic oppositeness between the p and k tendencies, the latter representing the need for separateness and relinquishment of object-relationships.)

It is most probably not by chance that it occurred to me to illustrate the needs inherent in the plus p constellation by quoting parts of a famous poem, since the need for artistic and creative productivity as such is mostly associated with plus p, especially the need for verbal, i.e., to a certain extent conceptualized, expression. Most writers yield plus p, as do a great number of individuals who feel the need to write without being able really to do it. This need for self-expression is the consequence of the "fluid" ego-structure characteristic of plus p individuals. The term *fluid* is used to denote the ease with which emotional material can reach consciousness, which implies the passing of this material through the psychologic system *preconscious,* which—according to psychoanalytic theory—consists of word-images. It consists of what was earlier verbalized material and can again be verbalized. This characteristic of the plus p constellation, namely that emotional material is perceived after having passed through the preconscious in which verbal concepts have been attached to it, accounts for the close link between plus p and the capacity for verbal forms of sublimation. One could also say that subjects with plus p have usually a high capacity for symbolizing their needs, by which is meant that some aspects at least of their emotional needs are actually perceived. This, however, does not mean that they are aware of all their needs or of the full meaning of the particular needs. In other words, subjects with plus p still have an unconscious; the plus p indicates only that the urging quality of emotions have risen to consciousness and have been conceptualized in some way, giving no answer to the question as to what extent the conceptualization represents the full meaning of the need.

The basic need implied in the plus p, the need for transgressing the limits of one's own ego, can also manifest itself in self-assertive, and sometimes actually aggressive behavior, in which case it appears in conjunction with plus s. However, even in these cases aggression usually does not imply physical aggression or seriously antisocial behavior; it implies, rather, aggression within the framework of a socially acceptable goal-setting. Primitive forms of aggression seem to be contradictory to the relatively high level of conceptualization implied in plus p. The fact that plus p is found infrequently in occupational groups which do not involve working on some sort of conceptualized material, points to the same aspect of this constellation. Plus p is most unusual in laborers (physical workers), but it is one of the most frequent p factorial constellations among college students.

The most important pathodiagnostic significance of this constellation refers to paranoid individuals, not necessarily in the form of paranoid psychosis, although plus p is characteristic for those forms of paranoia which show idealistic, religious content in the delusions. One cannot say more about the possible pathologic implications of plus p without being able to specify the corresponding constellation of the k factor. More will be said in connection with the various constellations in the *Sch* vector.

Plus p is a characteristic reaction for adolescents and young adults. It occurs most rarely in children of six to nine years of age, and in adults around seventy.

Minus p

Tension in the p factor in either direction is indicative of the need to demolish the boundaries of the individuality and to fuse with the outer world; however, in the case of minus p, this need is not recognized as such by the person. The more loaded the minus p is, the greater is the tension and the urgency of the needs demanding to be acted out. Indeed, there is acting out to a great extent with, however, a continual "short circuit" of recognition. Subjects with strong minus p do project their personality into the outer world through their actions; in other words, they structure their environment according to their own pattern of needs without, however, being conscious that this is what they are doing. Comparing this process with that described in connection with plus p, one could say that in case of minus p, the need-tensions are acted out without having first passed through the system of preconscious, thus, without their becoming linked to word-images. The results of the study

already quoted on various groups of artists, musicians, and
writers, can serve to illustrate these statements. While
minus p was practically nonexistent in writers, it was the
most characteristic reaction of painters. I think that the
difference between the creative processes involving the
manipulation of word-symbols, or that of expressing oneself
by means of visual images without necessarily being able
to verbalize the emotional content implicit in the final art
product, is what accounts for the significant difference
between the frequency of minus p within the above two
groups of creative subjects.

The frequency of minus p in the general population,
with the possible exclusion of any selective factor, is much
higher than that of plus p. According to our theory, that
would mean that most people act according to their emotional needs, which is to say that we are continuously engag-
ing in unconscious projection, which statement has been
our starting point in the discussion of the p factor, and
which sounds so simple and self-evident that it really takes
some time to realize its full psychologic implication. It
is exactly this common lack of understanding of the full
psychologic implications of our own actions, the lack of
recognizing the connection between everyday activities and
the underlying, deeper emotional needs, which accounts for
the findings that minus p is by far the most frequent p factorial constellation in any age group. Of course there are
certain age groups in which the difference between the frequency of the minus p and that of the second most frequent p constellation is smaller than in others, but in absolute amount, minus p leads throughout.

Besides this most general meaning of the unconscious
projection implied in minus p, more pathologic forms of
unconscious projection, in the real sense of paranoid defense-
mechanism, also can be implied in this position of the p.
If other signs in the test-profile series point towards psy-

chosis, the minus p might mean pathologic ideas of reference, suspiciousness, a tendency for false interpretations, and
a tendency to blame others, and to perceive needs originating
in the *self* as coming from the outside. Most probably
because of these potential "extra-punitive" tendencies,
minus p is even more frequent in groups of antisocial individuals than in the population at large.

Some of the possible positive manifestations of the unconscious projection inherent in this p position, have been mentioned in connection with artistic creativity of a nonverbal
type. Other forms of sublimation, characteristic for minus p,
can be thought-processes involving certain intuitive or mystical characteristics. This type of thinking does not follow
the accepted rules of logic, but proceeds rather by sudden
intuitive insights, in which there is felt no necessity to conceptualize the links leading up to the final results. (If intuition,
as such, is conceptualized as an accepted element in thinking, then the corresponding p constellation is no longer
minus, but *plus*.)

Some of the psychopathologic implications of minus p
already have been mentioned. Its frequency in all forms
of psychoses is far higher than the average frequency in the
general population. This is understandable on the basis
of the "prelogical," projective thinking of which minus p
can be an indication, and which can be found in practically
any form of psychosis; not only in paranoia. Of course,
another way to express this finding is to say that most psychoses represent mixed forms of various elements, and in
institutionalized cases there are usually paranoid traits, no
matter what the official diagnosis may be. This statement
is true particularly for cases of psychotic depression in which
paranoid elements are most well-known. The high frequency of minus p in antisocial individuals has also been
mentioned. It should be added, however, that in those

cases, minus p is associated with minus m, and mostly plus s, or plus h and open s. Thus, on the basis of our theory we are led to consider antisocial activity in these cases as the consequence of a process of projection, most probably in the form of attributing the blame for one's own frustration to specific objects of the environment, which objects can be "justly" punished as the source of disappointment. The whole question of objective or distorted social perception could be related to the function of the minus p. Examination of this topic is beyond the scope of this book: it is mentioned here because of its implications for research in experimental social psychology.

It is worthwhile to consider briefly the two groups in which minus p occurs least frequently—in which its frequency falls far below that found in any age group of the unselected population. These groups are represented by compulsion neurotics and hypochondriacs. Why minus p should be found rarely in these patients can be understood when we remember that in these two forms of neuroses there occurs the least displacement of one's own needs and conflicts to the outside. The symptom formations of both compulsive neurosis and hypochondria are carried out for the most part in connection with the *self;* i.e., the formations take place within the own personality without necessarily involving outsiders. This symptom formation is related to the function of the minus k rather than of the minus p which always indicates the subject's dynamic tendency to involve others in his own neurosis. Thus the neuroses associated with minus p are less private than those associated with minus k, the former having always a wider radius of effect. As we have pointed out earlier, minus p is always, in absolute number, the most frequent p factorial constellation in all age groups. It is, however, more frequent in children and the aged than it is in adolescents and younger adults. It is definitely least frequent in the

17–20 year old group, which apparently reflects the ages at which individuals are most aware of their needs. Children and individuals of advanced age characteristically project their needs upon the environment without awareness of their projection.

Plus-minus p

The plus-minus p constellation reflects an almost conscious conflict in regard to the need to fuse into the environment. The subject is in part aware of this need (plus p), and in part acts it out unconsciously (minus p). The outcome of this ambivalence depends so much on the accompanying position of the k factor that characterization of the plus-minus p, independent from the k, is almost impossible. Under favorable circumstances (when plus k occurs), plus-minus p can accompany a creative, or at least a productive, personality. In this case, the ambitendency of the p can be interpreted as showing the existing connection between conscious and intuitive (unconscious) thought-processes, which connection appears to be desirable in certain phases of creative thinking.

In other instances, however, plus-minus p is indication of subjectively experienced unhappiness, or helplessness. This, again, is one of the instances in which empirical knowledge has by far preceded theoretical understanding. It has been found that individuals undergoing a crisis in their relationship to their most important love object give plus-minus p frequently. By *crisis* is meant such well definable instances at which the person yielding plus-minus p feels abandoned by the object of his love. What the relation might be between the feeling of being abandoned and the plus-minus p constellation is not easy to conceive, although there obviously is a connection. It most probably accompanies the subjectively experienced conflict characteristic of this constellation. It appears logical that in times of crises, when fusion into the love-object encounters difficulties in reality, the need itself would be experienced more acutely, which is indicated by the plus-minus constellation of the p factor.

If fusion into an object does not cause any particular conflict, then the corresponding p constellation is either plus or minus, which expresses the subject's need to expand his own ego. The basic meaning of the p factor makes it apparently difficult to split one's attitude in regard to this particular need. One would expect that once there is any indication of conscious acceptance of this need (plus p), there should be no reason for an unconscious component relating to the same need (minus p) unless the unconscious (the minus p) component really refers to projection as a defense mechanism whereby the subject attempts to rid himself of unacceptable *own* needs by projecting them on objects of the environment. The situation is quite different when there is no sign of the person's inclination to experience his needs consciously; in other words, if there is no plus p at all. These cases may simply imply that the person's attention is not directed toward the perception of stimuli originating within himself; i.e., within his own organism. If, however, the person tends to perceive stimulations originating from within while there occurs unconscious projection sufficient to produce a minus p reaction as strong as the plus p, then the resulting feeling is that of indecision and doubt whether stimuli coming from within may be considered as acceptable and constructive, or alien to the organism. (These statements will assume a somewhat modified meaning following discussion of the corresponding k factorial constellations, which also can express acceptance or nonacceptance, although on a different level.)

In the general population, plus-minus p is the least frequent position of the p factor. The pathologic groups in which plus-minus p is relatively the most frequent are composed of those suffering paranoid forms of neuroses, latent homosexuals, and suicidal individuals. By paranoid forms of neuroses, I mean those forms in which the source of the conflict is projected into the environment, the subject suffering feelings of unjust treatment. Neurotic patients who feel abandoned or not wanted acutely enough by their love object fall in this category. The high percentage of suicidal patients who yield the same p constellation, can be understood on the basis of the same mechanism. The relationship between latent homosexuality and paranoid traits, which was first discovered by Freud * explains why plus-minus p is also frequent in this group.

The fact that plus-minus p appears least frequently among all the four possible p constellations has already been mentioned. Its frequency fluctuates between approximately ten to fourteen per cent in the various age groups, becoming even less frequent in ages above sixty. This decrease is due to the preponderance of minus p in old age, which in elderly individuals indicates the lack of even partially inward-directed perception and their lack of concern with conceptualizing their own emotional needs.

Open p

The open p constellation indicates that the dynamic tension of the subject's need to fuse his own personality into the environment has somehow been eliminated. This means that the subject no longer experiences the urgency of this need, which psychologic state of relative calmness might be due to various reasons. In this more than in any other connection, the p can not be considered without the k factor, since this elimination of outside object-directed need tension is usually due not to direct discharge but to the simultaneous function of the k factor. In these Sch configurations, in which the p factor is drained, the lack of tension usually

---

* Freud, Sigmund: Psychoanalytic Notes upon an Autobiographical Account of a Case of Paranoia. Collected Papers III.

means that it has been consumed by the k factor, either through the ego-mechanism of introjection, or through repression. However, in these cases, the activity of the end-result is quite far removed from the original emotional content of the p factor. Although the plus k factor aids in bringing about the unification between subject and object, which was the original goal of the p need, yet this unification is reached not by fusing *into* the object, but by introjecting the outside object *within* the *own* ego. In the course of this process, much of the primary emotional content of the original drive has been transformed into more intellectual content; or, in psychoanalytic terms; erotic libido originating in the id (in the test, corresponding more or less to the p content) has been transformed into narcissistic or ego libido (corresponding to the function of the k factor). Yet, this "neutralizing" process originating in the ego's (k factor's) wish to keep the organism possibly free from disturbing tensions, can actually succeed in its aim, which then is indicated on the test by the draining of the p factor; that is, by open p.

At other times, open p can indicate that the tension of the p-need has been eliminated through repression, or through a compulsive type of symptom-formation, which of course implies repression of the original tendency. Yet, in "ideal" cases of this compulsive process, the symptom itself represents the warded-off tendency, as well as the repression of the tendency; in other words, the symptom itself always can be regarded as a compromise.* It is due to this compromise-quality of the symptom that even this compulsive process based on repression of the id-drive can effect a superficial calmness in the ego by ridding the id-drives of their original tenseness—at least temporarily and superficially—thereby establishing some sort of a pseudo calmness

---

* Freud, Sigmund: Introductory Lectures on Psychoanalysis. New York, Liveright Publishing Corp., 1935.

within the ego.   In the event that this whole process succeeds
in reaching the above briefly outlined psychodynamic goal,
the corresponding p constellation—indicating that the tension of the id-drives have been eliminated—is again the
open p.

These interpretations of the open p hold true in all cases
in which the accompanying constellation in the k factor is
not open.   In other words, only when it is accompanied by
open k does open p mean elimination of emotional tension
by an actual living out of the need to fuse into an outside
object.   In these cases, it does indicate that strong emotional contact with the outside is a constant feature of the
personality.

The pathologic significance of open p refers first of all
to compulsion neurosis.   The psychodynamic connection
between the two has been discussed above.   Open p is also
relatively frequent in those forms of anxiety in which there
is a definitely structured symptom and *no* free-floating
anxiety; in other words, in phobic anxieties and hypochondriac anxiety.   The significance of open p in these groups
is most probably similar to that in compulsion neurosis.

The group in which open p occurs most rarely is represented by manic psychotics, which is understandable when
one thinks of the violent object-directed symptoms of this
psychosis.

The distribution of open p is fairly even throughout the
various age groups.   It is most frequent in prepuberty
(about 30 per cent), from which group it decreases gradually,
showing a sudden drop only in very advanced age, beyond
seventy years.   This sudden decrease is concurrent to the
frequency of minus p in those of advanced age.

The k Factor

The most general interpretation of the k factor refers to
the need to maintain the separateness and the integrity of

the ego. In terms of figure 8, one can say that the k factor functions as boundary-forces, acting in the direction against the outgoing tendencies of the inner-personal needs, thereby forming a barrier between the ego (or the *self*) and the environment, and also aiming to keep up the separation of the different need-systems within the individual. In this sense, the k factor aims at maintaining the rigidity of the ego by keeping the needs within the personality rather than by permitting them to flow out and cathect outside objects. At this point in our discussion it becomes obvious why we can call the k and the p factors opposites in the dynamic sense of the term, since the direction of their effectiveness is opposite; the p factor attempting to break down the boundaries to let the libido flow out freely in order to find objects adequate for cathexis, the k factor making rigid the boundaries to confine the libido. The p shows the person's need to fuse into his environment, while the k factor shows the extent and process by which the individual avoids emotional bonds with the world.

This process of avoidance of emotional bonds leads us directly into the explanation why pictures of catatonic schizophrenic patients can be used to "measure" the subject's ego on this dimension of rigidity and emotional detachment. In the context of this test, we think of catatonic patients as epitomizing rigidity of personality, in the sense of having the minimum of fluid emotional contact between libidinal energy and the environment. The well-known catatonic symptoms, apathy, mutism, diminution of all activities, lack of reaction to painful stimuli, verbal expression of emotions—sometimes even violent emotions—without corresponding feeling, and the generally exaggerated tendency for seclusion and lack of contact with persons of the environment, could be formally (or topologically) characterized as reflecting the exaggerated rigidity of the functional barrier surrounding the personality and also the rigidity of the inner structure of the personality.

Of course the same tendency which aims to keep up the separateness and the structure of the ego, is part of everybody's personality. One could not conceive of human character in general, without the existence of this need to differentiate between person and environment. Again, it should be remembered that the lack of choices in a certain factor does not mean a corresponding complete lack of tension in the respective need. Tension, or lack of tension, are relative concepts in the interpretation of the test, always taking the distribution of all possible choices within the eight factors as the frame of reference. Consequently, one can not conceive of anybody having no need to keep himself at least to some extent separate from the environment, even when there are no choices in the k factor. However, the difference in regard to this need between the subject who chooses no k portraits and the person who chooses five or six k portraits, is considerable. Yet, even the fact that a subject chooses all six k portraits—when they are chosen as "likes" as well as "dislikes"—does not indicate that the subject's ego is rigid to the extent of causing psychotic behavior, since the k factor is not the only force determining rigidity of the ego. There is always a simultaneous countertendency in the direction of the outgoingness, represented by the p.

The psychologic interpretation of the k factor, which can be applied in all cases—in so-called "normals" as well as in neurotics or psychotics—is narcissism, in the Freudian sense of the concept, or introversion in the strictly psychoanalytic sense and not in the manner it is used superficially, with a negative value judgment attached. (Introversion is used in the superficial sense in the usual pencil and paper personality tests.) Thus narcissism, or introversion, in the sense of the meaning of the k factor, is the tendency to keep within the person as much of the total psychic energy as possible. In other words, the "ideal" goal of narcissism is to rid the person of all those needs which tend to connect him to outside objects. This narcissistic desire can be carried out primarily through two mechanisms: (1) through introjecting the original object of the libido, whereby the object originally outside is internalized within the own ego (so that following a successful process of identification, the person can love himself rather than the environmental object); (2) through attempting to maintain narcissistic integrity of the person by repression of needs which would bring about the undesirable connections with the outer world.* It is not, of course, due to chance that the person resorts to one or the other narcissistic mechanism. The choice depends on a number of factors; mainly, the general personality structure of the person, and the more specific nature of the need which tries to manifest itself in connection with an appropriate outside object. Whether or not this narcissistic intention of the k factor has succeeded in a subject can be read in the test by the position of the p. In the discussion of the open p constellation, it has been mentioned that in cases in which the k has succeeded in consuming the outward-directed tension of the p factor, the p is found in "open" position.

I am aware of the fact that there is a great overlap between the Freudian concept of ego and what has been said about the function of the k factor. For some purposes, the p factor may be considered—although not quite accurately—as originating in the id, while the k factor may be considered as originating in the ego. For example, Freud's metaphor, given in his work *The Ego and the Id*, in which he compares the ego to a man on horseback, the rider holding in check the superior strength of the horse, can also be applied to the relationship between the k and p. Often, if the rider does not want to be parted from the horse, he has to guide it where it wants to go. In the same manner, Freud points out, the ego continuously has to carry out the wishes of the id as though they were its own.

* The connection between narcissism and repression is usually not pointed out in this manner in psychoanalytic literature.

This holding in check the dynamic tendencies implied in the p factor is really the function of the k factor. Yet the p represents not exactly the id, but—as we have said in the general characterization of the p—the more direct derivatives of the id wishes as they appear within the ego. If we associate the word *passion* with the id, and the word *reason* with the ego, then p is definitely the representative of passion, while k is that of reason.

Of course, all our difficulties in coordinating psychoanalytic concepts with specific factors and factorial constellations in the Szondi test, are unavoidable since originally these concepts are not meant to be strictly definable, even within the framework of psychoanalytic theory. Freud describes these concepts rather than defines them, and never fails to mention their partial overlap within his own system. The conceptual framework of the Szondi test was added later, on the basis of analyzing and conceptualizing empirical experience rather than on the basis of a preconceived system. Consequently, a single theoretical concept ultimately is represented by more than one factor or constellation, and one factor refers to more than one theoretical concept. Yet, returning to our discussion of the k factor, it is helpful to link its interpretation to the functions of Freud's concept of the ego. The individual discussions of the four possible k positions will doubtless help to clarify the general meaning of the k factor.

Plus k

This constellation in the k factor reflects the most clearcut narcissistic reaction, if we think of secondary—and not primary—narcissism. Secondary narcissism is implied by the subject's conscious attitude of acceptance of the need to maintain the self-sufficient integrity of his ego. The function of the k, as has been said, always is to reduce the outward-directed tension implied in the p factor; however, in the case of plus k, this elimination of tension is attempted primarily by the ego-mechanism of introjection.   Introjection, again, is not quite an unambiguous concept, demanding some further consideration.

Identification, as Freud describes it, permits the ego to cope with situations in which a love object has to be given up.* Following such situations, one can often observe in the ego a modification which can be described as a reinstatement of the object within the ego.   In other words, the ego, in order to reconcile itself to the loss of the love object, brings about changes within itself in order to become similar to the object.   The ego then may love the image of the object within itself despite the loss of the original.

This is, then, a mechanism which leads the ego to self-sufficiency, and makes libidinal satisfaction fairly independent of the outer world.   Discussion of this process is advanced here not as a recapitulation of Freudian ego-mechanism, but because the process is, exactly, the function of the plus k. The more loaded the plus k appears, the stronger is the drive for emotional independence in the person.   An individual giving plus k does not want to become involved in emotional relationships probably because he feels that it is unsafe to cathect an object he can lose.   Once the object is built up within the *own* ego, nobody can take it away: there is no more danger of losing it.

All this also fits in with the essence of narcissism; the tendency to direct the libido back to the self instead of investing it in outside objects.   Since the investment of the libido in outside objects is implied in the p, we are justified in saying that the aim of the k is to rid the organism from tension caused by the p, when p stands for the wish to have contact with the outside.   Szondi termed the function of the p factor *ego-diastole* (borrowing from physiology, in which diastole refers to the heart's dilating function), and the function of the k factor *ego-systole* (systole in physiology

* Freud, S.: Mourning and Melancholia. Collected Papers, Vol. III.

referring to the heart's contracting function). Actually these expressions are helpful only following elaboration of the meaning of the *k* and *p* functions. Otherwise, the terms may lead to misunderstanding, since it is questionable whether calling introjective mechanisms ego-"contracting" is justified. Introjection, as such, does not contract the ego; rather it enlarges it through the process of incorporating outside objects into the *self*. In another sense, of course, introjection *does* impoverish the ego, exactly because it rids the ego of dynamic, outgoing tension.

In one sense, projection (the *p* factor) and introjection (the *k* factor) are *not* opposite in that they both aim at destroying the boundary between subject and object. The difference lies in the manner in which the boundary is destroyed: by projection, the boundary is destroyed when the ego fuses into the outside object; by introjection, the boundary becomes non-existent when the outside object is taken in, to rest within the boundary of one's own ego. In a representation of the most extreme results of each of these functions, the visual symbolic representation would amount to practically identical end-situations. In both cases, of course, one would begin with two independent entities: (1) the person within, and (2) the outside world (fig. 9). At the end of a hypothetically complete projection (which, of course, never exists in reality), the boundary surrounding the person disappears since the total personality fuses into the environment. The corresponding symbolic representation would require only one circle, representing complete fusion. A hypothetically complete introjection means that the environment has been "eaten up" by the person, so that everything which had been outside is internalized. The corresponding symbolic representation again would be a single circle, representing now a total assimilation, by which the individual would reach a perfect state of self-sufficiency. He would contain the universe: for himself, he *is* the universe.

If the function of introjection is pursued theoretically to this unrealistically extreme degree, certain cases of catatonic schizophrenia which at first seem to oppose our original assumption that catatonic patients may be considered to represent the pathologic extreme of loss of contact with the environment, are no longer contradictory. For example, a catatonic patient described as having been in a typical catatonic rigid position for a considerable length of time was cited as proof against the theoretical explanation of the k factor that the catatonic may be regarded as the proto-type of those who close the defensive wall around their egos. After recovery from what seemed a catatonic "stupor," the patient explained that the reason for his immobility was that the forces of "good" and "evil" were having a fight in the universe, and his least movement would have influenced the outcome of this fight. The accompanying argument implied that many times a catatonic we consider rigid because he lacks contact with the environment is actually deeply concerned with universal happenings. This case, I think, not only fails to contradict assumptions which in the Szondi test refer to the nature of catatonic schizophrenia, but it is a beautiful illustration of the result in the ego of the most extreme introjective processes. I would interpret this example not as proving that the patient had contact with the universe, but as showing the psychotic distortion of the ego after it had introjected the universe, and thereby lost contact with outside happenings. This patient lacked even the paranoid's distorted interpretation of his environment; rather he experienced vague universal happenings within the boundary of his own *self* (or ego), not as something happening beyond the boundary. His fear of influencing the balance of forces by the least movement of his own, clearly indicates, I think, the completely narcissistic nature of his experience, and illustrates what we mean by the extreme functioning of the plus k, which I suppose this

276 Riverside Drive
New York 25, N. Y.

patient would have, although unfortunately we have no Szondi profile of him.

Another feature of the plus k is illustrated in pathologic form in the above example; that is, the person's egocentricity, which so many times is implied in this k constellation. The illustration is easy to understand, since egocentricity is almost the same as narcissism, except that the term is used in a sense more socially negative, implying the asocial consequences of narcissism in manifest behavior. However, in certain configurations of the total test pattern, the narcissism of plus k does not imply egocentricity in the above sense (for example, minus h, minus s, plus e, minus hy, plus k). In other cases, when the rest of the profile indicates the possibility of psychosis, the narcissism of plus k might reach the degree even of psychotic autism, as in the above example of the catatonic patient.

Character traits corresponding to plus k in so-called normal individuals may be the following: striving for self-sufficiency; striving to be unemotional by means of intellectualizing emotions. Subjects with plus k are likely to have good insight into emotional processes; they are willing to face their own emotions. However, in the very process of facing emotions intellectually, the individual absorbs the original emotionality, so that emotions become more the object of intellectual manipulations than the driving force for really emotional actions.

Plus k offers good possibilities for certain types of sublimation, mostly sublimation involving learning, logical thinking, systematizing, and reproducing learned material. In other words, plus k is linked with the less originally creative and less dynamic forces of sublimation. The synthetic function of the ego, as described by Nunberg,* can easily be linked with the function of the plus k, as manifested in thinking

---

* Nunberg, H.: The Synthetic Function of the Ego. Internat. J. Psycho-Analysis, XII, 1931.

processes. Nunberg points out that there is a specific force within the ego which functions as an intermediary between the inner and the outer world, attempting to adjust opposing elements within the personality. The functioning of this force is needed when a certain craving appears in the organism without being gratified by the environment. In these cases, Nunberg says, "the ego ideationally assimilates the id's objects; this is done by identification. Through identification, certain instincts and objects not consonant with the ego are not merely warded off, but united, modified, fused, divested of their specific element of danger." This process of assimilating and neutralizing cravings originating in the id, Nunberg calls the synthetic function of the ego, which could be applied word by word to the function of the k factor as related to the content of the p. Nunberg goes even as far as saying that our "need for causality" which is such a predominant feature of human thinking, is the intellectual manifestation of the same synthetic function of the ego. Findings of the Szondi test would certainly support this theory, and would also bear out the connection between this "synthetic function of the ego" and the plus k. Subjects with plus k are definitely inclined toward this kind of "synthetic" causal thinking, the logical derivations and systematization of thought-processes playing an important part in the thinking of these subjects. These systematic thought-processes are quite different from the more intuitive and "emotional" thinking characteristic of individuals with a much stronger p than k factor.

Certain data of a study on musical taste and personality * can be interpreted in the same sense, although the data do not refer to intellectual thinking processes, but to aesthetic judgments. The results of this study clearly show that the preference for strictly classical music (Bach, Mozart) is asso-

---

* Deri, Otto: Musical Taste and Personality. Unpublished M.A. thesis, Columbia University, 1947.

ciated with a strong plus k factor, while preference for romantic music (Wagner, Schumann) is found in subjects whose p factor is significantly more loaded than the k. Interpretation of these findings refers to the strict "logical" structure of classical music, versus the less clearly structured but more "emotional" character of romantic music. One more experimental finding in regard to the plus k needs mention. A series of test profiles obtained from patients undergoing psychoanalytic treatment, shows clearly the tendency of the k factor to become positive in the course of the analysis.

This could be interpreted as indication that the process of cure brings about an intellectual assimilation of emotional material, which actually is what takes place in psychoanalysis. Another meaning of the same finding may be that plus k reflects the process whereby the patient introjects the personality of the analyst. The two interpretations are by no means mutually exclusive. I am rather inclined to believe that both interpretations are simultaneously valid, and are also dynamically related, since through identifying himself with the analyst, the patient dares to face his own emotional problems.

The corollary to the above findings is that plus k is rarely found in those forms of neuroses which involve strong and "successful" repression of emotions. It can be found in character-neurotics who are intellectually aware of their problems, but who, due to the rigidity of their character, are unable or unwilling to change. Plus k is found relatively frequently in depressive psychosis. The connection between melancholia (depression) and the mechanism of introjection is described in detail in Freud's *Mourning and Melancholia* (op. cit.). On the basis of experiments with depressive patients before and after electro-shock treatments, I formulated a hypothesis in the light of which symptoms of depression are considered as being the consequence of unsuccessful attempts to repress certain emotional material. The supporting data on the Szondi Test were significant changes in the k factor from the plus towards the minus direction after completion of shock treatment.*

Plus k is most unusual in manic psychosis.

The age distribution of plus k shows that it is most frequent in young children between the ages of three and five. The frequency of plus k in this age group is more than twice the frequency in adults, probably because "physiologic" autism is characteristic of young children. The works of Piaget illustrate this autism in regard to behavior, to thinking, and to reasoning and use of the language. This is the age of stubbornness, and feeling of omnipotence, when children feel they understand and own the world. The frequency of plus k shows a sudden drop around the age of schooling, which might be interpreted in two ways: either as a consequence of enforced drill; or as the sign of a "physiologic" readiness to give up infantile autism. It should not be too difficult to explore this problem experimentally by comparing the profiles of six year old school children with profiles of children of the same age who, due to some reason, have not been sent to school. One might even get results by comparing children's test profiles from "progressive" schools with profiles from old-fashioned "drill" schools.

At approximately the age of puberty, the frequency of plus k again increases, and remains more or less constant (approximately 12–16 per cent) until old age. Beyond the age of seventy, plus k is found most infrequently, since at that age repression is used much more than introjection to eliminate emotional tension. Actually, repression is used more than introjection in all the age groups (which, in terms of the Szondi test means that minus k is more frequent than plus k) except that introjection (plus k) drops suddenly in ages beyond seventy.

* Deri, Susan: The Results of the Szondi Test on Depressive Patients Before and After Electric Shock Treatment. Chapter in Bellak, L., & Abt, L., Handbook on Projective Techniques. New York, Ronald Press Co., in press.

Minus k

The minus *k* also reflects the attempt to maintain the narcissistic integrity of the ego. The aim, again, is to eliminate the tension implied in the content of the *p* factor. However, minus *k* is an indication that whatever was the content of the *p* factor is not accepted by the critical part of the ego and by all means by the superego. Because of the intolerance of the ego and superego against emotional content which is implied in the tension of the *p* factor, the ego can not cope with the tension by using the mechanism of introjection. The emotional content or the object toward which the need-tension expressed in the *p* factor is striving is not permitted to be incorporated consciously into the ego, not even after divestment from its original emotionality and transformation into emotionally neutral intellectual interest. The minus *k* indicates that the id-demand represented by the *p* is neither wanted nor accepted into the ego: the ego does not want to synthesize its content, so that under these circumstances the only way to assure at least a relative harmony within the ego is to repress the forbidden impulses. The reason that these impulses clamor for acceptance into the ego is that the ego controls the motor system, and thereby controls the way excitations are discharged. Repression, on the other hand, aims exactly at the opposite; namely, to "encapsulate" the forbidden need so that it has possibly no communication with other parts of the ego, and certainly no access to the motor system: the main avenue for discharge must be barred. In other words, the ego does everything within its power to disown that particular part of the personality which corresponds to the forbidden id-demand. The real aim would be, of course, to make the tension caused by the id-demand nonexistent; however, without some sort of gratification a need cannot simply be extinguished. At best, the superego exerts pressure upon the ego to sever connections between the unwanted impulse and the rest of the ego. This is actually the structural meaning of the unconscious

dynamism of repression. The description of repression in
terms of the structure of the self helps to realize the structural unity of the function of the k factor, whether it acts
through introjection (plus k), or repression (minus k). In
each case the k acts as an organizing power, aiming to establish a firm structure of the ego by maintaining the boundaries around the personality as well as the boundaries between
the innerpersonal regions within the person.   Since we
assume that the content of the innerpersonal regions corresponds to various needs, it is obvious that maintaining the
structure means also reducing the need-tension.   Otherwise,
the increasing tensions would endanger the firmness of the
structure, because of the drive inherent in any need-tension,
which aims towards the outside in order to find the proper
object with which it can obtain gratification (this tendency
being implied in the p factor). Thus it is clear why we may
say that the "organizing power" implied in the k factor aims
at maintaining the structure of the ego through reducing the
tension implied in the p. Introjection and repression are
similar functions in that they both aim at keeping the ego
"tension-free" and detached from outside objects: yet they
are opposite because introjection—by definition—operates
through including something into the ego which had previously been an outside object, while repression operates
through excluding something from the personality; i.e., by
isolation excluding a need which had originated within the
organism.   In this sense one could refute the argument
raised recently that although, pragmatically, it has been
proved that the test is valid, any attempt to build up a more
or less unified conceptual framework to explain the validity
has failed. The question was asked: on what theoretical
basis could one accept the conclusion that repression is the
opposite of catatonic schizophrenia, which evidently follows
from the interpretation of the k factor, since the pictures
themselves represent catatonic schizophrenia?   I would agree

that repression can in a certain sense be considered the opposite of catatonic schizophrenia, namely in the structural sense described above. Catatonic schizophrenia seems to be the psychologic state following such a pathologically exaggerated degree of introjection whereby so much of the environment has been internalized that contact with the environment is no longer experienced as a need. The world is experienced within the person. All the typical catatonic delusions, which rather could be called body-hallucinations, could be interpreted as symptoms of pathologic introjection. In these body-hallucinations catatonics usually complain about experiencing strange happenings within their own bodies, happenings such as the shrinking of certain internal organs, the attachment of electrical machines to various parts of their bodies, etc. All these delusions are quite different from the classical paranoid delusions, in that in catatonics numerous unrealistic experiences are felt as taking place *within* the organism, while the paranoic delusions refer to misinterpretation of the environment. The case of the catatonic patient who experienced an abstract universal fight within himself is a good illustration of what may happen when the whole universe, with all its good and evil forces, has been included within the self. In the case of neurotic repression, however, the patient attempts to exclude parts of himself, and would like to consider at least some of his own needs as not belonging to him. This process then could be considered opposite to what happens in a catatonic schizophrenic. This, I think, refutes the argument, since our theory of interpretation, in this one point, at least, reveals no inherent inconsistency.

The character traits corresponding to minus k are again, of course, in many respects opposite to the character traits accompanying plus k, although the basic feature of rigidity and the aim to keep the person calm and detached are common to both groups of personality characteristics. The socially positive traits which accompany the minus k refer to the individual's willingness to accept limitations imposed by the environment; i.e., there is an optimum amount of ability and willingness to repress, which facilitates satisfactory adjustment to reality. The individual with minus k is much less a law unto himself than the individual with plus k. Minus k subjects do not dare to live out their individualistic needs openly, nor do they have the need to face what those needs really are. Standards and value judgments are readily accepted from the outside, with little questioning of their origin and validity. (It is interesting, that the typical age of endless *why's* in children coincides with the preponderance of the plus k.) It might be of interest here to note that the Rorschach records of minus k subjects show a high amount of popular answers, while plus k individuals give a relatively high percentage of good original F responses. In other words, the typically minus k person is willing to deny himself the privilege of open narcissism, and strives to be regular, to be like the others, while a plus k person strives to be an individual, disregarding popular standards.

I have noticed, although I have made no systematic study, that various schools of psychotherapy tend to affect different k constellations in the patients, depending on their explicitly or tacitly implied value-judgments in regard to social behavior. If facing one's own needs and accepting them despite the "prejudices" and in many respects hypocritical attitudes of our present culture is in hidden or open way implied in the interpretations, then the patient is likely to develop a plus k reaction. On the other hand, in those schools of psychotherapy which stress adaptation to our present social structure and the generally social aspect of personality adjustment more than the uniqueness of every individual's emotional conflicts, a stabilization of the ego in the minus k direction seems to result.

Except in the very youngest age group (3–5 years), minus k is the k factorial constellation appearing most frequently in the unselected population.

As can be expected, the psychopathologic significance of this constellation refers more to neuroses than psychoses. Most characteristically, it refers to those forms of neuroses in which the defense-mechanism of repression plays the most important role in the symptom formation. These are compulsion neuroses, conversion hysteria, and anxiety hysteria. Among psychoses, minus k is most frequent in mania, which fits in well with the findings that plus k is highly correlated with depression. In the pathogenesis of mania, introjection is of minimal importance; the symptoms of manic psychosis can be rather considered as the indication that there is no introjection of—and no identification with—environmental objects. The apparent contradiction between the raging symptoms of mania and the repression implied in minus k will have to wait for clarification until we discuss the various *Sch* configurations.

As we have said, minus k is generally the most frequent position of the k factor. Its frequency shows a more or less steady increase, being the least frequent in the youngest group of children, and most frequent in the oldest age group. According to our interpretation, this would mean that social learning results in increasing the extent of repression; or, one might call it, self-control.

Plus-minus k

The plus-minus k constellation in the k factor indicates that both "organizing" mechanisms, introjection as well as repression, are utilized simultaneously in order to keep up the tension-free integrity of the ego. Yet, the fact that both mechanisms are used simultaneously and to the same extent, results more in the subjective experiencing of tension and conflict in regard to this "need of independence" than either plus k or minus k would alone.   In fact, a plus-minus k is the typical reaction of those subjects for whom establishment of emotional independence from the environment constitutes a central problem.   In these cases, the k, by all means, wants to eliminate the tension caused by the p factor; however, by trying to reach this goal, through two—in some ways— opposing mechanisms, the result is usually that neither of the two methods can work really successfully.   In other words, subjects in this category are conscious of wanting to eliminate undesirable tensions from their personality; that is, the process of elimination is not—in a manner of speaking— automatic, but something they actually feel as performing. This experience results in a feeling of uncomfortable tension and often anxiety, even though the overt behavior of these subjects often gives the impression of strength, self-assurance, and goal-directedness.   This is, most probably, due to the fact that in individuals with plus-minus k, the need to be independent, rational, and detached in emotional matters is experienced consciously.   They can even verbalize this need rather easily.

Depending on the configuration of the rest of the test profile, this consciously experienced drive for emotional independence appears either in sublimated form and serves as a driving force for intellectual achievements, or it can result in a "cold," rational personality which forcefully strives to reach goals set for itself and is not disturbed if the goal is reached at the expense of others, since emotionality or "sentimental" feelings are almost ideologically disregarded.   (This interpretation holds only in cases in which plus-minus k appears with open p.)   Yet the subjective feeling of anxiety seems to be present in both behavioral manifestations of the plus-minus k mechanism.

The pathologic implications of this constellation are evident from the above discussion.   Plus-minus k is found with greatest frequency in anxiety states in conjunction with compulsive symptoms, and in such types of antisocial individuals whose antisocial actions do not involve physical force but rather stealing, cheating, and being generally unfair in an unobtrusive manner. A "workable" combination of sublimating plus-minus k in work, and at the same time living it out in an antisocial way, is scientific plagiarism, which is not uncommon with this k constellation.

It is worthwhile to mention that plus-minus k is uncommon in any form of psychosis. This negative finding reflects that plus-minus k, even though a conflict-constellation, still indicates ego-strength which most of the time is incompatible with psychoses. In this context, one could say that the ability to bear and to keep up ambivalence in regard to the use of two opposing ego-protective defense mechanisms is the dynamic antithesis to psychosis, which in all cases presupposes the lack of balance between various defense mechanisms.

Plus-minus k is given relatively rarely by the very youngest age group who can be tested (three to four years old), but appears about twice as frequently in the next age group, in the five to six year olds. This is actually the age at which children start the more or less conscious fight for their emotional independence. This tendency becomes even stronger, and certainly more conscious, around the age of puberty, which is also reflected in the additional increase of plus-minus k reactions at this age. From puberty on, the frequency of plus-minus k decreases, although in adolescence it is still as frequent as it is in children between five and twelve years old. The lowest points of the distribution curve are reached in young adults, at which age emotional tension, as such, appears most acceptable. In older groups, between fifty and seventy years, plus-minus k becomes again more frequent; or, in other words, intellectualization and repression of emotional needs increases with increasing age.

Open k

Open *k* corresponds to the state of primary narcissism. The original, psychoanalytic meaning of this concept refers to the psychologic state of infants, to the period when psychic harmony is still perfect because every impulse of the id finds direct fulfillment in the ego, if the term *ego* may even be applied to this earliest period of life.   Primary narcissism means that the infant or young child is concerned with nothing but himself, and loves nothing but himself. This. primary narcissistic self-love is different from the self-love of secondary narcissism, in that no outside object has ever been loved (cathected), so that the self-love is not a substitute for an external object, which has been loved, and from which due to frustrations the libido has been withdrawn and the object incorporated within the ego, which from then on becomes a secondary love-object.   In primary narcissistic self-love, there are no such complicated dynamic processes as cathecting outside objects, then transforming object-libido into narcissistic libido (which is what happens in plus *k*). In the period of primary narcissism, the infant loves himself simply because objects of the environment have not yet acquired any particular importance, since the gratification of needs has not yet met with frustration.   It is quite interesting to realize how closely taking cognizance of the environment is correlated to experiencing difficulties in the gratification of our needs: in other words, how the development of the ego is determined by the kind and amount of frustrations the organism meets during the course of life.   In a hypothetical case of continuous and complete gratification of needs, the needs would never be realized as such, nor would be subject and environment experienced as two different things.   Under such circumstances, there would be, of course, no ego in the sense of a coherent psychologic system which functions as an organizing power and decides the fate of the various id-impulses.   Id-impulse and ego would not be differentiated; there would be nothing to prevent the free flow of id-drives into the open, where they could be gratified without even the necessity of search for an outside object. In our hypothetical case, the object needed for gratification would automatically be at the place needed to facilitate gratification. Of course, this perfectly paradisiacal state of affairs is hardly conceivable after the minute of birth, and nobody really knows whether it exists before birth. However, we may assume that it does, and that all the needs of the embryo are automatically and immediately satisfied, in which case the embryo ought to give the open k reaction in the Szondi test. If we grant the same extent of absolute lack of frustration to the young infant, and assume that the mother's breast is available before he experiences hunger, so that the infant is not aware that his body has certain realistic limitations, then we would have to assume that this infant too gives open k, since there would be for him no necessity—and no possibility—to introject an object already at his disposal (no need for plus k). Further, this infant would not have to repress any need as long as pain and frustration were never experienced (no need for minus k). In other words, as long as need-gratifications do not encounter difficulties in reality, one can not talk about a boundary between the person and the environment, nor about such functions as taking a stand, being critical, trying to organize need-tensions. Consequently, there is no plus, minus, or plus-minus k function.

We offer this example of the hypothetical infant without ego-functions in order to facilitate the understanding of the open k constellation. Although infants cannot be tested, the ego-less state in which psychoanalytic theory assumes them to be would correspond to the prototype of the psychologic state represented in the test by open k.

Subjects with open k are actually infantile, in the sense that they give free reign to their needs without feeling the necessity either to neutralize the needs by introjecting the original object of the need, or to repress them. They accept their p impulses without much transformation, and seek to live them out in connection with whatever objects their needs want to cathect. In the above sense, the egos of these subjects can be called fluid, since libido can flow out freely into the environment. Thus, narcissism in these subjects does not refer to narcissistic self-sufficiency or rigidity, but to primary narcissism in the sense of love and acceptance of themselves as they are, with all their needs and expectations of environmental objects to facilitate without difficulty the gratification of these needs. Open k individuals are poorly prepared for frustrations, since there is no protective wall around their egos. They are ready to experience their emotional impulses with all their intensity, taking it for granted that living out the impulses will meet with no obstacles. Because of this self-understood, demanding attitude, open k individuals also can be called autistic and egocentric, yet one must be aware of the accurate meaning of these terms when they are applied to open k or to plus k constellations. In plus k, these terms indicate a much more conscious and defying attitude, while in open k, they refer to a completely spontaneous, "unpremeditated" attitude which is not even experienced as an "attitude" but as the most natural and only possible way of behaving. It is self-understood, for them, that the function of the world is to satisfy their personal needs. They expect to gratify these needs with almost the same ease as our hypothetical embryo and if reality does not fulfill this expectation, it is taken as personal insult, and can result in violent, vengeful reactions, since the ego is not prepared for any other defense. Reasoning, or arguing, with open k individuals is difficult, if not impossible, since the very process of reasoning, and the consideration of the opinions of others, is an introjective function. In order that verbal content may be communicated, the listener must

be able, for a short time at least, to incorporate into himself what has been said, compare it with his own content,
and draw conclusions on the basis of that comparison. If
the person is not willing to be receptive (i.e., introjective)
for any length of time there is no possible basis for intellectual arguments or explanation. This is often the case
with open *k* subjects. They do not want to "take in" anything from the outside; what they want is to *express* what is
in them. That makes social contact with open *k* individuals
often unpleasant, unless one happens to be interested in
"taking in" what *they* want to express. Whether or not one
is willing to apply the term *rigidity* to this type of unbending
character is a matter of defining the meaning of the word
rigid when it is applied as a personality characteristic. I will
commit myself quite definitely: in the Szondi test interpretation, I reserve the term *rigid* for the loaded *k* factor; i.e.,
secondary narcissism as shown in the lack of ability to let
one's own libido and emotionality flow toward the outside
world. According to this definition, a paranoid person is
fluid and *unbending,* but not rigid, because he is just too
eager to express his needs and attach his emotionality to outside objects. I feel it necessary to make this differentiation
explicit in discussing the open *k,* since the lack of precise
definition of the word rigid could give rise to misinterpretation of the *k* and *p* factors, especially because, in general
psychiatric usage, paranoids are usually characterized as
being the most "rigid" individuals.

The pathologic significance of open *k* refers mostly to psychotic states, and not to neuroses. This is to be expected,
since open *k* indicates practically no defense mechanism of
the ego. If open *k* appears within a series after a number
of test profiles with loaded *k* factor, then it has very special
diagnostic value, since one can suspect the breaking down of
the ego defenses and the appearance of prepsychotic or psychotic symptoms.

Open *k* can appear in epileptics immediately after seizure, in catatonic schizophrenics in the excited state, or generally after any sort of paroxysmal outbreak. In these stuporous, or coma-like states, the ego in its organizing capacity actually ceases to function. Open *k* is also rather frequently found in paranoid patients, most probably because of the dynamic relation described above, the paranoid patient having no need to keep up the boundary around, nor to repress his needs, but rather desires to "over-cathect" the environment and fuse into it.

The younger the age group we are able to test, the more probability there is to obtain open *k* reactions, in which case it means the really infantile form of primary narcissism, and indicates that practically no love object has yet been introjected. From the four year olds on, the frequency of open *k* decreases until we reach the age group of young adults, between twenty and thirty years of age. In this group, the frequency of open *k* is again about 20 per cent, and remains more or less the same until we reach the very oldest subjects, who are close to eighty or beyond. This seems to be the age at which lack of ego strength, in the sense of lack of organizing power corresponding to a loaded *k* factor, is most usual. The open *k* in this oldest group reflects, most probably, the lack of the need to be differentiated from the environment.

Sch Vectorial Constellations

The *Sch* vectorial constellations will be discussed from the point of view of ego development. The experimental findings have shown that certain *Sch* configurations are found with outstanding frequency in certain age groups. Again, as in so many other instances, the pragmatic knowledge came first, the understanding on a theoretical basis, and the conceptualization, later. As a general rule, I found that there are eight various *Sch* pictures which, on the basis of their frequency distribution, lend themselves logically to this genetic systematization. These eight $_3$o pictures comprise the developmental stages from birth (of course constructed theoretically on the basis of analogy) to young adults (early twenties). From this age on, the ego-pictures become highly individualized, and do not lend themselves to being systematized according to age until the variability of the ego-pictures decreases again, from about sixty years on, so that we are again able to talk about the most characteristic *Sch* configurations of old age.

In our discussion of the ego-developmental stages, we will refer to the single *Sch* configurations simply by referring to the respective constellations of the *k* and *p* factors, to preclude use of the elaborate letter-symbolic system which Szondi uses in his book.* Szondi needed the more elaborate system because he differentiates more stages in the ego-development than we shall, and he presents the material from viewpoints which will not be included in this book. In using Szondi's symbolization without including all his material or presenting the system in his manner, one could not justify the logic of the succession of the letter-symbols. For this more detailed systematization of the developmental ego-stages as well as for the corresponding quantitative data, the reader is referred to Szondi's book, pp. 129–207, and to the Psychodiagnostik Table Nr. IV, in the appendix of his book.

Stage I. *Open* k *with minus* p

Open *k* with minus *p* is the most primitive ego picture, in that it reflects the least degree of structurization (open *k*) and completely unconscious projections of the needs in the environment (minus *p*). We assume theoretically that this configuration corresponds to the completely fluid, undifferentiated ego of the youngest infant. The corresponding

---

* Experimentelle Triebdiagnostik. Op. cit.

experimental data are obtained from young children who are known to be fixated psychologically at a very early level of development, from deeply regressed psychotics, primarily schizophrenics, and also from severe cases of general paresis (dementia paralytica). Data were also taken from adults over the age of seventy.

In our theoretical construct, this *Sch* configuration reflects the first stage of infancy as that stage at which there is no differentiation between ego and id because there is no differentiation between subject and object, or between self and environment. Without the existence of these pairs of opposite concepts, the ego cannot be used as a frame of reference for psychologic organization, since the concept of the ego, by definition, presupposes differentiation between the self and the environment, between inside and outside, in that the ego is assumed to be the intermediary between the reality of the outer world and the wishes coming from the id. It is exactly this lack of differentiation which is implied in the interpretation of the open k, minus p as the first stage of ego-development. (Again it is necessary to point out that any such description as "complete lack of differentiation" is not meant to be taken literally, since not even a psychotic can be completely fused into the environment, and some remnants of the ego can always be found in any subject who can be tested. Yet the term helps to clarify the meaning of single ego-pictures when, for didactic purposes, we conceive of them in their most extreme form.)

The minus p component corresponds to the "reservoir" of unconscious needs, which are lived out by "immediate" projection. By "immediate" we mean that needs are satisfied so promptly that the subject is not even aware of the process through which he projected the presence of his needs, somehow, into the environment. He has no consciousness of having given a signal; the necessary object for need-gratification and the need seem to form a completely

continuous and harmonious unit. For a hypothetical example, we can refer again to the infant who feels at one with
the mother's breast, since need-tension (hunger) is never
experienced consciously because of the immediate gratification of the need. Consequently there is no need for the
ego (in the stricter sense of the word) to develop, since
there is nothing one must take a stand to so long as everything is perfectly harmonious. In discussing the later stages
of ego-development, we will mention the degree to which
frustration is the driving force for reality-testing, and thus
for ego-development. The *Sch* constellation under discussion now really should be termed the "pre-ego stage" and,
with reference to its place in ego-development, logically
should be given the rank number *o* rather than *1*. Yet we
are used to referring to this constellation as the first stage and
designate it as the "adualistic" stage of the ego, which in
fact means that there is no ego in the usual psychoanalytic
sense of the concept.

The term *adualistic*, or lack of dualism between subject
and object, has been borrowed from Piaget * who uses the
term to characterize the primitive state of undifferentiation
between the child and the rest of the world. This is the
stage at which the child "thinks" that the whole world feels
as he does. Pain is experienced not as something personal,
but as something experienced everywhere: the rest of the
world "hurts" too. He does not know the realistic limits
of his body; for example, there is no difference between his
relationship to his own toe and his relationship to his crib.
Even though this primitive, real confusion disappears rather
early in life—the differentiation being prompted by frustrations—much of this primitive animistic thinking can be
observed in very young children later, as it can be observed
in primitives of our age, and in certain psychotics. Sometimes this mystical animistic thinking can even be traced

* Piaget, Jean: The Child's Conception of the World. Op. cit.

in processes of artistic creativity. In strictly scientific thinking, such animistic features of thought supposedly play no
part, although there are some indications that they do enter
into the process of finding genuinely new insight into a
problem, more than is "officially" admitted. This genuinely new insight refers to those phases in thinking which
are unconscious—insights which occur suddenly and cannot
be derived logically. These are occasions on which one
just "feels" something is true. These "mystical" feelings
are typically functions of the open k, minus p constellation,
and are brought about by means of unconscious projection.
Logical explanations for these minus p intuitive insights can
occur later.

Individuals with open k, minus p—when they show no
symptoms of pathology—are extremely sensitive in their
reactions even to slightest environmental cues. They lack,
however, ability to verbalize the whole process. These
are the people who are guided by their emotions, the emotions being turned into action directly, without first passing
through the system of the *preconscious,* which would facilitate the person's conscious recognition of his emotions, and
help him understand why he acts as he does. In other
words, open k, minus p corresponds to the purest form of
projection, the term, again, being used in the broader sense
we have described in interpreting the p factor.

On the basis of our discussion of the ego-mechanism of
open k, minus p, it is clear that these subjects can be
described as autistic, in the sense of the "autism" as discussed
in connection with the open k constellation. Although they
react sensitively to subtle outward signals of the unconscious
of other individuals, nevertheless, because of their lack of
conscious insight and unwillingness for verbal conceptualization, they cannot readily be influenced by means of speech.
They act on the basis of "intuitive feelings" and show little
interest in rational reasoning.

The Rorschach records of subjects with this *Sch* configuration show extremely high numbers of FM (animal movement) responses. A comparative study from the point of view of types of movements seen of Rorschach records of subjects yielding open *k*, minus *p*, and plus *k*, plus *p* reactions, has been done by this writer.* The high frequency of FM's in subjects with open *k*, minus *p* is understandable from what has been said about this ego picture, and from what Klopfer says about the significance of FM. ". . . they (the FM's) represent the influence of the most instinctive layers within the personality, a hypothesis which would explain why children frequently see animals in action although they seldom see human action in their responses to the cards. . . . Invariably, where there is reason from other sources to assume that a subject is emotionally infantile, living on a level of instinctive prompting below his chronological and mental age, the Rorschach record of this subject shows a predominance of FM over M." †

The above description of the meaning of *FM* could hold, word for word, for the interpretation of open *k*, minus *p*. However, in the Szondi Test—and also in the Rorschach test—there are certain configurations in the total test pattern which indicate that this influence of the unconscious instinctive promptings can result in some forms of highly sublimated activity. It has been mentioned already that this configuration is not rare in creative artists, and even in some highly gifted musical composers. It is practically never found in writers, except in those preoccupied with mystical philosophy and mythology. Generally, however, this ego-picture is found much more frequently in subjects whose work does not involve any form of artistic or intellectual sublimation, but whose occupation is strictly on the level of physical activity.

* Unpublished paper read at the April, 1947, meeting of the New York section of the Rorschach Institute.

† Klopfer and Kelley: The Rorschach Technique, op. cit., p. 278.

The pathologic significance of this *Sch* configuration is great. It is found in cases of deteriorated schizophrenics, in dementia paralytica and in deteriorated epileptics. For all these groups the breaking down of the ego-functions is characteristic.

Open *k*, minus *p* is most frequent in the oldest age group, those persons of approximately eighty years. It also can be found with relative frequency, in young children who are emotionally, and sometimes even mentally, retarded. This primitive ego-picture is least frequent in adolescents and young adults, who seem to be representative of the age groups in which people are most consciously concerned with facing their own needs and strengthening their egos.

Stage II. *Plus* k *with minus* p

The plus *k*, minus *p* is the most characteristic *Sch* picture of the youngest group of children who can be tested, those at approximately the age of three. Theoretically, we assume that this configuration arises much earlier, in late infancy, when due to unavoidable frustrations, the child is forced to realize that he and the world are two things not continuously connected. This realization must first occur when an instinctive craving of the infant is not immediately gratified by the environment, so that a need-tension arises which makes the infant perceive that his need and the object which gratifies the need are not one. Thus, due to frustration, the child learns to differentiate between himself, from whom the needs originate, and the environment, from which they are gratified. The emergence of the child's personality as a differentiated unit is indicated by the plus *k* component of this configuration, coinciding with the use of the word *I* as reference to themselves. The plus *k* symbolizes the boundary around the self, but more than that, it also shows that the child is making use of the mechanism of introjection. (See section above on the interpretation of plus *k*,

p. 190). The primary meaning of this introjection might
refer to the infant's hypothesized ability for hallucinatory
satisfaction, as Freud describes it.* According to Freud,
after the infant has realized that the feeding breast does
not belong to him, he is able—at least for a short time—to
get hallucinatory satisfaction in case of hunger, by imagining
that the feeding breast is there. If this is really so—which
I doubt that we can decide—then this hallucinatory satisfaction could be considered to be the first instance of introjection. The imagining of the existence of the breast, then,
would be a form of ego-defense whereby the ego attempts
to cope with an environmental frustration first by projecting the object needed for gratification (minus p), then
by introjecting the projected image (plus k) into the ego,
attempting thereby to keep up the fiction of the lost self-
sufficiency (the fiction that the subject and the object of
the libido are one). Whether or not this complicated process of "double"-defense really takes place in the infant after
realization that the breast belongs to the mother is not of
primary importance in our discussion. The important point
is that this hypothetical example helps us to illuminate the
ego-mechanism of plus k, minus p.

The aim of this mechanism is to attempt to keep up the
omnipotence of the ego above the environment after the
child is forced to accept the fact that he is a separate entity
within the world. _This stage is called the "dualistic" stage
of ego-development, the term *dualistic* used to focus on
the difference between this stage and the "adualistic" stage.
In this "dualistic" stage the child is aware of himself as a
separate entity, yet he attempts to avoid the limitations
which the acceptance of an outside reality would naturally
tend to impose upon him. He can avoid submitting himself to the limitations of reality by using the mechanism of

* Freud, Sigmund: Interpretation of Dreams. London, Allen and
Unwin, 1915.

unconscious projection (minus p) and that of introjection (plus k) simultaneously. In terms of our interpretation, this means that the ego identifies itself with the unconsciously projected needs expressed by the minus p. The child structures the world in terms of his unconscious needs and then introjects the result, and actually feels that he is the world as he has structured it. This corresponds to the stage at which children feel able to do or to be practically anything. This is the mechanism of the playful fantasies which are still completely gratifying to the child. The child in this stage actually feels that he is the king, the queen, the elephant, the lion, or anything else he wants to imagine. This fantastic satisfaction presupposes the knowledge and the acceptance of the fact that there are elephants, lions, etc., in the outside world. However, the child's satisfaction does not depend on the realistic presence of these outside objects: if he wishes to have something he simply projects his wish in the form of an image (minus p) then incorporates this image (plus k) and thereby becomes himself the outside object. The difference between this mechanism and the adualistic one, in terms of the child's relationship to the world, is this: in the "adualistic" stage, the child feels that "the world is me, every object is somehow connected with me, I am *in* every object." The corresponding animistic way of thinking implies that the child or the primitive person attributes to lifeless objects of the environment his own personal characteristics, making thereby the whole world live and feel the way he does. (Of course in this stylized example, the term *I* is foreign to the person.)

The motto of the child in the dualistic stage could be paraphrased as: "*I am* the world. *I* can have the characteristics of any person or animal or object of the world. I do not need all these things because I can be them myself."

The children's poems of A. A. Milne express perfectly the psychologic state of this plus k, minus p period of childhood, and certainly it can not be by chance that children in this stage enjoy these poems tremendously, since the poems are really the "official" acceptance of autism. The following lines from the poem "Busy" * is probably the best expression:

> Perhaps I am a Postman. No, I think I am a Tram.
> I'm feeling rather funny and I don't know *what* I am—

This feeling of omnipotence is due to the ego's willingness and ability to incorporate anything the child's id dictates to project.

Besides this autism, there are other personality characteristics of children around the age of three which can be explained on the basis of this plus k, minus p mechanism: that is the well-known negativism an d stubbornness of children between three and five years of age. These characteristics, manifesting themselves in endless "no's," can be understood as the child's reaction against accepting the limitations of reality and his fight to keep the happy state of infantile autism. It is the reaction of the plus k against the parental or any other force coming from the outside and intending to change the plus k into minus k. From the psychoanalytic point of view, it is also interesting to note that the preponderance of this *Sch* configuration coincides with the height of the Oedipal period, in regard to which it can refer to the child's ability to identify with the respective parent. That is the period at which small boys consciously identify themselves with their fathers, wanting to be big and strong "like Daddy" and wear "masculine" clothes, while small girls love to play that they are mothers, and to put on mother's clothes. These games are also the product of the children's ability to project their wishes right into themselves, which mechanism corresponds to the plus k with minus p constellation.

In case this *Sch*-picture is given by adults, the detailed

* From *Now We Are Six*, by A. A. Milne, published and copyright, 1927, by E. P. Dutton & Co., Inc., New York (United States and Canada), and Methuen and Co., London.

interpretation described above still holds, although, of course, with appropriate modifications. Adults who give this configuration in the *Sch* vector are nonconformists and have the tendency to form autistic and unrealistic relationships toward the world. They are likely to make and follow their own laws of behavior which—depending on the remainder of their personality structure—might result in asocial as well as in socially highly valuable behavior. However, even in the latter case, subjects with plus k and minus p are likely to be "atypical" individuals who refuse to follow the crowd. They might, for example, rigidly insist on acting according to their convictions and their conscience, and cannot be deterred from an original course of action even when the course seems impractical and maybe even be undesirable. These are the people who may be fanatics in the good or bad sense of the word, depending on the rest of the test profile. The fanaticism of these subjects, however, is the fanaticism of the quiet introvert, who rigidly sticks to his convictions without attempting to convince others to think and act as he does. (This latter type is associated with a plus p reaction.)

Plus k, minus p individuals are self-sufficient and are found frequently in the so-called "professional" groups, which shows that intellectual activity is a good solution for persons with this ego-structure. This is also quite understandable, since one way to continue the childhood feeling of omnipotence lies in maintaining the projection of need followed by their introjection on the intellectual level. This continuation of childhood omnipotence can result in productive work, although the individual may not be aware of the real source of his emotional driving forces. (This is indicated by the presence of the purely minus p factor.) Yet the self-sufficiency desired can well be reached through successful intellectual sublimation and satisfaction in one's own work.

On the other hand, seriously antisocial individuals who

are "professional" criminals yield this *Sch* configuration with approximately twice the frequency of the unselected population. The underlying mechanism is the same: the person identifies himself with his unconscious projections; except that in this group the content of the minus *p,* that is, the content of the unconscious need which is lived out is quite different from the content of the latent need in the previous one. Plus *k* and minus *p* in this latter group is associated with plus *s* and minus *m,* while in individuals who use this autistic ego-mechanism for intellectual work, the *s* factor and the *h* is usually minus, and the *m* is plus.

This *Sch* configuration appears in psychoses to much greater extent than in neuroses. This must be due to the unrealistic autism and the lack of willingness to conform, implied in this ego-picture. Since outside forces are not accepted, only the own unconscious needs, the necessary predisposition for repression, which is the defense most often used in neuroses, is absent. Plus *k* with minus *p* can be found however, in nonconforming schizoid psychopaths.

The plus *k,* minus *p* configuration is also found frequently in schizophrenics and in psychotic depression. The latter finding bears out Freud's theory on the psychodynamics of melancholia, in that this ego-picture corresponds to the trauma of loss of connection with the primary object of the libido (loss of undisturbed unity with the mother) and to the attempt to make up for this loss by introjecting the image of the lost object. The process of mourning, which according to Freud is the prototype for what happens in depression in general, consists of exactly the same attempt to introject the lost object.*

The one age group in which this is the most frequent *Sch* configuration, of all the sixteen possible variations of *k* and *p* combinations, is made up of children between three and five years of age. Reasons have been elaborated above.

* Freud, Sigmund: Mourning and Melancholia. Op. cit.

The configuration is relatively rare in puberty, adolescence and young adulthood, and becomes again somewhat more frequent in middle age.

Stage III. *Plus-minus* k *with minus* p

In contrast to the plus k, minus p ego-picture, in which the child or adult feels omnipotent and unaffected by the limitations of outside reality, the presence of the minus **k** component in the plus-minus k, minus p ego-picture indicates that the undisturbed happiness of the period of independent autism is over. The minus part of the k factor symbolized the influence of the environmental forces upon the person, while the presence of the plus k with minus p constellation, which is also part of this *Sch* configuration, indicates that the autistic projectivity of the person is still operating. Developmentally, this is the third ego-picture, obtained in great numbers from children between the ages of four and seven, centering on the five year olds. Of course, to say that these *Sch* configurations correspond to developmental stages is as arbitrary as to characterize developmental stages in general. The overlap between the characteristics pertaining, theoretically, to a certain age, is as great as the overlap between the occurrence of the *Sch* pictures designated by rank order numbers to indicate the approximate succession of their appearance in the course of ego-development.

Yet, on the basis of our findings, we are justified in saying that plus-minus k, minus p follows the autistic stage of plus k, minus p, since the first time that it appears as one of the four most frequent *Sch* configurations is in the four year olds; and in the group of five year olds we already find it as having doubled its frequency. The sudden increase of this ego-picture in this age group corresponds to the children's increased reality testing, or in psychoanalytic terminology, it indicates the increasing power of the reality principle over the pleasure principle. This means

that the child has already discovered not only that he and
the environment are two different things (transition from
the adualistic to the dualistic stage) but also that the environment is something one has to adjust to, at least to some
extent, and at some times (transition from stage II to
stage III).   In stage III, the child is still able to indulge
in his phantasy-plays; however they no longer have the same
substitute value for reality as they did in the previous stage.
The mechanism of projecting any phantastic wish onto
oneself (plus k, minus p) no longer works, or if it does, the
child is much more aware than previously that "this is just
pretend, and not really real."   Anybody who has experience
in playing with children about the age of five, or even
somewhat younger, knows how consciously they verbalize
the difference between what is make-believe and what is
real.   It almost seems as if they would educate themselves
for testing reality.   Whether this change in their relationship to themselves and to the world has been brought about
by having been subjected to parental and other environmental "powers," or whether the change is based more on
some sort of an indigenous "law" of development, can not
be determined; at least not on the basis of our test data.
The fact is that their behavior as well as their test profiles
shows that something drastic is happening at this age in
regard to their relationship to reality.   The ambivalence
in regard to whether they should still attempt to free themselves from the limitations of the realistic world, or give in
and adjust to the limitations as unavoidable, is reflected in
the plus-minus position of the k factor.   On the other hand,
the fact that they are still living out their needs in actions
without being aware of what these needs really are, is shown
by the minus position of the p factor.   The outcome of
this ambivalence between autistic projection and realistic
adjustment manifests itself on the behavior level in restlessness.   Children in this "in-between" stage of Ego-develop-

ment are extremely active and restless physically; they are constantly "on the go," climbing, running, bicycling, etc. We assume that the driving force for this restlessness derives its intensity from the child's unconscious wish to free himself from the restraints of reality through activity rather than through the phantasy of the younger child. In any age group, plus-minus k, minus p is the *Sch* reaction most characteristic of subjects who are consciously fighting for the freedom of their egos, who, on the one hand rebel against external laws, and on the other hand, do not dare to ignore these laws. Even adults who are fixated at this level of ego-development show symptoms of restlessness at the physical as well as at the psychologic level. They like to change their environment, enjoy occupations involving travelling, enjoy changing their group of friends and sometimes even their type of work or profession. People with this ego-picture feel driven by undefinable forces and crave for change in general. Their behavior often seems inconsistent not only to the onlooker, but to themselves. They feel dissatisfied in any situation which seems to imply stability, but are unable to give rational reasons for their dissatisfaction. On the other hand, due to their wish to conform, they constantly drive themselves into exactly such situations which imply submission to some sort of rules and limitations, and from which they escape soon, only to start the whole vicious circle again.

The pathologic implications of this *Sch* configuration refer first of all to various forms of paroxysmal symptoms. Even the relatively well-adjusted subjects in this *Sch* category can best be described as paroxysmal individuals, because of their psychomotor as well as their physical restlessness. The pathologic manifestations of paroxysmality involve a wide range of possible symptoms from real epileptic grand-mal seizures to paroxysmal stuttering.

In children, this inner need for paroxysmal restlessness can manifest itself in periodic truancy, or in running away from home. These are the usual reasons why one finds so many children who are sent to the juvenile court giving this particular reaction in the *Sch* vector. Plus-minus *k*, minus *p*, is also frequent in certain types of antisocial adults, namely in the unstable vagrant who could also fit in the psychiatric classification of epileptoid psychopath (psycho-motor epilepsy).

As has been said, this *Sch*-picture is found most frequently in children between four and seven years of age. The frequency of this ego picture in adults is about a third of that in children. (about 4 per cent as against 12 per cent.) In subjects beyond the age of sixty, it appears again with increasing frequency, which Szondi believes is due to the frequent disturbance of the vasomotor system in this age, causing paroxysmal spasms in the blood vessels.

Stage IV. *Minus* k *with minus* p

Minus *k*, minus *p* is the ego picture of the child whose ego has been "successfully" broken down by the overwhelming strength of the environment. The picture's first appearance as the most frequent *Sch* configuration, occurs at approximately the age of schooling, and remains the leading configuration, among the sixteen possible variations of the *Sch* vector, through all the age groups. This means that the most frequently used ego-dynamism throughout life, in an unselected population, corresponds to that of the "broken-in" six year old child, who, on the basis of experience, has discovered that environment is stronger than he, and that the path of least resistance is conformity with whatever the environment expects.

It is worthwhile to recapitulate the manner in which changes in the *Sch* vector reflect this gradual process through which the child learns to accept reality as such: I. First there was the *adualistic* stage, (open k, minus p) which corresponded to the complete lack of differentiation between person and environment; i.e., the two were experienced as a continuous unit.   II. Then came the *dualistic* stage (plus k, minus p) the plus k component indicating the emergence of the ego, the feeling of I as an entity separated from the environment.   At this stage, however, the child still felt self-sufficient and omnipotent because, instead of dependence on environmental objects recognized as such, he felt the power of reproducing the characteristics of any of these objects himself.   III. There followed the stage of the breaking down of the omnipotent autism (plus-minus k, minus p), the minus k component being the first indication of recognition of the limitations of one's own ego in view of the realistic forces implied in the objects and persons of the environment. The result was a *restless paroxysmal* behavior, assumed to correspond to the child's unconscious wish to escape the limitations (by now recognized) of his own power.   This is the intermediate stage of half-autism and half-acceptance of reality.   IV. There then appears the minus k, minus p configuration, in which the lack of any plus k tendency shows that autistic (introjective) defense mechanisms have been given up completely. This could be called the stage of the *disciplined ego*.   Again it is an open question whether the willingness to submit oneself to discipline is brought about by education (i.e., environmental forces) or the more "natural" process of maturation, or whether it is the result of both factors. There is the further question: what is the proportion and relative role of these two sets of factors?   Most probably it varies greatly from individual to individual, but by all means it seems like a worthwhile and promising field for further research and appears to be within the range of possibilities for experimental investigations requiring longitudinal studies on children from various kinds of environment in regard to types and amounts of discipline imposed.   With the aid of the Szondi test, one could follow up and compare changes in the ego pictures in the respective groups.

The age at which minus k, minus p first appears as the most frequent *Sch* constellation coincides with the age at which children's behavior becomes quite realistic. Fantasy play and "make-believe" are given up almost completely, and there is also a noticeable reduction in the amount of physical activity for the sheer pleasure of physical motion. Children's games at this stage become more organized and goal-directed, and objectively measurable achievement becomes more pronounced. This feature of their games I believe also points to the fact that environmental standards of behavior and success have assumed greater importance. This is the period when children play games with set rules, when many times it seems that the most important approach to the game is to keep the rules. It almost appears as though they want to practice and enjoy their freshly learned ability of submitting to discipline. Children between six and nine are also at an age at which they become increasingly interested in factual knowledge and in learning to manipulate real objects. One could say that this age group is definitely object- and not ego-oriented. The presence of the minus p shows that there is a continuous unconscious projection of needs through action without, however, an awareness of this process; i.e., these children (and adults who yield the same *Sch* picture), acting according to their latent needs, are unaware of underlying sources of motivation and would be convinced that their actions are determined purely by the objective characteristics of their environment. This lack of insight in the underlying motivational sources of action is, indeed, characteristic for the so-called average person, which corresponds nicely with our findings that minus p, minus k is the *Sch* vectorial constellation appearing most frequently in all age groups from six years on.

It should be noted here that the appearance of the high frequency of this ego-picture coincides with the developmental phase at which we assume the child has gone beyond the actuality of the Oedipal period and enters latency. This would give us a psychoanalytic explanation why children of this age turn their interest primarily toward manipulation of concrete objects rather than entanglement in personal emotional relationships. Furthermore, conforming with reality and accepting authority are well-known characteristics of the latency period, and are implied in the interpretation of the minus k, minus p constellation. This concurrence of our experimental findings with findings obtained through wholly different methods justify to a great extent both sets of theories. The concurrency of experimental findings in regard to the stages of ego development on the basis of the Szondi test, the basis of psychoanalytic investigations, and the basis of the experimental investigations of Piaget and Charlotte Buhler furnishes an intrinsic consistency which, if it does not validate each theory in the strictest sense of the word, nevertheless makes the validation most probable.

To return to our characterization of the minus k, minus p configuration: since we have discovered that this is the most common Sch reaction in the unselected adult population, we must assume that the latency period is a point of fixation strongly favored for a great number of adults. Accordingly, a great number of adults must have psychologic characteristics similar to those of children from six to nine years old. I think that the generally accepted stereotype of the "average man" bears out this conclusion. Minus k, minus p—in the clinically symptomless population—is given primarily by those subjects who are extremely realistic, "down to earth" individuals. These are the people for whom "a spade is a spade"; that is, the people by whom the world is perceived and accepted at face value. They are overwhelmed

by concrete objects and by reality to such an extent that
there is no psychic energy left for introspection. Ego-
processes as such are not cathected; the person is occupied
with solving what to him seem to be "real" problems, and
he often considers preoccupation with one's own needs and
psychologic welfare to be a ridiculous waste of time.

Although we are not discussing systematically the most
frequent intervectorial correlations, it should be mentioned
here that minus k, minus p in the Sch vector is correlated
most frequently with plus h and plus s in the S vector, a
further corroboration of the realistic attitude of these subjects toward the world. The interpretation of this correlation between the S and Sch vector implies also that the
sexual attitude of these subjects is realistically goal-directed
in that their first desire is to live out their sexual need-
tension with the least possible complication. For these
individuals the sex act is more important than the specificity
of the love-object. In other words, they are not willing to
put off sexual satisfaction for the sake of waiting for one
specific love-object, but they can attach their "love" with
comparative ease to persons who are easily available in their
environment.

Among the various occupational groups, this Sch configuration is found most frequently among the nonintellectual occupations. It is most frequent (approximately 50
per cent) in the group comprising physical laborers, less
frequent in business occupations, and is quite rare in professions involving intellectual sublimation. Of all professional groups, it occurs with probably least frequency in
psychologists and psychiatrists. The low frequency of the
configuration in this group is to be expected since it is
comprised of professions which specialize in exactly those
problems which most subjects with minus k, minus p consider no problems at all.

Interestingly enough, it has been found that painters and sculptors yield this reaction in the *Sch* vector rather frequently, but musicians, practically never.   I was surprised to have obtained these results in my study, mentioned above, of various groups of artists and musicians, although these results can be understood when one considers that painters and sculptors are interested in representing reality by means of concrete, tangible material, and that the projection of their own personalities into their product occurs for the most part on an unconscious level.   Conversations with these subjects helped me to understand this process.   The artist (with the exception of representatives of nonobjective art who were not included among my subjects) while he works focuses attention consciously on the environment, and is definitely neither introspecting nor analyzing his own motivations for painting or representing an object in a certain manner.   The musical composer, on the other hand, focuses his attention on internal perception, and attempts, even consciously, to exclude perception of environmental stimuli.   In those few cases in which minus k, minus p was obtained from scientists, the subject's interest was also definitely focused on the objective environment, and the type of work consisted mainly of detailed observation of concrete objects (interest in morphology) with the least possible extent of theorizing.

The pathologic significance of this configuration is great if both the minus k and the minus p are loaded, and do not have those "counterbalacing" squares in the plus direction.   More than in any other pathologic group, it is found in manic psychoses, in the phase of manic rage.   It is found with the second highest frequency in organic psychoses (general paresis).   Minus k, minus p is also frequent in criminals, particularly in the most violent forms; first of all in murderers.   In this group the minus p is usually more heavily loaded than the minus k factor.

It is worth while to mention an apparent contradiction in the findings that on one hand minus k, minus p is the prototype of the disciplined and conforming ego, while its pathologic significance relates to the most antisocial forms of pathology, in psychoses as well as among the various forms of criminality. The interpretation of these data would imply that the conforming ego has achieved discipline by repressing (minus k) aggressive impulses with no insight into either the impulse or the repression. Thus the dynamic force of these impulses are at the outset inhibited from any open or sublimated discharge (high correlation with plus h and plus s) and thereby kept in latency which—as we know—increases rather than releases the dynamic urgency of the particular need which is forced into this latent position. At the time the dynamic urgency of the repressed need has reached a certain intensity, a sudden and uncontrolled outbreak of the impulses heretofore repressed takes place. For this reason, the more definitely negative the minus k and p factors are, the greater the probability for an uncontrolled antisocial outbreak in the near future becomes. The reason for the fact that antisocial outbreaks—in psychotics and otherwise—in subjects with minus k and minus p appear abruptly and are seriously violent lies in the complete lack of insight into the deeper layers of their *self* in these subjects (no plus k, and no plus p). Thus there is no way for the nonaccepted needs to be mitigated in their appearance by a previous process of intellectualization and transformation (lack of plus k function). The constellation reveals that the subject has reached no degree of the awareness of his socially dangerous needs which would be required for his mobilization of the most efficient forms of repression. More awareness would be indicated on the test even in the minus k, open p configuration, which would correspond to the typically compulsive ego-picture (the next developmental stage), indicating that the person takes an active stand in repressing certain needs with the help of a compulsive "substitute" activity, which even though in a distorted way—still satisfies to some degree the originally repressed impulses simultaneously to satisfaction of the critical instances of the ego and the superego.   There are, of course, enough cases which show that such strictly compulsive defenses can also break down under certain circumstances, in which case there might follow a breaking through of antisocial psychotic or criminal behavior; however, due to the continuous slight discharge of the repressed needs through the neurotic symptom itself, such sudden appearance of antisocial behavior occurs less frequently in the case of minus k, open p than it does in minus k, minus p, the ego-picture discussed here.   The presence of the minus p in this configuration is a memento that the intensity of the nonaccepted needs has not been really reduced at all; it has merely not been recognized consciously. That is why the loadedness of the minus p in particular determines the seriousness of the possible antisocial outbreak.   Criminals who yield this *Sch* configuration belong to that type of individual who for years lives the life of an ordinary and apparently well-conforming citizen, then in a day—to the great surprise of his community—commits a serious crime.   For examples of this type one need refer only to the headlines of daily tabloids rather than to textbooks of psychiatry.

Similarly, the outbreak of manic rage occurs usually without warning, and aims at destruction of objects in the environment.   Prior to this phase, the manic patient himself is, characteristically, not aware of his own latent aggression.   Rather, he might have impressed those in his environment as a hyperactive but friendly person.   In other words, the manic process as such takes place between the person and his environment, leaving the ego of the patient relatively intact, while in schizophrenics (primarily in catatonics and simplex) the psychotic process takes place primarily within the patient's ego, destroying the structure of the ego, rather than turning against the environment. Accordingly, minus k, minus p is found most rarely in schizophrenics while it is the most typical ego-constellation for the manics.

In cases of organic psychoses it refers, most probably, to the functioning on the concrete level (Goldstein) of these patients, and their apparent incapability for abstract behavior, a fact well-known by any clinical psychologist who has tested organic patients.

The age distribution of this ego picture has been discussed throughout this section. To recapitulate: altogether it is the most frequent Sch configuration appearing in all age groups from six years on. Its frequency is relatively less in prepuberty, puberty, adolescence, and young adulthood. From then on it increases steadily, the highest frequency being reached in the most advanced age group represented by the eighty year olds. The fact that this is the most frequently used ego-dynamism in the average population, as well as the seeming paradoxical findings that the very same picture is also the most characteristic for violently antisocial behavior, necessitated discussion of this stage of ego development in relatively greater length than the previous and following sections.

Stage V. *Minus k with open p*

The minus k, open p constellation in the Sch vector is, together with the minus k, minus p, the most frequent constellation in children between the ages of nine and twelve, and continues to occur quite frequently during puberty. The obvious difference of this configuration from the minus k, minus p is the lack of the minus p. This lack indicates that the repressive forces corresponding to the minus k are more effective in the present Sch picture, as revealed by the draining of tension in the p factor. The open p shows that this is one of the ego-constellations in which the k factor "fulfilled" its function in eliminating the subjective experiencing of a need-tension within the ego. Unconscious projection of the unaccepted impulses has been given up by subjects with this particular reaction in the *Sch* vector. Instead, the open position in the p indicates that some sort of discharge in connection with environmental objects takes place continuously, although the minus position of the k factor indicates at the same time that this discharge must occur necessarily through some "substitute" channels, since acceptance of the need is definitely declined by the ego and the superego (neither open nor plus k reaction). This *Sch* picture indicates that the process of counter-cathexis had been successful, and thus the original course of the id-impulses could be successfully deflected and redirected toward "acceptable" environmental objects with concomitant and appropriate changes being brought about in regard to the way in which the need is discharged.

In opening our discussion of this configuration, we would have been justified in using the brief term *compulsive mechanism*. However, the immediate use of connotative labels often hinders the full understanding or "re-thinking" of the dynamic process underlying a mechanism. Furthermore, the label often restricts meaning to strictly pathologic processes, ignoring the fact that similar mechanisms often take place in individuals who are clinically not compulsive neurotics. This becomes more evident when we consider the meaning of the minus k, open p constellation which, although a typically "compulsive" ego-picture, is generally the characteristic reaction of children between nine and twelve years of age, and not, particularly, of neurotic children. Of course, depending on definition, we would probably be justified in calling this the age of "physiologic" compulsiveness just because the mechanism described above is so characteristic for this age group.   The behavior of children in prepuberty shows many compulsive features. Children of this age are likely to be exacting and pedantic in regard to details; often there is a preoccupation with moralistic and religious problems which indicates the excessive functioning of the superego, and shows that the child is unconsciously fighting some "evil" forces within himself. Many children in this age show an eagerness for factual knowledge and learning about the world in general which, by its persistence bears the characteristics of a compulsive drive. One well-known manifestation of this "drive to know" is the excessive amount of reading during prepuberty; reading about practically everything: love stories as well as books on science, or descriptions of far-away countries and travels. The primary driving force, we believe—is the child's desire to "know" and to keep his mind occupied so that no disturbing thoughts and wishes are able to enter his consciousness. The emotional content which, at this age, is almost ready to overwhelm the consciousness unless the child resorts to particularly strong countercathexis, is most probably bound up with the sudden strengthening of the sexual impulses at this age. The conflict is due to the discrepancy existing between the newly acquired strength of the sexual impulses and the fact that the ego is still too weak to assimilate these needs on a more realistic level. This discrepancy results in the compulsive type of defense mechanism by which the child attempts to deflect his sexual curiosity into a general curiosity about the world. (This mechanism can lead to hobbies like stamp or coin collecting.) Yet even though this compulsive defense mechanism might be based on the same dynamic processes as are the symptoms of the compulsive neurotics, it cannot be called neurotic in the clinical sense of the term since there are very good realistic reasons why a child of this age cannot actually give way to his rising sexual drives. Thus, resorting to compulsive defense-mechanism, under these circumstances, can be considered an acceptable and realistic *self-*defense, indicating no particular tendency for neurosis at a later age.

A comparison between the dynamics involved in this stage of ego-development and the previous stage (minus *k*, minus *p*) has been made briefly in our discussion of the previous stage. It was pointed out that minus *k*, minus *p* implies much less awareness by the individual of those of his needs which may be dangerous socially or otherwise. His lesser awareness is indicated by his less energetic repression, or by the circumstance that *id* impulses actually have not been evacuated *from* the ego (since minus *p* is present); they simply have not been incorporated *in* the ego. In the stage of ego-development under discussion, however, it is just the appearance of open *p,* i.e. the forceful evacuation of the disturbing need from the ego, that demonstrates the particular care with which critical parts of the ego attempt to block dangerous needs from access to the motor system, indicating that in individuals yielding minus *k*, open *p*, the superego and whatever else corresponds to this critical aspect of the ego, has become more aware of the dangers implicit in id impulses. Whether this awareness is forced on the ego or superego by the increasing strength of the id impulses themselves, or whether it is brought about by an increasing sensitivity toward those needs cannot be decided with certainty on the basis of our test, although there are indications in the other factors pointing toward the probability of one or the other dynamism underlying different cases. A strong plus *s* factor, for example, would indicate that the compulsive defense has been brought about by the strength of the sadistic impulses; while a plus-minus *s* or minus *s*, minus *hy*, and the minus *k*, open *p* ego constellation points more strongly toward the inherent strictness of the superego precluding imminent danger of antisocial outbreak, even though compulsive defense mechanism is omitted. In the latter example, in addition to compulsive defense, the individual experiences acute feelings of guilt (minus *hy*, minus *k*). This constellation in the total test profile is not found in that group of children for whom the same *Sch* constellation is most characteristic. These children are warding off a more realistic danger, while in compulsive adults, the danger refers mostly to aggression on the phantasy level.

Adults who yield the minus *k*, open *p* configuration in the *Sch* vector have definitely compulsive features, even though not all of them can be classified as neurotics in the clinical sense. Apparent psychologic adjustment in spite of compulsive defense can be achieved with work which serves as adequate outlet for compulsive needs (if we may refer to a defense-mechanism as a "need"). Many occupations do serve this purpose, since compulsion refers more to the manner in which work is done than to the kind of work itself. Thus an individual yielding minus *k*, open *p* might find satisfaction in monotonous factory work requiring precision, or in devoting his interest to a detailed question in science to the exclusion of the context of which the detail is a subpart. These individuals are likely on a small scale to become experimentalists who, because of their precise work, are quite capable of reaching the limited goal they have set. They are critical toward their own work, as well as the work of others. They are likely to be slow and unimaginative. Scientists who are able to arrive at original approaches to complex problems, do not yield this *Sch* constellation. Sciences or professions involving relationships with human beings, and with emotional problems, are most rarely interesting to individuals with minus *k*, open *p*. Moreover, this constellation is rarely found in creative artistic work, although it can be found in individuals who are interested in artistic productions from a critical point of view.

Whether or not these subjects seem successful in their work, they are inhibited in their "private" emotional life. They are usually unable really to love because of their basic inhibition against allowing themselves to feel emotions at all. Since minus k is a sign of ability to conform with standards expected, these subjects often give the impression of living a "regular" life, exhibiting all the required constituents of "normalcy," such as family, home, job, etc. However the individual who yields this ego configuration is unable fully to participate in all these "normal" situations. Rather, he assumes his role as a duty, and with emotional detachment from everything he does. In certain cases, this feeling of emotional detachment approaches or reaches feelings of depersonalization, the basis of which is lack of identification with one's own latent needs.

The superficial appearance of normalcy is responsible for extreme difficulties inherent in the problem of validating studies on the basis of observable behavior or verbal or written questionnaires. Many basically unhappy individuals who are unable really to become emotionally attached to any person or object would rate extremely high on a written adjustment inventory, or on the basis of observation.

The most important clinical implication of this constellation in the *Sch* vector has been, practically, the topic of the whole general description of this ego picture. Most frequently the picture is found in compulsion neurosis, in conversion hysteria, hypochondriac anxiety (together with minus hy) and sexual immaturity in adults (the latter being many times the underlying cause for the first mentioned symptoms). The reasoning in regard to the underlying psychodynamics of why these forms of pathology should appear particularly frequently with this ego picture is also obvious on the basis of the previous discussion.

The age groups in which this constellation is frequent include first of all prepuberty, but also puberty and the

beginning of adolescence. From adolescence on, the frequency of minus k, open p decreases gradually, and occurs
least frequently in old age. On the basis of our findings, it
appears that this mechanism of active repression is probably
too energy-consuming for old age, when the use of the
"opposite" ego mechanism, namely the open k, minus p,
shows preponderance, this latter being a much more
"natural" mechanism involving no effort on the part of the
ego to inhibit the projection of one's needs into the
environment.

Stage VI. *Minus* k *with plus* p

Roughly speaking, the minus k, plus p *Sch* configuration
follows the minus k, open p, although there is a great deal
of overlap between the occurrence of these two ego pictures.
The interpretation corresponding to these two constellations
is also similar in many respects. They both reflect a situation within the ego in which the critical and organizing
aspect of the ego, the k factor, fights against acceptance of
the needs represented in the p factor. Both configurations
show that the person has accepted the overwhelming power
and the limitations of the environment, and no longer
believes in his own omnipotence (minus k). Accordingly,
certain personality characteristics in individuals giving
minus k, open p, and minus k, plus p are identical; characteristics such as willingness to conform with expected
social norms, and accentuated self-control. The difference,
however, is in the degree of repression of disturbing emotional content: the previous picture indicating successful
repression, while the plus p in the minus k, plus p configuration shows that tension of the emotional needs has become
so strong that despite repression the needs break through
to consciousness, or close to consciousness. This conflict
situation in the ego is found most frequently in late puberty
and in adolescence. It reflects the additional strengthening

of the id impulse (primarily sexual) in this age, while the
ego is still too weak to cope with these needs consciously.
To a certain extent, it corresponds to the "marginal" character of young people of this age, in which there is experienced the intensity of their growing needs for expansion
with a simultaneous inhibition of self-assertion. This is the
age at which the individual still does not dare to "live his
own life" because he is not sure of his own strength in
realizing plans, although the wish is there and is experienced
as such. The tension between internal inhibition and the
desire for self-expansion is greatest at this age in the so-called
clinically "normal" population. The behavior of subjects
in this age group exhibits certain features which could be
called compulsive, although they differ from the type of
"physiologically" compulsive behavior described in connection with the minus k, open p Sch constellation, and the
age group of prepuberty and early puberty. Even the compulsiveness of adolescents is more expansive than that of the
younger age group. They are less "bookish" and there
is a lesser degree of displacement of the libido from its
original object. The concept of sexuality has broken
through barriers to consciousness, and children in late
puberty and early adolescence enjoy talking about it. Their
conversation, however, shows many mannerisms which
border sometimes on compulsiveness. It seems as though
they would attempt to dispel their deep-seated anxieties
through the "magic" of the words. The discrepancy between
their verbal "wordliness" and their actual awkwardness in
many real life situations is considerable. This discrepancy
refers not only to the sexual sphere; it can also be observed
often in the adolescent's attitude toward the world, and
toward life in general. Puberty and adolescence represent
the ages at which the ego is inflated with great ideas and
plans, coupled with the feeling of inability to obtain them.
In this sense, it is the phase opposite to infantile autism,

the plus *k*, minus *p* (the visual configuration itself is opposite) when the child is unconcerned about the exact content of his needs but feels able to carry out anything he might conceive of. In other words, during the elapse of time between the second and the sixth stage of ego development, the child makes a complete reversal in regard to his attitude toward himself. Immediately after his ego has emerged as an entity separate from the rest of the world (after the adualistic stage) the child experiences his newly acquired ego as omnipotent, and does not perceive the limitations imposed by the environment. Slightly more than a decade later, the situation is exactly the opposite, in that now (during the minus *k*, plus *p* period) he is consciously concerned with his own needs but feels overwhelmed and inhibited by reality in carrying his needs into action. The period represented by plus *k*, minus *p*, typifies "no conflict in regard to one's own potentialities," while the period of minus *k*, plus *p* typifies "conflict in regard to one's own potentialities."

If obtained by adults, this ego picture still refers to the same adolescent-like personality characteristics. It is given by adults who feel that they have not lived up to their own expectations. Their level of aspiration is always higher than their level of achievement. The corresponding feeling of failure is independent of the realistic value of their achievements or of their success as judged by their environment. For individuals with minus *k*, plus *p*, the characteristic trait is just this feeling that whatever they have achieved is not enough. Accordingly, in their behavior they often drive themselves to extreme performances, in order to pursue the ego-ideal they have set for themselves and which they are unable to reach. The compulsive character of such behavior is obvious. The underlying feeling of insufficiency is due to the fact that these subjects experience the process of repression as an alien force operating within themselves, even though they would not be able to verbalize whatever it is they repress. Yet the presence of the plus p indicates that these subjects are sensitive in regard to their own psychologic processes. Thus, among others, they "feel" that they are repressing something, and experience a lack of balance in their ego-structure. This feeling of discomfort within themselves often drives them spontaneously toward seeking help in some form of psychotherapy. This is many times the beginning picture of patients who undergo psychoanalysis. It is the "typical" representation of the fight between the superego and the representatives of the id impulses. Accordingly, the behavior of these subjects is usually highly social and they consciously attempt to conform. However, the conforming behavior of these individuals is dynamically quite different from that of subjects with the "disciplined" ego (minus k, minus p). Subjects with the "disciplined ego" do not experience the process of conforming as a burden. They take it as the most natural course of events, and do not experience their own contradictory tendencies until—occasionally—these tendencies break through in a crude form. Subjects with minus k, plus p are aware of the continuing fight between impulses warded off and the inner agent responsible for this process. In this case, the subjective experiencing of conflict is acute, but there is seldom an antisocial breaking through of the denied tendencies. This might be due to several reasons: it might be due to the fact that the continuous awareness of the existing conflict acts in itself as a prevention against a crude form of outbreak, but it might also be due to the difference in the content of the need in the minus p, plus p positions respectively. The fact that the p factor is able to rise into the plus position might indicate that the corresponding needs are—at least to some degree—more acceptable socially than the needs of those adults whose p is kept continuously in the position of latency; yet even in this latent form the ego has to fight against them (minus k).

This theory is partially borne out by our clinical findings that the latent need in the "disciplined" ego refers mostly to sadistic needs, (to plus *s* needs), while in adults who yield minus *k*, plus *p*, the content of the *p* refers mostly to *h* factorial needs. Latent homosexual and latent incestuous wishes form many times the basic conflict inherent in this *Sch* configuration.

The distribution of the minus *k*, plus *p* ego-picture is fairly even among the various occupational groups. Among various pathologic groups this *Sch* configuration is found most frequently in compulsive neurotics. It is also found frequently in psychosomatic symptoms, in disorders of a primarily sexual nature mainly based on repression of intensive but still latent homosexual tendencies. It is found also in various types of anxiety symptoms and in stutterers. Although characteristically a neurotic picture, it can be found in schizophrenics; not, however, as a constant constellation within a whole series of ten profiles, but as one of the varying *Sch* configurations. This is particularly true of series in which the minus *k*, plus *p* constellation immediately follows or proceeds its opposite: the plus *k*, minus *p* configuration.

As we have pointed out, the most characteristic age for this *Sch* picture is late puberty and adolescence. Following these ages it decreases gradually in frequency until it is one of the rarest *Sch* reactions of the oldest group. The explanation for this most probably hinges on the fact that this ego-picture, because of the acute conflict situation inherent, is too energy-consuming to be tolerated beyond a certain age.

Plus-minus k *with* plus p

In our discussion of the previous *Sch* constellation, the minus *k*, plus *p*, characteristic for adolescents, the presentation of the typical stages of ego development as reflected in the succession of the *Sch* configurations in the various age groups has been more or less completed. We say more or less, because in psychology any developmental pattern expressed in terms of succeeding stages is of course a somewhat arbitrary conceptualization. Yet, up to the adolescent age group we were justified in designating the *Sch* configurations described above with consecutive Roman numerals since the quantitative data of frequency distributions have shown not only that the highest points of density of those *Sch* constellations lie in the respective age groups, but also that those configurations are either the first or the second most frequent ego picture in the respective age groups. This could be due to the fact that up to adolescence the variability of the ego pictures within the single age-groups was relatively limited. In other words, the age-patterning was more pronounced than the individual patterning. From eighteen years on, however, the situation changes, and the development of the ego—as reflected in the changes in the *Sch* vector becomes a highly complex matter of individual development. The result is that—with the exception of the minus *k*, minus *p* constellation, which stands out with its high frequency from the six to the eighty year old groups— there are no specific *Sch* configurations which show particularly close correlation with any single age groups. If, on the other hand, we begin with the various ego-constellations and observe the age groups in which the *Sch* configuration appears most frequently, we are then justified in coordinating the constellation with its representative group. On this basis we will discuss the plus-minus *k*, plus *p* constellation as that following stage VI of ego development (minus *k*, plus *p*).

The plus-minus *k*, plus *p* configuration reflects a complex and highly structured ego, which is found very rarely in the unselected population (in about three per cent) but appears with more than twice its average frequency in the 18–22 year old group. In this age group it is approximately the fourth most frequent ego configuration.

When we compare this stage with stage VI, we see that the plus-minus k, plus p constellation shows that the individual no longer feels compelled to repress all his needs; the reappearance of the plus k component indicates that he is able to identify himself—at least in part—with his needs. It should be remembered that, although the characteristic ages for this constellation lie between 18 and 22, this constellation is not characteristic of the "average" eighteen to twenty-two year old individual. It presupposes a much too complex ego organization to reflect the average reaction of any age group. The long range maintenance of this divided and selective attitude toward one's own needs, particularly if these needs have already inflated the ego, necessitates a well-developed and differentiated personality. This is one of the few constellations in the test profile which has a high correlation with intelligence above average. The fact that late adolescence and young adulthood are the characteristic ages for this complex ego mechanism must be due to the relatively strong organizational power of the ego at this age. Those subjects who give this particular reaction in the Sch vector feel strong enough to accept at least part of their needs without becoming autistic (the willingness to conform being indicated by the minus k component). They have an extremely strong need to organize their egos, the plus-minus position of the k factor showing that they are aware of this need in themselves. This organizational process is carried out half by introjection (see the section on the mechanism of plus k) and half by repression (minus k). However, neither of these k factorial mechanisms of ego organization, or the two together, succeed in eliminating the emotional tension corresponding to the plus p component of this constellation. The presence of the plus p indicates that the person experiences the need to cathect objects, which means he experiences the need to invest his libido into environmental objects, while the plus-minus position of the k factor indicates that simultaneously he fights for his narcissistic independence, which means that he fights for his emotional detachment from the environment.   In other words, there are two different types of ambivalence reflected in this configuration: first, the ambivalence in regard to whether to cathect outside objects or to withdraw the libido from the environment (conflict between the plus p and the k factors); second, the ambivalence between the two opposite kinds of ego mechanism in order to eliminate the emotional tension implied in the plus p (conflict between plus and minus k mechanisms).   Any individual who is able to make use of such a complex and apparently contradictory set of ego-dynamisms is—by definition—a highly differentiated person, or he would not be able to function under the emotional strain of these ambivalences.   Again, it should be remembered what a close dynamic relationship there is between the concepts of "conflict" and "synthesis" or "integration."   One definition of a mature personality could be that he is able to bear the coexistence of contradictory tendencies, without collapsing under the strain.   In the context of the Szondi test this definition holds true in regard to the *Sch* vector, which reflects the person's more integrated attitudes toward his partial needs, but not in regard to the other factors which reflect the state of tension resulting from the partial needs themselves.   A complex organization of the ego reflects flexibility in regard to dealing with the partial needs, whatever their state of tension or the position of these needs is, as indicated by the other six factors.

Accordingly, the plus-minus k, plus p configuration corresponds to such a flexible and conscious handling of the partial needs that it shows that the person is—almost consciously—able to decide which needs may be "let through" in their original form, which needs should be introjected, and which should be repressed.   The presence of the minus k shows that, despite their strong narcissism, these subjects

are willing to conform with environmental standards and
expectations. The goal which these subjects set for themselves in regard to their own ego is so high and complicated
that it necessarily results in subjectively experienced tension
and anxiety. The source of anxiety is most probably the
feeling that something might go wrong in the course of this
complicated mechanism: something they intended to repress
might break through to the motor system and thus appear in
open behavior; or, the outwardly-directed libido of the p
factor might gain the upper hand and thus destroy the
narcissistic integrity of the personality. A person with plus-
minus k, plus p is conscious, or fairly conscious, of all these
possible dangers, due to the functioning of the plus k, plus p,
both of them indicating that the awareness of his own needs
and the tendency for introspection is great. The ego processes as such are highly cathected in these subjects.

The breaking through of the repressed impulses is actually
quite probable in these subjects, since the plus p indicates
that the isolation of the unwanted needs is not complete in
that the plus p factor acts in the direction of breaking down
the walls surrounding the innerpersonal regions (corresponding to needs), thus facilitating their access to the motor system. Yet even in case of unsuccessful repression these subjects do not exhibit antisocial behavior. This is even more
true of subjects yielding this Sch configuration than it was
in the case of minus k, plus p. Again, as in the case of the
previous Sch configuration, we can hypothesize two reasons
for the lack of antisocial behavior in this group of subjects.
A sudden antisocial outbreak might be prevented either by
the continuous functioning of the plus p and plus k (which
means the original intensity of the id-impulses might be
mitigated by the individual's continuous awareness of those
needs (plus p) and the integrative process of the ego ($-$plus
k) or the needs themselves might not be primarily antisocial.
The fact that this Sch configuration usually is associated

with either minus h or minus s, or both minus h and minus s in the S vector and with plus m in the C vector, would support the second hypothesis.

Individuals giving this reaction in the Sch vector are usually highly social and well-sublimating. It is most rarely found in the lower occupational levels. Most of the time it is given by "intellectuals" who are productive, but who feel "driven" to work by their subjectively experienced anxious tension. They attempt to overcome their internal panic by work, and because of their strong organizational powers they are able to hide their anxiety from the outside observer. However, due to their introspective ability they are well aware of their problems, and thus often go voluntarily for psychoanalytic help. The same ability for dissecting emotions intellectually leads them often to professions dealing with the emotional—and psychological—growth problems of others. Accordingly, this ego picture is found frequently in psychiatrists, psychologists, psychiatric social workers, teachers, and educators in various fields.

Usually, if this is a stable Sch reaction within a series of profiles, there are no obvious open symptoms which are particularly characteristic for these subjects. However, it is a typical picture for subjectively experienced anxiety states, without apparent symptoms. Due to the narcissistic surface barrier ("character armor," according to Reich*) which these subjects are able to utilize in order to camouflage their underlying anxiety, they could be rather diagnosed as character-neurosis. Despite, or perhaps because of, their good intellectual insight into their own problems, their analysis is usually of long duration.

It is hard work to restructure the ego of such highly organized and realistically rather well-functioning individuals, for whom analysis gives relatively little heuristic insights,

* Reich, Wilhelm: Character Analysis. Orgone Institute Press, New York, 1945.

and who have long-developed subtle mechanisms at their disposal to avoid too strong emotional involvement in any human relationship. However, the presence of the plus *p* factor is still a good sign that in the long run a transference relationship can be established.

It has been mentioned at the beginning of this section that by far the most frequent age for this complex ego picture occurs at the close of the teens and the beginning of the twenties. These years appear to represent the age at which there is most interest in the own ego functions in these individuals who become interested in their own ego at all. It is rare to find this *Sch* configuration in middle-aged subjects, and is practically nonexistent in ages beyond sixty.

Plus k *with plus* p

The plus *k*, plus *p* is another complex and highly differentiated ego picture which occurs rarely in the population at large, (in somewhat less than 3 per cent) but is found with almost three times its average frequency in the age group between twenty and thirty. Thus we can consider it as following the previously discussed *Sch* configuration, the plus-minus "*k*" with plus *p*, with which the present configuration has many characteristics in common.

The disappearance of the minus *k* component of the *k* factor shows that these subjects identify themselves more completely—if not quite completely—with their emotional needs* and do not feel the necessity for conforming with standards imposed from the outside (lack of minus *k* component).

This picture reflects an extremely tense situation within the ego because the intensity of the outwardly-directed object libido is as strong as the person's narcissistic need to introject the objects of the *p* factorial "libido," achieving thereby the

---

* The expression "emotional need" is used because we also refer to the *k* factorial striving for unemotionality and narcissistic independence as corresponding to a "need."

autistic self-sufficiency of the personality. The plus position of the p factor shows that the person is aware of his need-tension, while the plus position of the k factor shows that the organizing aspect of the ego, completely identifies (consciously or unconsciously) itself with these needs. Identification—as indicated by the plus k—means that the person continuously attempts to face and understand his needs intellectually, hoping to absorb thereby the emotionally urging character of these needs. In other words, there is a continuous attempt to transform the object-libido into narcissistic-libido; however, the presence of the plus p indicates that this goal has never been reached.

One could call this ego "over-worked" because of the unconditional attitude of wanting to solve all of one's psychologic problems on the conscious level. Not only are the emotional problems of these subjects cathected, but one could say they are "over-cathected," so much of the psychic energy is used up for introspection and attempts to understand oneself. To be sure, this "attempt to understand" is usually successful in individuals who yield plus k, plus p. This is again an Sch configuration which usually is indicative of above average intelligence and strong drive for intellectual achievements. The continuous and uninhibited flowing in of emotional needs to the *preconscious* and *conscious,* with simultaneous striving to intellectualize these needs, gives these subjects the feeling of acutely experiencing their own intellectual and productive potentialities, yet they experience difficultes in translating these vague feelings of "being able to do something" into realistic actions since the "thinking out" of the problems involved takes up too much psychic energy. The difficult problems for subjects giving this Sch constellation are centered in a paradox: on the one hand, a lack of repression permits practically every emotional content to rise into consciousness, striving thereby to expand the ego by fusing into the appropriate objects; on the other hand, the plus k factor tends to digest intellectually all the emotional impulses, to conceptualize and systematize them, and thereby to utilize the psychic energy within the ego rather than to invest it in the environment. However, the k factor with its systematizing and intellectualizing function is—figuratively speaking—always "behind" the ·new emotional contents coming up in the plus p. Dynamically, the subjectively experienced psychologic effect of this undecided "fight" between two equally conscious yet opposing tendencies within the ego is a feeling of "disorder" or "chaos" within the ego with the simultaneous feeling that actually one would be able to make order and organize oneself if only the new emotional contents and ideas would not always interrupt the process of systematization. However, the fact is that so long as the person gives this particular reaction in the *Sch* vector, the newly intruding emotional contents and ideas—the proper description could be "emotional ideas" do always interrupt the k factorial process of systematization and organization. Yet the k factor does not give up its attempt to intellectualize the content of the p and thereby "liberate" the person from emotional involvement with outside objects. As long as the person gives this reaction in the *Sch* vector, he lives under a constant state of tension and conflict between "intellect" and "emotions," between fusing in an outside object or detaching himself from his environment. Characteristic of these subjects is the fact that they are quite conscious of the exact nature of this conflict themselves, and not only are they able, but they actually do, enjoy conceptualizing this conflict with all its constituent elements. They feel extremely "potent" and productive, and inhibited at the same time. Many times they experience something similar to anxiety, only one cannot quite call it that, because of its being so highly intellectualized and consciously accepted that it became practically an integrated character trait of the personality rather than a pressing anxiety. The concept of real anxiety presupposes more repression, more defense on the unconscious level, than can be found in the present *Sch* configuration, in which it is practically nonexistent. What these subjects do experience is a conscious feeling of tension and an "anxiety" of disintegration; the idea of a potential psychosis is not foreign to many of them. My hesitation to call this feeling "anxiety" results from clinical observation that these subjects are on such almost "friendly" terms with all their pathologic potentialities that sometimes it approaches the symptoms of depersonalization. Intellectually they accept their anxieties, and conceptualize them until the concept becomes void of most of its original emotional content. The similarity to symptoms of depersonalization lies in their ability to look at their own psychologic processes as an onlooker from the outside. This again is due to the fact that all psychologic processes and conflicts take place on the plane of consciousness. The subjects are "emotional" but at the same time they are able to alienate themselves from their own emotions, even being aware of this process of alienation. This awareness contrasts to the symptom associated with the minus k, open p constellation, in which depersonalization and alienation from emotional content also take place without the subject's awareness of the ongoing process of repression. Plus k, plus p subjects frequently experience painfully, despite their need for emotional attachment, their inability actually to "lose" themselves in any emotional situation. It seems to be the function of the plus k factor to make these subjects always aware of what is going on so that they conceptualize their own roles in any interpersonal relationship, as well the structure of the situation itself. In this way, the plus p factorial needs, as well as the plus k factorial needs, are satisfied (unless, under a different definition of satisfaction, one might say that neither of them is really satisfied). In other words, these subjects do enter emotional relationships with persons and objects (many times to objects of art), while at the same time they avoid complete fusion into the object through their constant mental and intellectual "recording" of what is going on. This psychologic make-up lends itself well to various types of intellectual and artistic sublimation. The plus k, plus p configuration is practically never found in nonintellectual occupations. It is a typically "intellectual" or "artistic" (usually both) ego picture, although the subjects belonging to this group are not the most productive members of these professions. It appears that lack of repression to the degree discussed counteracts real productivity, since productivity appears to require the ability to disregard certain contents in order to pursue those which are most important and fruitful within the given context. The intellectual interest of subjects with plus k, plus p, is usually too widespread and all-inclusive to permit the systematic development of one given problem. They usually have many and frequent "good ideas" and sudden insights without following them up or working them out in detail: the intrusion of a fresh idea bars the development of the original. This process is due to the continuous identifying of the ego (plus k) with whatever content comes up in the plus p factor.

There is much of the "Faustian" conflict and Faustian searching for rational solutions in these subjects; "Faustian" because, in whatever field they work, they feel torn between the desire to approach the problem emotionally through their "intuitive" feelings, and the desire to force themselves to act and reason on a highly rational and intellectual level. The product of their work, as well as their way of working, reflects this dual attitude. The accompanying subjective feeling is dissatisfaction with either approach, leading to attempts to integrate the two, in which attempts they might be more or less successful for short periods. Many times, however, their realistic productivity stagnates because of this conflict.

Usually in the test profiles of subjects with plus k, plus p, there is another sign which points toward the tendency to intellectualize emotions: that is the minus h, minus s in the S vector, with which this Sch constellation is most frequently correlated. In terms of their sexuality this correlation means that, for these subjects, the specificity of the love-object is far more important than the carrying out of the sex act itself. They are able to bear frustrations (indeed, they might even "look for" frustration) rather than to compromise in the choice of the love-object. "Love" is more important than sexuality for these subjects. One could say that their primarily sexual needs have been drawn into the ego, and lived out on a higher conceptual level of "love." The great sensitivity and appreciation of these subjects for products of art, literature, and music can be intepreted as another sign of the same phenomenon.

It should be noted that the characteristics of individuals who yield plus k, plus p are diametrically opposite to the characteristics of subjects giving the disciplined ego, the minus k, minus p. The briefest recapitulation of the oppositness of these two groups of subjects would be that those giving minus k, minus p are realistic in their daily lives but irrational in regard to their own psychologic processes and in conceptualizing the phenomena around them, while those giving plus k, plus p tend to be unrealistic in their daily lives, but are highly rational in regard to their attempts to conceptualize the phenomena within themselves as well as outside themselves. Subjects with minus k, minus p live on a concrete level, while those with plus k, plus p live on an abstract level of symbolization. Subjects with minus k, minus p, are "regular" and conforming with "average" patterns of behavior, but in case of a break-down they become violently antisocial. Subjects with plus k, plus p

are likely to live "atypical" lives, being more concerned with the integration of their own egos than with conforming to social rules. They are highly narcissistic, and in this sense, asocial, because so much of their attention is centered in their own *self*. Yet they practically never will turn against society or indulge in any violent activity. The percentage of criminals giving this *Sch* configuration is zero. Subjects associated with the configuration have a great need to assert themselves, but only on an intellectual or "symbolic" level.

Strangely enough, serious psychopathologic breakdowns of subjects with plus k, plus p are also rare. The plus k, plus p constellation (which is usually associated with a minus block, minus h and minus s in the S vector) is a counterindication for any serious forms of pathology. It seems that despite the acutely experienced conflict caused by the simultaneous acceptance of two contradictory tendencies, the two opposing factors have a mutually tempering effect on their respective manifestations, thereby avoiding the breaking through of any extreme forms of manifestations. Another possible explanation for the apparent lack of serious symptoms with this *Sch*-picture is that these subjects by continuously facing and intellectualizing their pathologic potentialities, actually succeed in diminishing the dynamic power of their most dangerous needs. They practically live in a constant process of self-analysis.

The pathologic symptoms which can be found with this ego picture refer to cases of preschizophrenic, or characterneurotic "pseudo geniuses" who always talk about the great things they are going to produce, and indulge in their own eccentricities. They enjoy being "atypical" and do everything to exhibit their difference from the rest of humanity. They usually have a sort of "sectarianism" whereby they voluntarily ostracize themselves from society and look down at the "average and common people." One can usually spot them visually by their unusual hair-do and obviously unusual

selection of clothing. Not seldom they live a rather para-
sitic life, since taking care of and exhibiting their own
ego takes up all their time and energy, and what is left is
spent on talking about "great things." Ideologically they
look down on a regular way of living. Anybody who has
been in the cafes of New York City's Greenwich Village is
familiar with this type. They are the grotesque caricatures
of people who live on an "abstract" level; grotesque because
their satisfaction in exhibitionism, rather than their real
experiencing of a conflict, perpetuates this mode of behavior.
There is usually a deep underlying sexual frustration and
strong latent or open homosexuality. However, even these
subjects do not turn antisocial in the active sense of the word,
nor do they break down into an open form of psychosis (or
at least very rarely). Many times there is a sort of "spontaneous recovery" around the end of the twenties.

At any rate, this ego picture decreases steadily beyond the
age of thirty and is never found in old age. The psychic
energy needed to keep up this intricate constellation and the
ability to bear the emotional tension of living in an acute
state of conflict on the emotional as well as intellectual level,
is too much for most subjects to keep up as an ego mechanism
for more than a few years between twenty and thirty, which
are the most consciously formative years for ego development.

Plus k with open p

The plus k, open p configuration is again not frequent in
the general population (occurring in about 4 per cent), but
as far as developmental sequence goes its discussion fits here
following the discussion of the plus k, plus p pattern since
it is one of the two most usual outcomes of the previous *Sch*
constellation (the other is the open k, plus p). In the period
of young adulthood the plus k, open p reaches its highest
frequency, and is given usually by the same subjects who,
previous to that stage, gave the plus k, plus p reaction. The

latter, as has been described in the previous section, is an extremely tense ego picture, containing many contradictory elements which are simultaneously, and with equal force, fighting for manifestation, since both tendencies have reached the same level of consciousness. This was a critical situation for the ego, because of the strain imposed on it by the coexistence of the plus p (object directed libido) and the plus k (tendency to withdraw object-libido into the ego.) Although a critical and in a sense self-contradictory psychologic state, under favorable circumstances and for a limited period of time, this highly complex ego structure could have a constructive effect upon the further development of the personality because of the continuous ego building process inherent in it, a process of ego building without a complete withdrawal of the libido from the outside world. In the plus k, plus p stage, this means primarily emotional and intellectual processes were being experienced simultaneously.

This critical situation, however, even in case the person makes use of it constructively, is not usually kept up for a long period in anyone's life. After a period of undecided "fight" between the plus k and the plus p factors, there comes, usually, a period when either the introjection of the k wins over the outside directed tension of the p factor, or the dynamic strength of the p succeeds in breaking down the rigidity of the k.

The plus k, open p constellation corresponds to the process under which the k factor succeeds in eliminating the emotional tension caused by the p to the extent that the p factor is completely drained. Usually, in the period during which the person yields the plus k, plus p reaction, one can predict on the basis of the profile as well as by the subject's behavior, whether the "instinctual dilemma" will be decided according to the forces corresponding to the k or to the p factor. On the test profile one can see still before the clearcut open k, plus p or plus k, open p occurs, whether the k or the p factor has the tendency to be more loaded, and in the behavior of subjects yielding the plus k, plus p pattern, one can distinguish between those in whose observable behavior the characteristics corresponding to the k factor are dominating from those who impress the outsider as primarily p factorial persons, who only themselves are aware how much they must fight against the "rigidifying" effects of the plus k. On the other hand, there are subjects at this particular stage of ego development who want to impose—and are many times successful in this desire—as rigid and unemotional individuals, while underneath this surface calmness they experience emotions intensively. They may give the impression of being unattached and self-sufficient individuals, while actually they experience the strongest emotional attachment to a particular environmental object, or even several objects (in this case, "objects" meaning, nearly always, persons). It is this type plus k, plus p individual who is likely to change his *Sch* reaction into plus k, open p, indicating thereby that his wish to appear self-sufficient and calm has been achieved not only on the behavior level but in deeper layers of his personality. Whether or not this emotional self-sufficiency is actually as genuine and deep as the plus k, open p subject would like to believe, is another question.

Nevertheless, this *Sch* constellation indicates that object-libido has been transformed "successfully" into narcissistic libido, by way of making extreme use of the mechanism of introjection. This means that the original object of the libido has been incorporated into the ego (see section on plus k) thereby making it possible to give up the original environmental object and love one's own *self*, which by then means loving the incorporated image of the love-object once actually needed. Because of this "identity" of love object and the subject himself, the need inherent in the p factor, driving to establish fusion between subject and object, can

be lived out continuously, as indicated by the open position,
since the goal of fusion has been achieved, only in the direction opposite to the original intention of the p factorial
need. Instead of the person fusing into the object, the object
becomes incorporated within the person, which in fact
is the only place for the object where it can be "loved" continuously—in the literal sense—since it is the only way to
"carry" the love object wherever one goes. Thus, in this
configuration, the open p means that the need for object
love has been lived out continuously because the ego itself
became the love object.

In subjects with this *Sch* configuration, the process of
introjection takes place usually by way of the intellectual
process of thinking. The person faces his emotional needs
consciously, thinks them over, conceptualizes them until
very little—if any—of the original emotional feeling of the
needs is left. At the same time the original object of the
libido is thoroughly examined from an intellectual point of
view. The goal of these subjects is to be objective under
any circumstances, which in terms of psycho-dynamics is
equivalent to saying that these subjects want to increase the
distance between themselves and the actual object. One
can be objective only when one considers the object as
separate from the observer; that is what the word "objective"
(as against "subjective") means. Thus, by being objective,
they alienate themselves from the real outside object while,
at the same time, by the very process of thinking *about* the
object, they incorporate it on an intellectual and conceptual
level. (Sense of humor and the attempt to see things in a
grotesque light is a frequent manifestation of this basic
need of keeping distance between oneself and the environment.) Now that they own the conceptual image of the
object, they can think about it and practically "feel" its
existence within themselves, instead of needing the real
contact with the real object. This process of intellectual

introjection leads many times to sublimating a need originating in the id, in appropriate types of professions. Professions lend themselves well to channelization in the form of intellectual and "objective" interests, such "instinctual" needs which—in their original form due to one reason or another—could not be accepted by the critical parts of the ego (superego). As a matter of fact, this is not one way but *the* way of sublimating through professional work. This is the process for which Freud uses the metaphor of the horse and the rider corresponding in our context to the p (equals horse, equals id) and the k (equals rider, equals organizing and critical function of the ego) which states that if the rider is not to be parted from his horse, he is obliged to guide the horse where it wants to go. In terms of the present *Sch* configuration, this means that the k factor has to guide the person to such type of acceptable work to which the "instinctive" drive of the p factor leads it, a work which satisfies the socially high standards of the superego, the narcissistic requirement of self-sufficiency of the ego, and the instinctual demands of the id, simultaneously. As can be seen, the compromise character of sublimation is very similar to that of compulsive symptom formation (indicated in the test by the mirror picture of the present constellation: the minus k, open p) although there is a great difference in terms of libido-economics. The compulsive symptom is neurotic because its primary function is to ward off the unaccepted id demand while giving no real satisfaction to the person as a whole, accumulating thereby frustration over frustration and necessitating the mobilization of always stronger repressive forces if the need should indeed not break through. This is a most "uneconomical" way of using psychic energy, and after a time results necessarily in a number of additional symptoms and an increasing inability of the person to use his energy for productive adjustment and useful work, since gradually all his energy is used up for the purpose of repression. In other words, warding off an id impulse by the minus k mechanism brings about neurotic symptoms because of the lack of gratification for the total personality, which is inherent in this process. Sublimation on the other hand— indicated by the elimination of the p tension by plus k— wards off the unacceptable id impulse by substituting a truly gratifying activity. Repression works by establishing barriers around the need to be warded off, while sublimation establishes channels for discharge on a highly socialized level. How we know that this sublimated activity is "truly" gratifying can be answered only in a pragmatic way: by the observable fact that the person functions well, is able to adjust to reality, and seems to get emotional satisfaction from his work. There are undoubtedly "borderline" and "mixed" cases, in which although the person appears to be engaged in a sublimated activity, he indicates in his behavior the symptoms of continuous frustration, which shows that in this case the individual drives himself compulsively to sublimate, in which case the corresponding k constellation is usually plus-minus.

One of the most interesting aspects of the Szondi test is the way it reflects in a perceivable and "tangible" form, the dynamic relatedness between seemingly opposite dynamisms, such as in the present case, both the oppositeness as well as the close relationship between repression and sublimation is revealed by the experimental findings that the corresponding difference in the *Sch* vector is the turning of the minus k into a plus k, while the similarity between the two dynamisms is indicated by the open p constellation in both instances, reminding us that the function of either mechanism is to lower the intrusion of the id-tension within the ego. I do not think that any of the other projective technics fulfills this important function of making the psychologic dynamisms known from psychoanalytic theory, actually visible, demonstrating thereby the manner of their operation in an empirical and experimental fashion instead of describing them verbally on the basis of case material.

The frequency of the plus k, open p constellation is about a third of the frequency of minus k, open p, (and less than a sixth of the most popular ego picture: the minus k, minus p), bearing out Freud's contention that only relatively few people have the "ability" to sublimate successfully. This "ability to sublimate" means the readiness to exchange one mode of attaining gratification for another (and not the renouncing of gratification), to accept one object as a satisfactory substitute for another. In this sense we can say that successful sublimation presupposes a relatively great power for symbolization, the term being used in its most general meaning to denote the process whereby one object acquires the significance of another to the extent that for the person (the third entity in the process) the two objects—the original object and the symbol of this object—have the same phychologic meaning.*

Plus k, open p subjects have this ability to derive gratification from symbolic activities to a greater extent than subjects with any other reaction in the Sch vector. According to this definition, emotional satisfaction derived from professional or artistic work, is "symbolic" as far as it serves successfully as a substitute for more "instinctive" and less socialized activities. These subjects "love" their intellectual or artistic work, or such products of others, with practically the same intensity as other individuals love a person. For subjects with plus k, open p reaction, this attitude towards their work is very characteristic. The possibility is not denied that some "residual" frustration is always implied in so extensive an attempt for "symbolic" or sublimated satisfaction, yet if this frustration does not go beyond a certain "optimal"

* For a detailed description of the meaning of symbolization, see Susanne K. Langer: Philosophy in a New Key: A Study in the Symbolism of Reason, Rite and Art. Penguin Books, Inc., New York.

point, then it can manifest itself—instead of causing neurotic symptoms—as a constructive driving force for further sublimated activities. The question of how much frustration is desirable for the productive functioning of the person, and when it does become the source of neurotic motivation, is one of the most delicate questions in the realm of psychodynamics, having something to do with subtle differential quantities of psychic energies as well as with fine shadings of qualitative differences. In the case of the *Sch* configuration under discussion, the experimental findings which show that plus *k*, open *p* is correlated most of the time with minus *h*, minus *s* in the sexual vector, gives us a further insight into the psychodynamics of these subjects, showing that the transformation of the primarily sexual energy has taken place at a very basic level of energy-organization, so that the task of sublimating sexual libido is not burdening the *k* factorial ego processes alone.

At this point, reference to psychodynamic concepts outside the framework of the Szondi test becomes very difficult, because of the lack of one hundred per cent overlap between any one psychoanalytic concept and specific factorial constellations in the test. Thus, we have to resort to dynamic explanations in terms of factorial and vectorial correlations. The dynamic correlation I want to point out here is that all the three exclusively "plus" constellations in the *Sch* vector (the plus *k*, plus *p*, the plus *k*, open *p*, and the open *k*, plus *p*) occur most frequently in conjunction with complete minus reactions in the sexual vector (with minus *h and* minus *s); while all three exclusively minus reactions in the *Sch* vector (the minus *k*, minus *p*, minus *k*, open *p*, and open *k*, minus *p*) are correlated most frequently with complete plus reaction (plus *h*, plus *s*) in the sexual vector. This clearcut opposite correlation in the general direction of the reaction in the *S* and in the *Sch* vectors shows that sublimation as indicated by the ego vector occurs typically when there are signs of the primarily sexual component—needs having undergone a certain "desexualization," as indicated immediately within the sexual vector. On the other hand, the ego vector indicates the person's making use of the defense mechanism of repression and unconscious projection in case the primary sexual drives appear in an unmodified form in the sexual vector. To what extent the modification of the sexual drives—as indicated by the minus h and minus s constellation—is a primary process in itself, and to what extent it might be considered as the result of the sublimating processes within the ego, is an open question. Yet it seems— at least to me—that these two main indications of sublimation on the test profile are not simply reflecting two aspects of one and the same process, but correspond to sublimating (or desexualizing, or symbolizing) processes taking place in different layers of the personality or, one might say, at different levels of energy organization the processes indicated in the minus reactions in the sexual vector, corresponding to the more primordial function, being related more directly to the handling of the sexual energy *per se*. The plus k and the plus p factors reflect a more inclusive type of sublimation at a "higher" level of energy organization, referring to the socialized transformation of all the component needs of the personality which are contained in the remaining six factors of the profile, and not exclusively to the sublimation of the primarily sexual needs. Yet the vicissitudes of the h and s needs seem to exercise a specifically strong influence on this more generalized sublimation taking place within the ego vector, deciding to a great extent whether or not the ego will be able to resort to the more conscious and constructive dynamisms, which imply the person's facing his own needs, or whether the ego will be forced to resort to the more unconscious types of ego defenses.

Among the ego pictures, the plus k with open p (together with the previous picture, the plus k plus p) is the prototype

of the "introspective" and not-repressing ego mechanisms—
or "defenses," to use the term in its most general meaning.
Their correlation with the minus h and minus s pattern,
seems to indicate that those subjects are able to face and to
accept their "instinctual" needs, whose sexuality, to start
with, is relatively "desexualized" and lends itself thereby
more easily to being channelized toward asexual and idealistic goals. Just what the basic characteristics of this type of
sexuality are cannot be answered yet, but it appears that
there is something essentially inherent in the quality of the
sexual energy of those subjects who can readily deflect it
from primarily and physically sexual goals to sublimated
activities without neurotic symptom formation. (The
intensity of the pregenital and latent homosexual component
drives is most probably a decisive factor in the process of
directing sexual energy towards idealistic goals.) Even
though we cannot define these inherent qualitative peculiarities of the primarily sexual energy more precisely, it should
be remembered that this flexible and "directable" kind of
sexuality is most characteristic for subjects with plus k and
open p reaction in the Sch vector.

Subjects with this ego picture seem to be able to live
without much primary sexual gratification rather easily. In
interpersonal relationship they often seem cold and unemotional. The ambivalence between being "emotional" or
"rational" which was characteristic for the subjects with the
plus k and plus p configuration, seems to have disappeared
in the present configuration, the subjects in this group
impressing their environment as being purely rational
beings. In interpersonal relationship these subjects are
unable really to give themselves; they are always on guard
against getting involved emotionally. Deeper analysis of
these subjects reveals, usually, the defense character of this
apparent coldness and self-sufficiency. In many ways this
reaction can be compared to the reaction of the "burned

child" not daring to invest emotions into persons because of having been forced once to give up a most important love object. The time of the occurrence of this "basic" trauma seems to vary from person to person, within the group giving this *Sch* reaction. In some cases it seems to refer as far back as the necessary giving up of the most intensive attachment to one parent or the other, while in other cases the traumatic loss of an object might have occurred later in life. In all cases, however, _characteristic_ for these individuals is the _way they react to this trauma_; namely, by passive withdrawal rather than by any form of dynamic revolt or attempts to gain back the object. On the contrary, the person exerts great efforts to rid himself of the need of needing objects altogether, and—by the above described mechanism of introjecting the lost object—attempts to restore the narcissistic integrity of his own ego, and establish emotional calmness within himself. The frustration tolerance in regard to realistic loss of objects is high in these individuals, due to the quick—at least on the surface—regenerative effect of introjection. However, the frustration tolerance in regard to being able to bear the subjective experiencing of suffering and emotional tension is extremely low in these subjects. In every day life these individuals are often described as "being too proud to suffer"—which is quite true to a large extent. In some ways they resemble the state of the autistic children, who gave the plus *k*, minus *p* configuration, and who felt able to project all of their own wishes directly upon their own ego, establishing thereby their emotional independence from their environment. Actually the plus *k*, open *p* constellation expresses the same need, only on a more conscious level, and at a higher level of personality development, with a correspondingly higher degree of social adjustment, and with more awareness of the whole process, and of the fact that what they are doing is a reaction forma-

tion against the dangers involved in case they dare to give
free reign to their emotions.

The steady occurrence of this *Sch* picture is a counterindication against serious forms of pathology. It is given
frequently by rigid character-neurotics, who are able to
function well on the behavior level, but are unable to form
satisfactory emotional relationships. The same type of subjects are often called "schizoid" individuals, who are not,
however, actually psychotic. It can be found also in the
beginning stages of depression (indicating the immediate
effect of the loss of an object), particularly in cases in which
one hesitates between the diagnoses of incipient schizophrenia or incipient depression.

It has been mentioned that the characteristic age for
this *Sch* constellation is in early adulthood. It is unusual
to find it in children, and even more so in old age.

Open k, plus p

The frequency of the open *k,* plus *p* ego picture in the
general population, as well as in the age at which it appears
with particularly high frequency, is the same as the frequency of the previously discussed *Sch* configuration, the
plus *k,* open *p.* As mentioned above, both these configurations can be considered as derivatives of the plus *k,* plus *p*
pattern; the critical instinct-dilemma of that ego constellation being decided once in terms of the secondary narcissism of the plus *k,* while in other cases it is the dynamic
power of the plus *p* which wins over the rigidity of the
k factor. The open *k,* plus *p* corresponds to the latter case.

The plus *p* in this configuration indicates the dynamic
strength of the needs, driving them up "into the open,"
toward conscious forms of manifestation, and toward cathecting outside objects with the libido, so that finally the need-
tension can be released in connection with objects of the
environment (see section on plus *p).*

The open k in this configuration shows the person's *primary* narcissism, i.e. the ego's accepting and lenient attitude towards the dynamic urgency of the needs inherent in the plus p. In this constellation the open k indicates that there is no internal barrier which would intend to handicap or to modify the needs implied in the plus p. Contrary to the situation in the previous two *Sch* configurations, in which the presence of the plus k indicated the ego's intention to modify and intellectualize the emotional content of the plus p, attempting thereby to free the ego from the need to fuse into the actual love object, the lack of any measurable tension in the k factor in the present configuration indicates the person's willingness freely to submit himself to the emotionality of the p factor, without intellectual neutralization of the respective needs. This means that these subjects experience a strong need in regard to finding the proper environmental objects to be cathected, which objects finally will serve their function by facilitating the reduction of the need-tension. Subjects with open k and plus p constellations have to be in love with somebody or something; many times they are "in love" with idealistic concepts. Whatever the object of their need is, whether it is a person, or an ideal of humanity at large, their attitude toward this object is the same. It is the diametric opposite to the attitude of the plus k, open p subjects who intend always to increase the distance between themselves and the realistic object in that the open k, plus p subjects do everything to decrease the distance between themselves and the environmental object which attracts their libido (or psychic energy in general). They want to approach complete fusion into the object as much as possible. Since one hundred per cent fusion into anything environmental is—by definition—impossible, these subjects are likely to feel frustrated no matter how successful they seem to an outsider in establishing object relationships. What they want is complete lack of resistance on the part of the object, so that nothing is in the way of their "need to fuse."

The child with open k, minus p reaction has lived out this "need to fuse" without being conscious of the existence of the need. At this early stage of ego development the emotional content of the need was still unconscious, yet in this—or rather, because of this—latent position, the dynamic efficiency of the needs was stronger. The needs as such were not perceived and conceptualized, since they had not passed through the system of the preconscious; however, they still possessed their full magical power, which prevented the recognition of any realistic resistance on the part of the environmental objects. Because of this all-powerfulness of the unconscious needs, we could justly designate this as the stage of "adualism," meaning thereby the experience of uninterrupted continuity between subject and object.

The subject with open k, plus p is the person who consciously experiences the above described need; he wishes he had magical power whereby he could re-establish the continuity, by then disrupted, between himself and the object cathected. (Interest in such phenomena as hypnosis, or scientific interest in problems of extrasensorial perception, which is found frequently with this Sch pattern, might be the expression of the same need to establish continuity between subject and environment.) The fact that the p is in plus position indicates that needs are perceived and conceptualized (at least some needs) after having passed through the $preconscious$. This whole process, of course, presupposes a rather highly developed personality structure, at which stage the differentiation between object and subject has—naturally—taken place a long time ago. Yet, the open k, plus p individual makes conscious efforts to re-establish this prehistoric adualism, an effort which at this stage of ego development necessarily leads to nonfulfillment. However, at the encountering of realistic barriers (which might seem as barriers only to such extremely demanding individuals), the open k, plus p individual does not withdraw as his dynamic opposite, the plus k open p subject would do. Rather, he revolts against the unyieldingness of the environment. The readiness for projection, in the sense of positing the blame for subjectively experienced failure in the outside rather than within the person, is characteristic for these subjects (the tension in the p factor indicates readiness for projection in whatever position it is). Open k, plus p individuals are likely to be intensively and hopelessly in love, without retreating from such an unrewarding situation. It appears as though they would want to experience the last drop of emotional potentialities of any situation, whether it means pleasure or suffering. Contrary to the plus k, open p subjects, they do not want to save themselves from any sort of emotional experience. Rather, they seem to derive some masochistic pleasure even from frustrating experiences, nor are they opposed to "exhibiting their wounds" to others.

In Rankian terms, one could describe these subjects as having never accepted, emotionally, the reality of the birth-trauma, insisting on considering the world in general as an enormous uterus, the function of which is to fulfill all their needs. Anything contrary to this function is taken as personal insult. To a certain extent, this characterization does hold for the plus k, open p subjects as well, since they might also be described as suffering from the trauma of birth, or of being weaned, all their lives; yet they attempt to avoid actual suffering by pretending that they themselves can be their own benevolent "uterus" and the rest of the world does not count emotionally. The open k, plus p individual, on the other hand, does not pretend emotional self-sufficiency, but fights actively against—what seems to him—rigid resistance of the environment. The ambivalent character of this type of subject is obvious from the above description, since love and aggression is so closely linked in them. They love intensively and aggressively, feeling always that their love is not sufficiently reciprocated. They do not experience conflicts consciously within themselves, but rather between themselves and the environment. Their ability for introspection is limited, in spite of their being aware of many of their needs. They—almost ideologically—accept emotions as the "raison d'etre" of human beings, and reject detailed intellectual analysis of emotions. Despite experience to the contrary, they believe in the omnipotence of their own emotions (not of themselves, as in the case of the plus k, minus p subjects, who feel the complete "autoplastic" omnipotence) in the sense that if only they try hard enough, they will be able to overcome any resistance imposed on them by the environment. This tenacity in pursuing their goals makes them often productive in their work, as well as genuinely creative.

In the previous section, it has been mentioned that open k, plus p is also one of the three *Sch* configurations which most usually are correlated to the minus h, minus s reaction in the sexual vector. This should remind us of the fact that the basically sexual energy of these subjects is directed many times toward highly idealistic and, seemingly, impersonal goals, such as social, political, or religious ideas for which they fight in action as well as in written words. Writers preoccupied with social problems frequently give this reaction in the *Sch* vector. In the lower occupation levels, this ego picture is practically nonexistent. Yet even the sublimated activities of these subjects have, usually, a strongly emotional coloring, which is much more apparent in the surface behavior, as it is in the case of the plus k, open p individuals. In subjects of the open k, plus p category, the basically sexual origin of their energy can be detected even by the clinically untrained observer. These are the individuals who are often described in common terms as doing everything as "if their life would depend on it," and that is actually the feeling they experience themselves. It should be mentioned that this ego picture, besides being among the three most frequent ones correlated with the minus h, minus s reaction, is also found as the most frequent Sch configuration in conjunction with minus h, plus s, in which group the plus k, open p configuration is one of the least frequent. The open k, plus p appears also relatively frequently in conjunction with configurations in the sexual vector in which either the h or the s is open. This means that open k, plus p is not so typically correlated with sublimation and symbolization of the sexual libido as indicated directly within the sexual vector as was the plus k, open p reaction. Thus, it is understandable why, in subjects giving the present Sch picture, the need expressed by the plus p is more closely related to primarily sexual goals as well as to open aggressive behavior (high correlation with plus s) though more in the form of aggressive self-assertion than in actually antisocial behavior. This constellation in the Sch vector is counter-indication for criminal behavior. What it does indicate often is the aggressive type of social reformer who has no doubts in regard to the correctness of his convictions. These form the type of individuals who were described in our discussion of the plus p constellation as being actively fanatic; i.e., trying to impose their own ideas on others without being willing to listen to the opinions of others. They have an enormous need to express themselves rather than to take in the ideas of other people. In interpersonal relationships this exaggerated need for self-expression and self-assertion might be resented by others (particularly by individuals with minus k, plus p ego constellations, who experience the same need for self-expression, yet are inhibited in their behavior); however, if channelized in professional work, it might manifest itself in real productivity. Scientists who give this Sch reaction experience no difficulty in producing work, express themselves readily, and write easily because of their full conviction of the correctness and originality of their ideas. Whether or not their ideas are actually original is of little or no interest to a typically open k, plus p type of person. Because of the lack of the introjective function of the plus k, they are much less interested in reading the work of others than in expressing what they feel are their own ideas, which attitude, depending on factors outside the realm of the Szondi test, can lead to fruitful new ideas as well as to enthusiastic rediscoveries of generally known facts or viewpoints. Whichever is the case, the open k, plus p individual feels creative and confident in his own work.

This again is an *Sch* picture which, if stable within a series of profiles, is rarely associated with serious clinical symptoms. It is most rarely found in any kind of neurosis, a finding which could be expected on the basis of the complete lack of repression and acceptance of emotions. It is found in so-called paranoid individuals, who, despite their energetic activities and realistic successes in life, feel handicapped by environmental factors. (This is very different from the feeling of insufficiency of minus k, plus p individuals who feel that they were actually unable to live up to their own potentialities because of their inner inhibitions.) They feel not duly appreciated in their intellectual work, and not satisfactorily reciprocated in their love-relationships. Sometimes this paranoid trend reaches the extent at which the impression is given that they actually succeeded in mismanaging their lives, so that realistically they do not get enough love, and become involved in one hopeless emotional relationship after the other.

Sometimes this *Sch* picture is given by real paranoid psychotics, with idealistic and religious types of delusions. However, in this case, the position of the p factor changes within a series of profiles.

This configuration is given about twice its average frequency by young adults and from then on decreases in frequency gradually. It is practically never found in children nor in adults beyond the age of sixty.

Plus-minus k, with plus-minus p

The plus-minus k, plus-minus p configuration is one of the most rarely occurring ego pictures in the general population. Its average frequency is approximately between 2–3 per cent. Yet, it should be mentioned because it represents the coexistence of all the ego mechanisms described previously, together with those omitted (because of limitations of space) from our individual discussion of the single *Sch* configurations.

To point out the pairs of contradictory ego mechanisms inherent in this configuration, which is the most complex of all, will be practically sufficient to make evident the immense psychic energy needed to keep up this ego picture of multiple ambivalence.

The subject who gives this ego picture is simultaneously autistic (plus k, minus p) and self-controlled (minus k, plus p). He concentrates his libido on integrating his ego processes consciously (plus k, plus p), and subjects himself simultaneously to generally accepted social standards and to environmentally imposed discipline (minus k, minus p). He has the characteristics of the "fusing" type of personality experiencing acutely the need to fuse with the object of his libido (plus-minus p), while at the same time he gives the reaction of the person who wants consciously to get rid of any emotional ties with which he might be bound to persons of his environment (plus-minus k).

The coexistence of so many contradictory tendencies, particularly within the ego vector which is assumed to represent a more organized "frame of reference" for the individual's dealing with the drives corresponding to the other six factors, results necessarily in the subjective experiencing of an extremely strong tenseness, to the extent that subjects for whom this ego-picture is characteristic feel "ready to explode" at any time. Their egos are actually overstrained, and they know it. They expect almost inconceivable achievements from their egos (or their *selves)* which even in cases in which the series of test-profiles indicates that they have succeeded in their efforts (indicated by the steadiness of the plus-minus k, plus-minus p configuration) consumes practically the total amount of the psychic energy at their disposal. In these subjects almost all the energy from the drives corresponding to the rest of the factors is somehow "strained through" and concentrated in the ego. They are highly differentiated personalities, aware of their inner processes as well as the processes and requirements outside of themselves, yet there is a certain aloofness in their interpersonal relations despite their need to establish such relations. They are aware of the fact that objects and persons of the environment are needed for the purpose of serving as "props" to enable them to live out their own ego needs so that most of the spontaneous "warmth" of interpersonal relationships is absorbed by this process. The situation is different from the plus k, open p individual, who also tends to appear cold in human relationships because of his constant intellectual analysis of what is happening. However, the plus k, open p person tends actually to keep himself away from relationships which appear as though they might necessitate the mobilization of emotions, and succeeds to a great extent in eliminating the need for such relationships in himself. The plus-minus k, plus-minus p individual, on the other hand, does not use mechanisms which aim at the elimination of any need (he rather wants to conserve the existence of his needs), but uses, instead the mechanism of mobilizing opposing forces of the same strength simultaneously, calling thereby in the extreme upon the *self-regulatory controlling processes* of his ego. This is the *Sch* configuration which indicates the person's making maximum use of conscious and unconscious control within his ego, which results not in the elimination but in the neutralization of the effect of any one need in open behavior, while the subject himself experiences the presence of all his contradictory tendencies.

The task of continuous self-integration has been also characteristic of the plus *k,* plus *p* configuration, in which self integration was simpler to fulfill than it is in the plus-minus *k,* plus-minus *p* configuration. The plus *k,* plus *p* individual can allow himself to disregard the realistic requirements of his environment, which cannot be disregarded by subjects whose *Sch* configuration comprises the minus *k,* minus *p* pattern.

If the plus *k,* plus *p* constellation can be called the stage of conscious self-integration, then the plus-minus *k,* plus-minus *p* constellation must be called the stage of conscious integration of the self within the realistic setting of the environment.

The behavior of these subjects is harder to characterize than was the behavior associated with any of the *Sch* configurations previously discussed because of the neutralizing effect of the coexisting contradictory tendencies. The word "neutral" would be quite appropriate, actually, to describe many aspects of their behavior. "Oscillating" would be another term to characterize the behavior of these subjects in interpersonal relationships, the oscillation between extremes taking place within such short time units that the end-effect approaches neutrality. For a short time they might give the impression of a person who is emotionally deeply involved in a situation, while immediately after, without any outside motivation, they act in the most rigid narcissistic manner, taking the role of the person who fights for his independence and wants to get rid of any emotional obligation. Sometimes this double role is lived out with two different persons, sometimes with the same one. The same duality of behavior can be observed on the dimension of social conformity. These subjects are the most autistic individuals in some aspects of their lives, being concerned with nothing but their own psychologic welfare (plus k, plus p), while in other aspects of their lives they willingly (or unwillingly) submit themselves to rules and standards prescribed by their society (plus k, minus p). Due to their manifold psychologic potentialities, they are able to attract and to get along, to a certain point, with a great variety of personalities without, however, feeling really satisfied in any one of their personal relationships. This feeling of dissatisfaction drives them to establish numerous such relationships, so that in succession, and in connection with various individuals, they live out, at least partially, their own self-contradictory needs. They are usually described as "colorful" and "dynamic" personalities, who attract the interest of the environment. They themselves get easily interested in others; however, with all the reservation of real emotion described above. Nevertheless it should be repeated that in cases of this *Sch* configuration, this emotional reservation is not evident in small units of behavior, but only in longer spans of the subject's life. The process of intellectualizing emotional experiences does not take place immediately during an experience (as in the case of plus k, open p subjects), but following the experience.

This exceptionally controlled and integrative ego picture is strongly correlated with the above-average intelligence and is found rarely in nonintellectual occupations. Subjects with this ego picture are many times not only intellectual but definitely creative in an original way, more so than are subjects with either plus k, open p, plus k, plus p, or open k, plus p constellations, for whom intellectual sublimitation was also characteristic. Actually nothing but the intellectual creation is a real emotional discharge for these subjects, whose ego needs are too manifold and too contradictory to be satisfied by any more realistic experience. By virtue of their ability to draw upon the resources of their unconscious (existence of the minus p within the configuration) they are more creatively productive than subjects with such *Sch* constellations (the three mentioned above) which indicate that the preconscious and conscious processes of intellectualization of needs have reached such an extent that the individual can no more draw upon the emotional reservoir of his own unconscious (lack of minus component of the p) for the sake of creative work.   This intimate connection between unconscious and conscious processes (indicated by plus-minus reaction of the p) seems to be the most fruitful p factorial constellation from the point of view of original creativity.   In other words, this means that too strong attempts at strictly conscious and logical thinking counteracts real creativity, which always seems to retain something of the genetically more "primitive" intuitive way of thinking.   The person with purely plus p reaction experiences the need for such thinking, yet extinguishes its real effectiveness by the very process of conceptualizing it and approaching the problem of "intuition" logically, which is a contradiction in itself.   Not seldom, open k, plus p individuals are the most emotionally violent opponents of anything which reminds them of "intuition" in scientific work, insisting on the dychotomy of "scientific" as against "intuitive" thinking—the emotionality of their standpoint deriving its intensity from their own wish to be able to allow themselves—sometimes—to use their "intuition."   A plus-minus k, plus-minus p individual is not afraid of making use of whatever power he feels to exist in himself, yet he attempts to integrate his "intuitive" insights into a scientifically acceptable system (the latter being the function of the plus k, plus p in the configuration).   Another characteristic feature of the intellectual sublimation of plus-minus k, plus-minus p subjects, is that neither theoretical nor practical approach alone satisfies them, but, again, only the integration and the coexistence of these two approaches. The subjective feeling accompanying their work is much less unambiguous than it was in subjects with open k, plus p, who feel consciously so certain about their being right. Individuals with the *Sch* picture under discussion live in constant doubt about everything they are doing, since, due to the complexity of their potentialities, they can always think of another way (or many other ways) in which the respective work could have been done. It is hard for them to part from their own product, and they have the tendency to do the same work several times, always changing their methods of approach.

The pathologic significance of this *Sch* configuration refers to the same subjective uncertainty which in turn derives from the unusual stress imposed upon the ego by the simultaneous existence of the manifold ambivalent tendencies. The pathologic manifestations of this feeling under stress, are various symptoms of anxiety, mainly hypochondriac anxiety. The tenseness of the psychologic situation is perceived in physical terms, and is actually many times the cause of physical heart symptoms (paroxysmal tachycardia). In other cases, the subject's experiencing of having made excessive use of the ego-controlling mechanisms, results in an almost phobic anxiety of a psychologic breakdown. They have a premonition of an approaching psychosis. The occurrence of psychotic breakdowns is actually more frequent in cases of plus-minus p, plus-minus k, than it is in cases of plus k, plus p, in which the anxiety of psychosis is also frequently present. In those cases, however, the stress upon the ego was actually less, since the ambivalence within the k and within the p factors was absent. The ambivalence in regard to whether the needs should be faced, whether anxiety in itself should be faced and integrated consciously as a personality trait (which was the case in the plus k, plus p subject) or should be repressed from consciousness, seems to be more connected dynamically with an actual predisposition for a psychotic breakdown; while the more manifest but subjectively accepted "prepsychotic" behavior of some plus k, plus p subjects has very little correlation with a real psychotic breakdown.

The plus-minus k, plus-minus p configuration is found rather frequently in individuals with relatively weak sex-drive, since these individuals attempt to channelize even their sexual impulses through their egos. They get some sort of sexual satisfaction from primarily nonsexual relationships, but experience difficulty in establishing satisfactory real sexual relationships. From the strong correlation of this Sch configuration with minus d, minus m, in the Contact vector, we can interpret a basic fixation upon a realistically unavailable love object, with no attempt actually to secure this object. The analysis of such subjects has shown their usually unresolved simultaneously positive and negative Oedipal conflict. Their overall ambivalence in their egos might be a later elaboration of this basic unresolved ambivalence, with all concomitant "double" attitudes in their interpersonal relationships, and also their simultaneous masculine and feminine identification, which in these subjects, is many times a conscious source of conflict. This conflict could not be adequately characterized as latent homosexual conflict, because of the essentially asexual character of these subjects.

This Sch configuration is found in no age group among the four most frequent ego pictures. Most frequently it occurs in puberty and adolescence. It can also be found in adults, but practically never in very old subjects.

Open k, *open* p

The underlying similarity between this and the previous ego picture, the plus-minus *k,* plus-minus *p,* is greater than one might think after the obvious visible differences between these two *Sch* configurations. The similarity refers to the overemphasis of the ego processes in the plus-minus *k,* plus-minus *p* constellations as well as in the open *k,* open *p.* In both cases the subject intends to solve all his "instinctual" tensions and conflicts through making extreme use of his ego functions. In fact, the aim of both of these ego-dynamisms is to deny the importance of any of the drives corresponding to the rest of the factors, and to try to live through nothing but the ego. In dynamic terms, this means that subjects with either of these *Sch* pictures intend to manipulate their partial drives consciously, by allocating to them the channelization through the ego as the most desirable way of discharge. The result in both cases is that much of the "instinctual" (or spontaneous) character of the drives are being absorbed by the time they appear in manifest behavior. In whatever way, and to whatever extent, these subjects act, they do it consciously; they con-sciously direct their own actions, the ego fulfilling almost consciously the role of the "stage-director," and actor simul-taneously. This is probably more or less the role of the ego in any case; however, in the present two *Sch*-configura-tions, the subject's experiencing this function of the ego gives a strongly schizoid character to the picture; namely, the subjective experiencing of being split into a "driving" and an "executive" system. This deeply seated schizoid character of subjects with either of these two *Sch* configura-tions, can be detected by thorough analysis of their per-sonality even in cases in which the surface presentation of behavior seems smooth and well-functioning. Whatever has been said until now about the characteristics of the subjects giving open *k* with open *p,* refers only to those

cases in which this is a steady *Sch* reaction within a series
of ten profiles.

Besides the above described similarities between the
dynamics of the open *k*, open *p* configuration, and the plus-
minus *k*, plus-minus *p* and the *Sch* configuration, there are
considerable differences, resulting in behavior patterns dif-
fering enough to be rather easily discernible by an outside
observer. The obvious dynamic difference is that while
the plus-minus *k*, plus-minus *p* individual operates by calling consciously upon the self-regulatory controlling forces
within the ego (plus-minus position in both ego factors),
without attempting to eliminate the extreme tension which
thereby is brought about within his ego, the open *k*, open *p*
individual is acting out his drive through his ego to such
an extent that the tension within the ego is completely (as
far as the test can indicate) eliminated. These subjects
are unable to bear the subjective feeling of such controlling
mechanisms which imply a state of balanced tension within
their egos. It might be that they feel that their controlling
mechanisms are too weak to function efficiently, or they
might feel that the tension in their partial drives constitutes too much danger to be discharged directly, yet they
have to discharge them somehow, thus the relatively least
harmful way is to let them be discharged after they have
passed through the modifying channels of the ego.

The high correlation between this *Sch* configuration and
the completely ambivalent, bisexual reaction in the sexual
vector (plus-minus *h*, plus-minus *s*) points toward the probability of the second hypothesis. By all means, the ego
of these subjects acts out continuously something, often on
the verbal level. The behavior of these subjects is characteristically active (still with reference to those cases in
which open *k*, open *p* is a constant *Sch* reaction), many times
to the extent of compulsive activeness, yet never in the sense
of a definite compulsive-neurotic symptom formation. These

individuals simply experience an urge in regard to doing something all the time; they must fill up time with some activity; if there is nothing else to do, then with talking. The dynamic explanation of this behavior lies in the connection (or perhaps in the partial identity) between the ego and the motor-system; thus in order to alleviate the organism from unbearable tensions, the ego resorts to making excessive use of the motor-system. This strong drive for activity in subjects with open k, open p has many times socially positive manifestations, since the fact that primary drives are not released directly but through the ego implies, most of the time, socialized or sublimated forms of discharge. Not the type of activity, but the manner in which these subjects drive themselves to be active all the time, gives the impression of compulsiveness. These are often the people who, one feels, want to lose themselves in whatever they are doing; in fact, the exaggerated activity is often motivated by this unconscious, and sometimes even conscious, wish to lose their own identity. Depending on the accompanying constellation of the s factor, this activity is really active or passive in nature. By *passive* activity, I mean such manifestations as excessive reading, movie or theater-going, by means of which the activity of others are experienced through identification. In open k, open p subjects, these activities are frequent. These are the persons who take from the library one book after the other for the sake of the activity of reading, with little concern about choosing specific works they want to read. Their movie-going has the same character; they go for the sake of filling up time and their minds with whatever is offered, with no particular enjoyment. The function of these activities is again to permit them to lose themselves by identifying with a great variety of various characters. What they do not want is time to experience themselves the way they really are. Yet this "running away" from themselves, in the case of open *k,* open *p* subjects, does not imply repression in the sense of the minus *k,* open *p* configuration. In that case, the subjects were repressing successfully, which means that they were not aware of the process or of the content of what they wanted to repress. In the present *Sch* configuration, however, the subjects have usually fairly good insight into their own personality (no sign of active repression), and exactly because they know what they do not want in themselves, they try to fill up their time with activities which "take their mind off" themselves. Most probably it is just this lack of actual repression which helps them to avoid real neurotic symptom formations. Subjects for whom this is the characteristic *Sch* reaction, "act" continuously, either professionally or in their daily lives. They are exhibitionistic through their ego, which means on a more conscious level than the exhibitionism as was described in connection with the *"hy"* factor. Many times it is an intellectual or consciously artistic exhibitionism, being conscious of their wanting to impress people as a certain "interesting" type of personality. At other times, there are definite types of personalities whom they want to impersonate throughout their lives, with every action of their life. For example, they might be consciously "charming" in interpersonal relations, in which case the psychologically trained observer can definitely sense the compulsive-defense character of the almost exaggerated "charm" This particular "role" is chosen usually by those subjects who feel their strong basic aggressive tendencies, and make a conscious decision of not wanting to be aggressive. Again, the process is different from simple repression, and is not unusual in individuals who have, at least for a while, undergone psychoanalysis, whereby they were faced with their own drives and given the possibility to choose consciously which they wanted to accept or reject.

On the basis of similar mechanism, this *Sch* configuration is given often by basically masculine types of women who decided to live in a definitely "feminine role." These are often women with strong intellectual drive, as well as with physical characteristics of masculinity, whose actual life, however, is completely "feminine," in that they throw themselves compulsively into the role of efficient house-wife, and self-sacrificing wife or mother. The results might be fairly successful, since they get multiple emotional "rewards" if they fulfill the chosen role well. They might win appreciation from their environment as well as from themselves because of the feeling that they were able to live up to their own ego ideal, yet, at the very bottom of their consciousness, they are aware of the unrealness of their lives. Despite the impression they give of complete loss of themselves in their activities or their roles, there is a kernel of their personality which is encapsulated, and which remains their "private property" no matter how sociable and how "fusing" they appear on the surface. (In this respect they are similar to the plus-minus k, plus-minus p individuals.) To use a quantitative metaphor, we might say that 90 per cent of their ego is extremely flexible and adjustable to environmental requirements, but the remaining 10 per cent is completely rigid and narcissistic, resisting change by any environmental influence. Again we have arrived at the fact that these subjects are basically strongly schizoid because they are able to live and function as "split" personalities. In Jungian terms, one could characterize them as having a strongly developed "persona" inside of which there is a basically autistic and nonadjusting part of the self. The definition of the term _persona_ is the following in Hinsie and Shatzky (quoting Jung), _Psychiatric Dictionary_, Oxford University Press: " 'Mask for actors; impersonated character. . . .' With this term Jung denotes the disguised or masked attitude assumed by an individual, in contrast to the more deeply-rooted personality com-ponents. 'Through his more or less complete identification with the attitude of the moment, he at least deceives others,

and also often himself as to his real character. He puts
on a *mask*, which he knows corresponds with his conscious
intentions, while it also meets with the requirements and
opinions of his environment, so that first one motive then
the other is in the ascendant. . . .' " This definition of the
"persona" coincides so perfectly with the interpretation of
the open k, open p configuration that practically nothing
more has to be said about it except that, in a case in which
this configuration appears in a series of profiles suddenly,
following more loaded and changing *Sch* configurations, it
is often the indication of a sudden break-down of the more
repressive defense mechanisms, and can indicate the beginning of a psychotic process. In nonpathologic cases, the
sudden draining of the whole *Sch* vector can be found in
the artist immediately following the "draining" of his ego
through a creative act.

The pathologic significance of this *Sch* configuration in
cases in which it appears as a steady feature of the personality, refers primarily to symptoms of depersonalization
which can appear in cases of severely compulsive characters,
without specific symptoms. The corresponding complaints
are usually that they "act without feeling"; that is, they go
through the routine of life in a perfunctory way, without
an accompanying feeling of "emotional significance" of what
they are doing. They do not suffer particularly, but they
cannot enjoy either, and because of sudden feelings of aim-
lessness they might voluntarily seek the help of a therapist.
The analytic work with such patients is extremely hard, just
because of the lack of specific symptoms, because of the
surface calmness and efficiency of their behavior, and mainly
because of their stubborn defense against transference,
although they are very polite and "well-behaving" patients.

The age-distribution of this *Sch* configuration is similar
to that of the plus-minus k, plus-minus p.

CHAPTER XI

Syndromes and Case Illustrations

WITH THE discussion of the open k, open p configuration we have finished as much of the presentation of the theory of interpretation as we intended to include in this introductory book. As thoroughly as I have tried to indicate the varying meanings of the single factorial and vectorial configurations, pointing out the way in which they depend on the total pattern of all the eight factors and the entire series, this method of discussion, in which we examine the single constellations in succession, falls short, necessarily, of an integrated picture of personality interpretation based on test findings. Nevertheless, this method is the only feasible introductory step to a test involving so manifold and complex a series of assumptions and reasonings accompanying each of the eight basic factors. It may be that a more pragmatic introduction, hinging on immediate presentation of a great number of concrete examples and deriving from actual case histories the corresponding syndromes on the test profiles, would have seemed more practical and more satisfactory to many clinical practitioners. Dwelling less on the dynamic implications of interpretation, and listing more "signs" and syndromes with accompanying one-sentence interpretations, the book would have approached more the character of a manual which could be used as a "dictionary" to find the "meaning" of specific test profiles. However, this is exactly the use I wanted to avoid, although I am aware that the book might have been more "popular" that way. As has been said, the aim of this introduction is to reproduce, as closely as possible verbally the dynamic processes which are assumed to underlie the specific choice reactions made in the test. In other words, its aim is to remove as far as possible the "mystic" character of the test and to account for the various meanings of the various reactions in terms of dynamic psychology, which in this case often means psychoanalytic theory.

I know that my hope and my aim is to convince at least a few of those skeptical psychologists and psychiatrists who readily think in terms of dynamic and psychoanalytic psychology but for whom interpreting "deep" psychologic-characteristics on the basis of a peculiar pattern of red and blue squares seems absolutely unbelievable, if not completely ridiculous. Whether or not this book will succeed in reaching this aim, even to a minimal extent, I cannot judge myself. I know only that it seems to me more important to convey, at least to some degree, the thinking implied in interpretations to a few clinicians who are concerned with what, essentially, a new projective technic is "all about," than it is to compile a practical and easy-to-use manual to facilitate the production of a great number of fairly accurate interpretations by less skeptical psychologists whose main concern is the addition of a new test to their battery, and who would be ready to use the test by means of reference to various plus and minus reactions, "signs," and syndromes, without worrying about the reasons for these interpretations so long as they appear to be clinically valid.

Now that we have reviewed the "basic processes" of interpretation, it is clearly necessary to discuss more in detail the involved interfactorial correlations, the normal personality, and clinical "syndromes," with ample illustrative case material. This will be the content of the forthcoming second volume. In the framework of this introduction, we shall have to limit ourselves to the brief presentation and discussion of a few cases, chosen as representative of characteristic constellations and "syndromes." In order to cover, at least briefly, more varied and extensive material, some of the cases will be illustrated with only one or two profiles which duly represent the subject's basic personality structure; in other words, cases in which reactions are fairly stable throughout a longer series. Yet it should be remembered that such a presentation and interpretation on the basis of one or two profiles, can be done only for didactic purposes on the basis of external evidence that these profiles *do* represent the subject's basic personality pattern, and not to illustrate habitual clinical practice, in which one can never predict the possible range of variability of reactions within a series of ten profiles, and in which one can make gross misinterpretations from consideration of only the first few profiles as reflecting the subject's basic personality structure. (See Chapter IV in regard to the meaning of changes.)

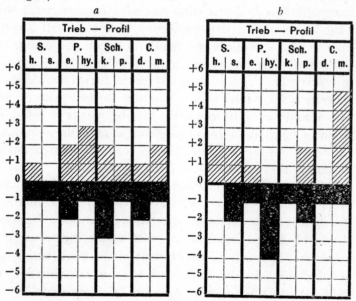

Fig. 9. Interpretation 1. *a.* T. T., 23 year old husband
b. N. T., 23 year old wife.

The profiles in Figure 9a, b have been chosen first because of the specific constellations of the reaction in the *Sch* vector. We have not discussed the plus-minus *k*, open *p*, and the open *k*, plus-minus *p* configurations under separate headings since the interpretation of either of these configurations is so much related to the meaning of the other, in that individuals giving these two reactions are found many times to form a special type of unhappy couple. Consequently, it seemed to me more adequate to discuss these two ego pictures in their relationship to each other in connection with a concrete example.

The obvious characteristics of profile (a), (the husband) are the following:

Most loaded factor is the *k*, in plus-minus position.

Interpretation: Dynamically the strongest need is that of keeping up the narcissistic integrity of the personality. For that purpose, both mechanisms, introjection (plus *k*) as well as repression (minus *k*) are made use of. The person is conscious of this narcissistic need to keep himself "free" and detached from any emotional bonds to other persons (plus-minus position).

Open reactions are found in the *h*, the *s*, and the *p* factors. These are the "tension-less" areas of the personality.

Interpretation: Open *h*, with open *s*, if it is a recurring pattern, indicates sexual immaturity if given by an adult; no sexual need experienced subjectively; fixation at an infantile level.

Open *p*, (with plus-minus *k*) means that the tension corresponding to the object directed libido of the *p* factor has been absorbed by the function of the *k* factor. In other words, object-libido has been transformed "successfully" into narcissistic libido. The person no longer feels the need to cathect (love) objects of the environment, because, in the present case in which open *p* appears with plus-minus *k*, the original id impulse has been partially desexualized through intellectualization (introjective process indicated by plus *k*) partially repressed (minus *k*). This ego picture indicates the most conscious fight against any sort of "unmodified" emotional attachments to persons of the environment. More important than anything else is the need to keep up the "organization" of one's own ego in persons with plus-minus *k*, and open *p*. Emotional independence from their environment constitutes their central problem. The fact that they have to employ two mechanisms, which in some ways are opposed to each other, results in subjectively experienced anxiety, this constellation representing to a certain degree the failure of the introjective mechanisms as well as that of repression. Yet in their behavior they appear calm, "organized," and able to pursue their own goals without being disturbed about the possible effects of their behavior on others (no tension in the *p* factor always indicating the lack of such projective manifestations as sincere "sympathy" or "empathy," psychologic processes underlying these phenomena presupposing the existence of unmodified object-directed libido). Individuals with this *Sch* configuration combine the characteristics of the subjects with plus *k* and open *p*, and those of subjects with minus *k* and open *p*. In other words, these are the subjects who compulsively drive themselves to sublimate. Their behavior is really similar to that of compulsive neurotics, except that the kind of activity they feel as compulsive is often of a sublimated nature, which dynamically implies that despite the existing feelings of anxiety, they are able to derive some "real" emotional (that is, in this case, narcissistically emotional) gratification from their work. Since the plus-minus *k* reaction is relatively least frequent in the age group comprising young adults (see section on plus-minus *k*), it deserves specific consideration as an "unusual" reaction in cases in which it does appear in the age between twenty and thirty. Reactions which are atypical for the chronological age of the subject, as well as factorial correlations which are "atypical" are always useful as starting points to interpret the specifically unique and individual personality pattern of the subject in question.

The most loaded vector as a whole is the paroxysmal vector, in profile (a), giving plus-minus e, with plus hy.

Interpretation: Emotional control is a "tension" area in this person. He experiences conscious conflict in regard to the manner in which he might deal with his aggression (plus-minus *e*), while his exhibitionistic needs are accepted subjectively without causing any conflict (plus *hy*). The fact that the plus *e*, plus *hy* pattern is implicit in the present vectorial configuration shows that the emotional exhibitionism of the plus *hy* is prevented by the superego (plus *e*) from having truly antisocial manifestations, while the fact that the configuration also implies the minus *e*, plus *hy* constellation points towards the existence of more ruthless exhibitionistic drives. Correlating these findings in the *P* vector with the open *s*, we can assume that the person is discharging aggression in the form of steady activity, which more or less remains within socially acceptable limits; yet one can also find manifestations of a basically asocial or antisocial nature in the person.

Interpreting the loadedness of the *P* vector in the light of what has been stated about the ego picture of this 23 year old man, one can say the following: direction of emotional inflation through strictly narcissistic channels is attempted (and successfully so). The coexistence of the plus *hy* with a plus *k* reaction (at least one part of the *k* factor being positive in the present case) is always a "sign" for strongly narcissistic-exhibitionistic drives. In other words, emotions are not directed toward objects but toward the ego, and persons of the environment are needed only insofar as they constitute the "audience" for the person's exhibitionistic manifestations (plus *hy*). The relative successfulness, or rather, the strength of these narcissistic-exhibitionistic drives, is shown in the fact that the p factor is drained, which means that the person no longer experiences the need to fuse into objects of his environment.

The Contact vector (C) is the most balanced area in the entire profile, as indicated by the fact that neither of the two factors is strongly loaded or quite open. The twin factors of the C vector are treated alike in this case, both showing an average reaction of three choices, distributed in the most balanced way: two in one direction, with a counter-balancing one choice in the other direction. Also, the association of a mildly minus d reaction (rejection of the need for "anal" hoarding and mastering of material objects) is most harmonious with the mildly plus m reaction (acceptance of the need to enjoy objects of the environment).

Interpretation: Despite all the previously mentioned conflicts and immaturity of the personality, this man is able to establish and maintain a satisfactory relationship with his environment. He is able to enjoy whatever relationships he establishes (the kind of relationship he does establish being indicated by the constellations of the other factors and having been interpreted above as exhibitionistic-narcissistic type, with aggressive characteristics, and asexual in character).

The minus d, plus m configuration indicates a basically optimistic attitude toward the world, considering the environment as a source which can offer possibilities for "oral" type of gratifications. Minus d, plus m persons are usually faithful to a specific object of the libido, the object for subjects in this C vectorial category being usually an idea, to which they cling with the same intensity as a child clings to his mother. The plus m indicates that there is actually something (whether person or idea) to cling to, and the fact that the plus m is not loaded (just mildly positive) indicates that the person feels rather secure in regard to his relationship to this "ideal" object. Minus d indicates that no physical effort is required to bring about this satisfactory relationship. It also shows that the person is "sticking" to his particular object. This constellation is found mostly in professional groups (see section on minus d, plus m configuration) for whom the kind of work they do represents the "ideal" object, the work they can enjoy, and to which they are faithfully adhering. It is an idealistic picture, given by persons for whom the kind of work they do is more important than the financial reward for the work, but who, on the other hand, do not like to spend the money earned. The steady pleasurable object relationship in these subjects is usually due to their ability to establish object relationships by way of thinking; in other words, their power of symbolization is usually high. Ideas for them can have the same emotional value as realistic objects do for other types of subjects. This is a typically "adult" picture, given by basically mother-fixated individuals, who however, do not suffer frustration from being forced to give up attachment to the mother. In reality, they were able to transfer the same intensity of the feeling "to be attached" to more symbolic forms of attachments (science, art, political ideals).

Integration of the part-interpretations: T. T. is a sexually infantile, strongly narcissistic individual. His aim is to be detached emotionally from his environment, yet he needs persons for the sake of having an "audience" for his exhibitionistic drives. His superego is developed but not functioning in a quite reliable way. Due to the strength and the efficiency of his ego, his id impulses are kept under control and are never allowed to appear in behavior, unless modified and neutralized by the ego functions. This is achieved by the simultaneous use of repression and introjection. Despite some compulsive characteristics, this person is able to derive considerable satisfaction from his ability to sublimate, as indicated by his optimistic and friendly attitude toward the world. It appears as though he were able to find ways to live out his exhibitionistic-narcissistic needs in reality, in a fairly sublimated form, although there is still a drive of sufficient strength to get more satisfaction of this sort. Despite his experiencing anxiety, most probably in connection with his need to obtain visible indications of success, he seems to function successfully as far as arranging his own life is concerned. In interpersonal relationships, however, he must be cold and unconcerned about the feeling of others, just as a young, egoistic child must be. His basically asexual personality also helps him to keep himself organized and to concentrate all his efforts on his ego needs. Egoistic pursuit of some sort of professional success is most probable, with actual success achieved. Without reviewing his case history now, we can add that he most probably fulfills his role as husband in a very unsatisfactory way, since all his libido is used up for narcissistic purposes, precluding a sincere need for heterosexual relationship. As far as one can judge from this profile, the only function of his wife he really needs is that of audience to appreciate his intellectual achievements.

Profile (b)

The most loaded reaction is in the *m* factor, the subject having chosen all the six *m* portraits, five as liked, one as disliked.

Interpretation: Dynamically, the strongest need in this young woman is her need to *cling* to objects of the environment for the sake of obtaining love and support from them. The extreme loadedness of this factor indicates the *anxious* quality of this clinging. It shows that the subject feels helpless and insecure unless there is something or somebody to cling to, yet she feels the danger of the possible loss of the love object. She has a strongly "oral" character, and possibly exhibits a great variety of oral characteristics, such as talking, eating, smoking, drinking, or, on a more sub-limated level, a drive to cling to objects for intellectual or artistic enjoyment. In the case of such extreme loaded-ness, one has to think of some neurotic manifestations of this oral need for dependency, although that does not exclude the possibility that oral characteristics of a more sublimated nature are also present in the same person. Nevertheless, it does indicate that sublimated activities do not quite satisfy the basic oral need, otherwise we would not get this reaction of choice of *all* the *m* portraits, which in either direction indicates frustration in this area. The fact that the choices are for the most part positive shows her still optimistic attitude in regard to the possibility of satisfying this need in a socially acceptable, positive way. She still expects "help" and love from her environment, and does not turn against the objects which cause her frustration. It also indi-cates her own willingness to give affection to others.

Open, tension-less reactions are in the *e, k,* and *d* factors.

Interpretation: Open *e* means that emotions are discharged readily; if this is a recurring constellation, then it shows that she is an irritable person who easily gives vent to small amounts of aggression rather than accumulating aggression and discharging it in antisocial forms. Psychosomatic symp-toms can be indicated in open *e* also; however, in this case it is not probable because of the open *k* factor (psychosomatic symptoms usually accompanying open *e* and minus *k*). In addition, the fact that the open *e* in this profile consists of one positive and one negative choice is a counterindica-tion of serious *e* factorial (epileptoid) symptoms.

The open *k* reaction shows that the organizing power within the ego is weak, the person is poorly differentiated as a separate and integrated unit from the environment. She does not make use of the mechanism of secondary nar-cissism, which means that she does not withdraw, in case of frustration, her libido from the love object. She has no strong boundaries around her *self,* and thus exposes herself to be hurt in the event of frustration. She does not experience herself as an individual who can stand alone, but only in connection with another person. At this point we have to explain this specific constellation of open k with plus-minus p in its relationship to the plus-minus k with open p. The open k, plus-minus p configuration is the "par excellence" reaction of individuals who feel, and actually are, rejected in a specific personal relationship; namely, in the relationship which for them is the most important, and which they are not willing to give up even in view of obvious signs of rejection by the "partner." Neither do they deny to themselves the fact that they *are* rejected (no minus k). Yet they insist on attempting to fuse into their "love object," despite all the objectively perceived difficulties. The plus-minus constellation of the p factor reflects the conscious conflictual character of the need to fuse into an object. Our subject is aware of her conflict, but not of the real nature of the need which drives her to this one particular person and not to another (minus p). Analysis of subjects giving this particular *Sch* reaction has shown that these are individuals who have never overcome the trauma of having been weaned from the mother. They became fixated at that particular stage of ego development which corresponded to the trauma of weaning, and were not able or willing to make the next step which would have led them to the development of a plus k reaction, i.e. to a narcissistic withdrawal of the libido from the frustrating object, which would have been a necessary step toward developing the integrity of their own egos. Instead, they insisted on remaining in the frustrating situation, which hardly would be conceivable unless they derived some sort of masochistic gratification from the experience of suffering. In fact, adults giving this particular ego picture have always concomitant masochistic personality characteristics. They seem to drive themselves into situations in which the "primary" trauma, that of being rejected by the mother, can be relived. And here we arrive at a possible dynamic explanation of the reason subjects with the open k, plus-minus p reaction invest their libido so many times in individuals with plus-minus k, open p reactions. They attach themselves to persons by whom they least can hope to be really accepted and loved. Our open k, plus-minus p subject clings with all her force to her plus-minus k, open p husband whose main goal in life is to rid himself of any personal attachments and redirect all his libido toward himself.

The "trauma of weaning" has been, we hypothesize, extreme for subjects with either of these two ego pictures, yet their reaction to it is diametrically opposite. While the individual with the plus-minus k, open p reaction "sets out" never to let himself become emotionally involved again in a situation in which he can be the person to be abandoned, the open k, plus-minus p reaction reproduces the primary trauma over and over again in all his later relationships. The question in regard to what the decisive factors might be in determining which of these two types of reaction the person will develop cannot be analyzed more deeply within this context. Yet discussion to this extent gives us enough insight into the otherwise paradoxical findings that two individuals with such incompatible ego structures should be found regularly forming a couple of any sort—husband and wife, unhappy yet close friends, or parent and child who seem unable to live either with or without each other. In such unhappy relationships, the perpetuating factor is most probably the narcissistic and the sadistic satisfaction on the part of the plus-minus k partner, who is gratified by constantly proving to himself that he is able to keep up his unemotional integrity despite the efforts of the other person to fuse into him. He is now undoubtedly the person who is "stronger" in that he is the more self-sufficient. On the part of the plus-minus p partner, the perpetuating force which makes the person stick to such apparently unrewarding relationship is some sort of a complex masochistic satisfaction derived from the primary association between the feeling of love and rejection; conditioned, as it were, by the first experience of that sort in connection with the mother. There is some clinical evidence that this masochistic reaction is likely to develop in the person whose mother has been actually a sadistically forceful personality, and in whom the feeling of being rejected was based on realistic experience in the subject's childhood.

Returning to the profile of N.T., and correlating those two aspects of her profile which have been thus far interpreted, we can see that the dynamics of the open k, plus-minus p ego picture seem to be borne out in this specific case, as indicated by the extreme tension in the need for dependence and clinging $(m$ factor$)$. In the section concerning the p factor, it has been said that the specific content of the need which demands expression through the p has to be read off in the rest of the test profile, namely in the most loaded, i.e. the most dynamic and tense factor. In the case of N.T. this means that it is the need for oral dependency which is most frustrated and which has inflated the ego to cause consciously experienced conflict (plus-minus $p)$ in her need to fuse into an object. The loaded plus m defines for us the specific character of the relationship she unsuccessfully strives for. She wants to establish a relationship in which she can be the passively clinging person who needs an excessive amount of motherly love and support from her love-object. She still needs to be "nursed."

The open d reaction in this case might mean that she is weary of looking for an adequate object, although she knows that the old object is really not worth holding on to.

This means she is not interested in the "anal" type of possessive and mastering kind of object relationship; there is no "anal" tenacity in her actively pursuing an object. She merely tries to cling to the object nearest to her, without having the strength to change realistically the status-quo. It shows an easy-going attitude in regard to material objects and wanting to enjoy them, rather than to accumulate and master them (open d, plus m). Yet, faced by tension to this extent in the m factor, we cannot imagine a really happy, easy-going person except as a person who is "easy-going" in an apathetic way.

It has been mentioned in the section concerning the open d constellation that in a certain configuration the open d might mean an actually depressed mood, as a surface symptom. Open d, with this anxious clinging indicated in the strong plus m, and with the open k, plus-minus p configuration in the Sch vector, is a typical pattern in which open d must be interpreted on this level of manifest symptoms of depressed mood. It also has been mentioned that this is always an apathetic—and not the worrying—type of depression (the latter being indicated by plus d). Subjects with open d and plus m have been described as characteristically passive in their relationship to objects, having no drive to manipulate objects and situations actively. In social contact they are pleasant, nonaggressive, and desirous to please (all in the hope of getting some love in return). The open d indicates that although our subject is unable to initiate change in her situation, if such a change should be forced upon her due to external circumstances she would be able to adjust to it fairly easily, although in the present case, as long as her ego reaction remains the same, she would most probably find another similarly frustrating object relationship. The open d, plus m configuration shows also her drive to sublimate her orality, yet the lack of success of such efforts is indicated by the existence of extreme tension in the m factor.

After the Contact vector, the second most disproportionately treated is the Paroxysmal vector. Besides the open e,
there are four negative choices in the hy.

Interpretation: Although this configuration has not been
discussed separately among the P vectorial configurations, the
open e, minus hy does represent a characteristic emotional
reaction; namely, that of acutely experienced anxiety, not
of the diffuse kind which would be indicated by minus e,
minus hy, but a more systematized and objectified anxiety.
The minus hy shows that this person is rather reluctant to
manifest her emotions openly—not any kind of emotions,
but specifically her tender object-directed feelings. She
hides her real feelings and exercises control over her exhibitionistic needs, although the loadedness of the hy factor
indicates that she does not experience such needs. This
reaction is usually a sign of a well-functioning superego,
which does not allow the person to live out her childish
need for narcissistic-exhibitionistic satisfaction. (It should
be remembered that her husband gave exactly the opposite
reaction; namely, he completely accepted these exhibitionistic-narcissistic needs.) The lack of plus e in the case of
N.T. shows that her emotional control is not so rigid that
it prevents her from actually experiencing her inability to
live out her exhibitionistic needs, thus the corresponding
frustration must be experienced as such, and the irritability
as indicated by the open e reaction might be a consequence
of this frustration. Other effects of repressing the open
and visible manifestations of the libido are increased indulgence in phantasy life, daydreaming, feeling of anxiety. The
fact that minus hy is strongly negative, while its "twin"
factor, the e is discharged—if recurring in a series—indicates that repressed exhibitionistic drives are *the* most dangerous latent needs in the personality, "dangerous" in that
they are the underlying driving force for actual neurotic
symptoms, just because they are unaccepted so that they
are forced to influence behavior in a round-about (neurotic)

way. Anxiety hysteria is one of the most frequent symptoms occurring with this *P* vectorial configuration. In the case of N.T., such real neurotic anxiety symptoms are made probable by her reaction in the *C* vector which also pointed toward such symptoms.

N.T.'s reactions in the Sexual vector are also relatively the most balanced: there is no disproportionate loading of the two factors, and no strong discrepancy in their direction. She reacted with two positive choices to the *h* portraits, and with exactly ambivalent reactions to the *s*.

Interpretation: Despite all the neurotic symptoms in the other three vectors, and despite the fact that this young woman feels subjectively much more unhappy than her husband (profile *a*) she has reached a much higher degree of sexual maturity than he. Of course that is partially responsible for her unhappiness, since she does experience heterosexual needs, yet is unable to form object relationships which would satisfy her sexual needs. (In the case of her husband, the fact that he was shown to be practically "asexual" facilitated his getting satisfaction from his "sterile" narcissistic activities.)

The plus *h,* plus-minus *s* configuration shows that N.T. has basically identified herself with the passive and feminine role in sexuality, although she is undecided in regard to whether she should be completely passive and submissive or not (plus-minus *s*). Yet this ambivalence does not pervade her whole sexuality, since the completely plus *h* reaction shows her unambiguous need for physical tenderness. The coexistence of the plus *h* and plus part of the *s* factor is also a guarantee against sadistic manifestations of the plus *s;* the simultaneous acceptance of the two opposing needs exercising a certain self-regulatory and mutually modifying effect on each other's behavioral manifestations (see chapter on the interpretation of the formal characteristics of the test profile).

The plus *h* reaction in conjunction with such a strong plus *m* reaction is a typical "syndrome" of a person who needs an enormous amount of personal love and tenderness. In this configuration—with plus *h*—the possibility to sublimate successfully the oral need indicated by the strong plus *m* through intellectual or artistic activity or

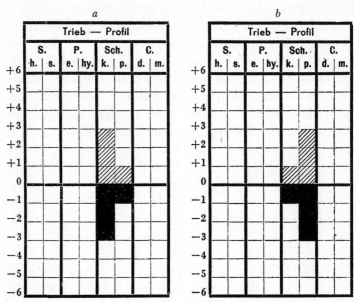

Fig. 10. Frequent but typically unhappy, yet close, relationship between two people. *a.* Rigid, narcissistic partner who is unwilling to "fuse." Self-sufficient. Also the picture of a compulsively sublimating person, with outward success. Reproductive rather than creative. *b.* The passive, "fusing" and unhappy partner. Not self-sufficient.

enjoyment is counterindicated, since the plus *h* is a sign of the person's inability to transform her primary need for physical tenderness into more conceptualized forms of abstract love. On the basis of the total configuration of the test profile, we have to assume that the plus-minus *s* in the case of this subject is connected with her crisis in her object relationship, indicating a "clinging" to the object of such intensity that it approaches "violent" clinging. It indicates a sado-masochistic object-relationship—correlating it with the ego reaction—referring to the "sadistic" gratification she obtains from her "masochistic" clinging to a hopelessly narcissistic partner. This is not an unusual mechanism in "martyr" characters.

In conclusion we can say the following about the profile of this 23 year old woman: she has a passive, strongly dependent oral character, frustrated in the gratification of these

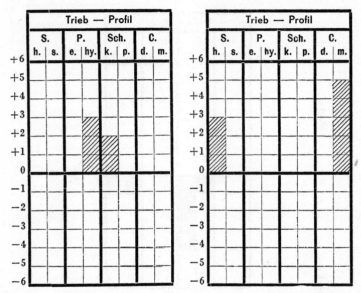

FIG. 11. *a.* Exhibitionistic narcissism. *b.* Excessive need for affection; clinging.

needs. Her ability for successful sublimation is limited, and by no means sufficient to provide satisfaction for these needs on a "symbolic" level. At the present stage of her ego development she is bound to remain in essentially frustrating situations, even though she realizes the unsatisfactory character of her object relationships. She is apathetic and unable to bring about changes actively. She is depressed and anxious, her anxiety being manifested most probably in definitely structured and objectified symptoms. Her basically healthy heterosexual drives form a good factor from the point of view of prognosis. In interpersonal relationship, she most probably is pleasant and eager to please, yet frequently she is irritable, although never without exercising control over the ways in which she discharges aggression. She is basically a sensitive person who does not want to hurt others, and who feels lost if left alone. Most prob-

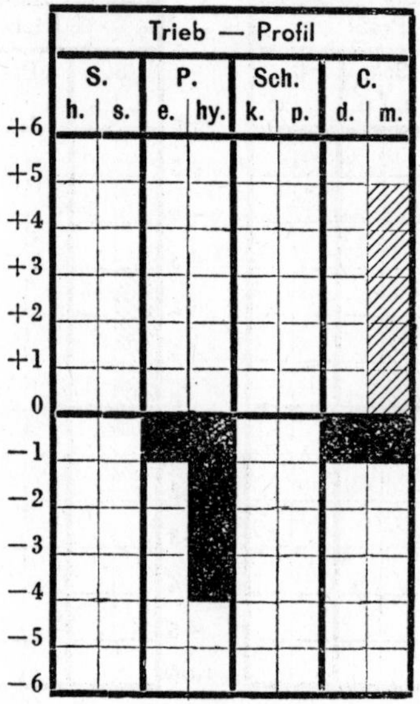

FIG. 12. OBJECTIFIED ANXIETY

ably she indulges in phantasies and daydreaming to the extent that it impairs her efficiency in whatever work she does.

Now that we have analyzed to this extent the test profiles of this couple, a short abstract of their case histories will be sufficient to round out the picture and to furnish objective, independent data which then can be compared with the personality pictures gained on the basis of the test profiles. The coordination of the details of the case histories to the corresponding test findings will be left to the reader.

N.T. and T.T. had been married for several years at the time these profiles were obtained. The girl felt the need to seek psychoanalytic help because of the following complaints: she felt unhappy due to frequent anxiety attacks, accompanied by attacks of vomiting and complete loss of appetite. These attacks occurred regularly whenever she was in the company of certain people, usually her mother. At the beginning, whenever she mentioned the word "mother," in whatever context, she started to weep. Weeping was frequent with her anyway. Her worst attacks of vomiting took place whenever her mother gave her a present. Her mother was actually torturing her with eating, always forcing her to eat, like a small child who is a feeding problem. The mother was an aggressive, forceful personality, used to dominating everybody around her. She was the main financial support and the head of the family, the father being a weak, submissive person. N.T. felt always neglected as a child, and actually she *was* neglected. The worst period came with the birth of a younger brother, when she was eight years old. At that time the financial status of the family was more secure and the second child actually got more attention and time from the mother, who by then was not required to work so much in the office. From then on, she consciously disliked her mother, although she tried always to be "good" in order to please her mother. N.T.'s feeding difficulties started early, but were intensified in this period. In school, N.T. was well-liked by children and teachers alike. She was and is a talkative, friendly person. She decided to marry immediately after her graduation from the gymnasium (which in Europe, is the equivalent of the high school, usually completed at the approximate age of eighteen years). She actually did marry soon. Her anxiety and vomiting attacks started during the honeymoon. She was the partner who forced the marriage, and immediately after the wedding felt guilty about it. At that time, she also developed a habit of "grimacing" which was almost like a facial tic, and resembled a sucking movement with her lips. Originally she had "dreamed" about a stage career (she had some real talent for acting), which she abandoned before a start to support her husband, who was at the time of their marriage a university student of history. She was proud of the intellectual success of her husband, but sexually quite dissatisfied. Her psychologic insight into her husband's personality was fairly good. She knew that spontaneously he would never have married her, and that he had practically no sincere sexual needs. He lived only to be the best student, appreciated by all his professors, and he was actually able to reach this primary goal of his. He had no real interest in anything but his immediate studies, which were narrowly limited to a neglected period of medieval history. He "liked" his wife insofar as he was able to like anybody. His studies took practically the twenty-four hours of the day, including week ends. There was no originality in his work, but he was extremely conscientious and ambitious. Most of his work consisted in reading. After he completed his work at the university, he began to teach himself, getting satisfaction to an extreme degree from this activity. There was still no more time left for his married life, because of his preparations for his classes. He carefully selected only those "friends" who duly admired him, and he expected to be admired for his intellect by his wife as well. Even in this respect he was gratified, because she did admire his intellect, although she realized the shortcomings of the rest of his personality. Yet N.T. was unable to leave this man who gave her no gratification of any sort, except, probably, that of being proud of his success. She wept, and complained, and analyzed the reasons for her frustrations in detail, but she never made a move to rid herself of this situation. Her reasoning was characteristically that "who knows that another husband would be better." Although extremely pretty, she had no self-confidence in regard to attracting men. Another reason for not wanting a divorce was her concern about her mother's reaction to her daughter's divorce. She continued daydreaming about "once getting on the stage," but did nothing about it, and kept her secretarial job for years, although she admitted that she hates the work. She was not an efficient worker, often becoming confused through daydreaming. Since neither of these subjects was my patient in analysis (the husband, of course, never thought of analysis) and because I left the country, I was unable to follow up the later development and changes which must have taken place in this girl during analysis.

The factorial correlations in Figures 10 to 12 can be abstracted from the profiles in Figures 9a, b as representing generally valid and rather frequently occurring syndromes.

Figures 13a and b, two profiles of a nineteen year old boy, are presented despite the fact that I know practically nothing about him as an individual; I know only that the profiles were taken in a state prison in Hungary, to which G.Y. was sentenced for four years for a case of attempted murder, and because of his part in arson against a synagogue in company with a gang of boys of similar age.

Unfortunately, profiles of severe criminals are not usually available until after commission of the crime, when the profiles are taken during custody, thus possibly introducing a modifying factor the effect of which cannot be separated from that of the underlying personality pattern. Yet the "typical" reactions of criminals in jail are meaningful in terms of our theory of interpretation of the various factorial positions, so that we assume that even though possibly somewhat modified through the effects of confinement, these test profiles may be regarded as representing the reaction pattern of antisocial individuals.

In the two profiles of G.Y., we see the following char-acteristics: most loaded factor is the *s*, all six pictures of sadists in the second profile having been chosen as five liked, one disliked.

Intepretation: Greatest tension lies in the area of physical activity, which in this case of extreme loadedness in an adult, must be interpreted as physical aggression ready to be dis-

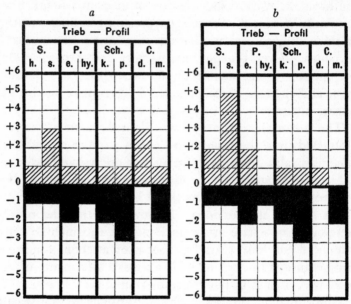

FIG. 13. *a, b.* G. Y., 19 year old male, sentenced for attempted murder.

charged. There is a need to manipulate aggressively environ-mental objects. No power of abstraction. No intellectual interest. Impulsive character. Childish reactions.

Open reactions: h (once), hy (twice), d (once).

Interpretation: Open *h*, in conjunction with plus *s*, is a typically "bad" constellation. It indicates dissociation in the two main component factors of sexuality, whereby each of the two tendencies is likely to appear in pathologic form of behavior, since the mutually "mitigating" effect of the two opposing factors is lacking. (The pathologic effect in a case of this type of dissociation of the two factors in the sexual vector is more apparent in behavior when one of the factors is open while the other is in plus position, than it is when the factor which is loaded is in the minus position next to the open reaction. Neurotic, hidden pathologic manifestations can be expected in this latter case, and *not* antisocial pathology, since a minus reaction in either the *h* or the *s* factor implies sublimation too strong to allow antisocial behavior.) In the present case, in which open *h* appears with plus *s*, one can assume that childish sexuality, perhaps actual homosexuality, and sadism are both pathologically apparent features of the behavior. This is a usual *S* vectorial picture in sexual perverts and criminals (the two not being mutually exclusive).

The open *hy* reaction by itself can be interpreted only as lack of control in regard to exhibiting emotions. By itself it has no particular socially negative or positive significance; however, in conjunction with this poorly integrated and extremely sadistic sexuality, one can definitely attribute a socially negative significance to the lack of emotional control as indicated by the open *hy*. Something is always "acted out" in individuals with open *hy*, with this strong plus *s* (and as we will see with the other socially unfavorable factorial constellations) it means that a criminal role has been acted out. It should be remembered that the percentual frequency of the open *hy* among the various pathologic groups is the highest in the group comprising antisocial individuals. The open *d* reaction indicates a lack of concern about the specificity of objects in the environment. There is no strong attachment to any object; whatever is closest and easiest to obtain is taken. Its significance in terms of social behavior can, again, not be interpreted except in relation to the *m*. Open *d*, with minus *m*, is socially the least favorable constellation of *all C* vectorial configurations. These are the subjects who have the most negativistic attitude toward the world. There is no attempt at socially positive adjustment, not even in the sense of "neurotic" adjustment. In behavior there is a socially desperate attitude of indifference and aggression against the frustrating environment. This not unfrequently takes the form of destructive activities in order to "secure revenge" and evoke some "pleasure" from the frustrating environment. Highest in frequency among the pathologic groups, this configuration is found again in criminals, and next in manic psychotics.

Changing factors are the h, *the* e, *and the* d. None of these changes is great—from one to two squares only (counterindication against psychosis). The tension in the *h* factor shows parallel increase with the tension in the *s* factor, resulting still in the same degree of discrepancy in their relative loadedness as was seen in the first profile. The interpretation is similar, except that a slightly more balanced sexual picture occurs in the second profile. Nevertheless, the subject is a strongly sadistic, outgoing, nonintellectual person. He has no ability to sublimate. (This statement is borne out also by the rest of the factors, primarily in the *Sch* vector.)

The change in the *e* factor is more interesting. Although only one additional picture has been chosen as *liked,* still the balance within the *e* factor has changed considerably from 2 minus and 1 plus (twice as many minus choices), to ambiequal position. Minus *e* is the typical reaction of individuals with poor control over aggressive emotions, and this is particularly true if minus *e* appears with open *hy,* which configuration represents the poorest emotional control conceivable. Yet on the second profile there is some indication of the presence of a controlling agent (superego) which, although in a conflict situation, nevertheless indicates a lack of unconcerned spontaneity as far as open behavior is concerned. It is an indicator for the appearance of some guilt-feelings. (This, for instance, seems to me a possible "jail"-induced reaction.) It is interesting to note that the plus *e* component increases parallel to the extreme increase in the plus *s* tension, which might be in dynamically causal relationship, the guilt-feeling being the consequence (the increasing inner tension in regard to physical aggressiveness).

The change in the *d* factor shows a draining of the plus *d*. Plus *d*, plus *s* is the typical picture of the anal-sadistic individual: plus *d* indicates the need to accumulate and master concrete objects, and plus *s* indicates that this need is carried out in a ruthless way. If minus *m* is also present, there can be practically no doubt about this socially negative implication of plus *d*, plus *s*. The alternation of plus with open *d* points toward the person's slightly changing attitude toward the value character of the environment in general. Plus *d*, in this constellation, indicates that objects are still valued; it is worthwhile to hoard them and to fight for them sadistically; while open *d* indicates an even more cynical, not-caring attitude, in which destruction for the sake of revenge becomes more important than any material gain from an antisocial activity. (Setting a temple afire fits in well with the second constellation, while robbery is more common with plus *d*.)

The ego picture is one hundred per cent stable within the two profiles, giving both times the childish "drill" picture of minus *k* with minus *p*, the minus *p* being in both cases the more loaded.

Interpretation: The forced control character of this ego configuration has been discussed in the corresponding section in the chapter on ego development. It also has been pointed out that although most of the time this ego constellation accompanies disciplined behavior, it represents the socially least reliable way of arriving at controlled behavior, since it implies the lack of recognition of any of the latent destructive forces operating in the deep-repressed layers of the personality. "Breaking-through of the repressed" in an unpredictable way is most common in this *Sch* configuration, particularly if the *p* factor is the more loaded, and undoubtedly if it is associated with an otherwise as socially negative a pattern as this test profile (plus *s,* minus *e,* open *hy,* plus or open *d,* minus *m).* Theoretically, I would assume that during the time the criminal act is performed, there is a draining of the minus *k;* however, I have no supporting experimental data of "criminals in action."

Summary: The two test profiles of this 19 year old boy show a sexually immature, anal-sadistic personality. There is no possibility for sublimation in any of the possible channels represented by the eight factors. He is disappointed in the world and turns against it. His emotional control is seriously deficient, there is a tremendous amount of motor excitability without adequate control. His ego is childish, in a "nebulous" state in the sense of his indifference to his own psychologic processes. His interest is strictly and aggressively concrete. He is capable of some sort of disciplined behavior however motivated wholly (or almost wholly) by the realization of external punishing agents. As long as external punishment for antisocial behavior seems imminent, he can restrict himself; however, there is no inner control. He gives the picture of the child who is "good" only as long as the parent or the teacher sees him. In the case of the adult, the parent or teacher is represented by the police. However, if this constellation is obtained by adolescents or adults, it implies typically antisocial tendencies.

Figures 14–16, typical syndromes, can be pointed out on the basis of these profiles:

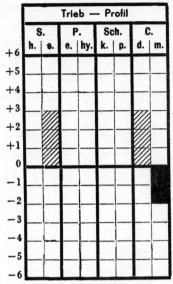

FIG. 14.   UNMODIFIED ANAL-SADISTIC TENDENCY

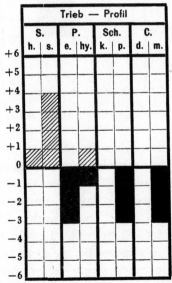

FIG. 15.   Murderous impulses (not necessarily carried out in reality).

These two profiles of another boy, approximately the same age as the adolescent discussed above, have been chosen for presentation because, in most respects, the factors constitute the constellation opposite to those of the two profiles of G.Y. Accordingly, the two subjects of the same age and sex show opposite types of personality, although the adjective *aggressive,* if taken out of context, could characterize both

Fɪɢ. 16. Nonsublimating "average" person. Interest is exclusively in concrete, tangible environment. Physically active but not necessarily aggressive.

of them. However, while in the case of G.Y. this meant actual physically sadistic impulses, as well as behavior manifestations, in the case of T.R. the aggression is a purely "intellectual" aggression, having no other manifestation than an extreme wish to "know" and to achieve success in his studies as a medical student. I could have chosen profiles more completely contradictory to those of G.Y., profiles in which actually every single factor shows diametrically the opposite position to those of G.Y., so that the personality of the two subjects would have been more nearly one hundred per cent opposing. Yet I rather chose the case of T.R. just because he has in some ways also an "aggressive" personality, giving us the opportunity to demonstrate the way in which the same constellation in a single factor can have completely different implications for behavior in an otherwise completely different test pattern.

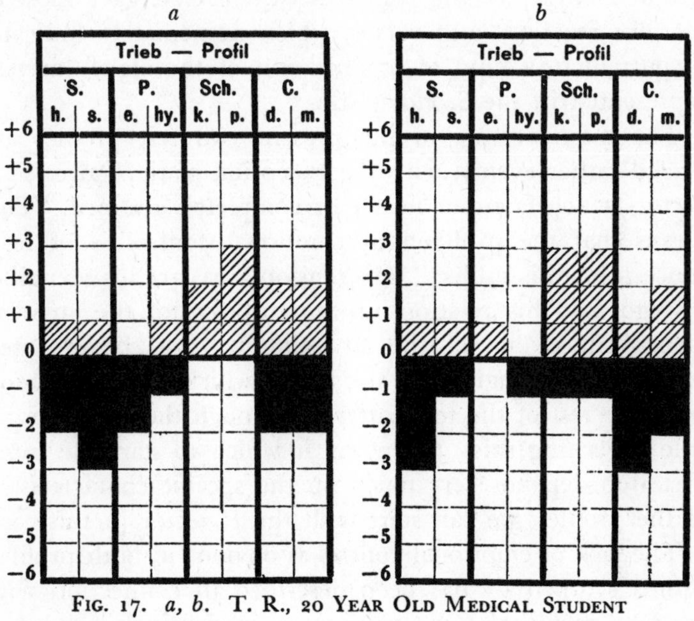

FIG. 17. *a, b.* T. R., 20 YEAR OLD MEDICAL STUDENT

The first difference we can notice in the two pairs of profiles is that in the case of T.R. there is no factor loaded with more than four choices, and even when there are four, one of them has the position as the "counterbalancing one" square, opposite to the direction of the other three choices in the same factor. (G.Y. chose all six pictures in the *s,* with five in the plus direction.) This alone is an indication of the fact that T.R.'s profiles correspond to a rather well-balanced type of personality.

The next structural difference we can see is that T.R.

gives three ambiequal reactions in the two profiles, while
G.Y. gave none. Without even considering in which factors
these ambiequal reactions are found, we can say that they
are indication of more self-control and more awareness
of psychologic processes than G.Y. showed.

The third general comparative remark can be that in a
quick overview we see that T.R.'s minus reactions are distributed mostly in the factors in which G.Y. gave most of
his plus reactions and versus, which immediately indicates
a contradictory kind of organization of the eight "drives"
represented in the Szondi test.

The main vectors in the present two test profiles are
loaded rather evenly, with the exception of the Paroxysmal
vector, which is either nearly or completely drained. This
means that the problem of emotional control is of least
concern for this subject. His tension areas are his sexuality,
his ego, and his relationship with objects of the environment. Since one of the advisable ways to begin interpretation is to begin with the vector which stands out most
from the rest of the test pattern (although there is no rigid
rule governing this: the point at which to start the interpretation depends very much on the specific characteristics
of the profile), we can start with the P vector in this case.

The lack of emotional control is obvious in both profiles.
Minus e, open hy has been described in connection with
the first profile of G.Y., who gave—interestingly enough—
exactly the same configuration. We said that this suggested
the poorest emotional control, indicating irritability, readiness to discharge aggression, and some sort of exhibitionistic
outlet. However, the meaninglessness of attaching schemes
of interpretation to positions *per se* is clearly illustrated in
this case. Can we expect that this boy will be ready to
discharge aggression and display exhibitionistic characteristics in a manner similar to G.Y.'s? A glance at the other
six factors will give us clearly the answer "no." It is true

that he *must* have some sort of an exhibitionistic outlet, and that some sort of aggression must break through easily; however, the minus *h*, minus *s*, plus *k*, plus *p*, and the presence of minus *d*, and plus *m* part reactions, is a guarantee that whatever this boy does is strictly within socially acceptable limits; even more, the rest of the pattern indicates that he is a typically idealistic, sublimating individual. Thus, within this context, minus *e*, open *hy* has more the meaning of emotional spontaneity; actually there is no reason for him to invest much psychic energy in controlling emotional manifestations, since at the outset his drives appear within his psychologic organization in socially sublimated form. The basic sublimation of the primary drives and their integration within the frame of the ego are the psychologic functions utilizing most of this boy's psychic energy. There is no indication of forced, constrictive-control in any of the factors (primarily, I refer here to the lack of minus *k*). The modification (or channelization) of the basic drives takes place at a more basic level of organization. Thus, the lack of emotional control in this young man is psychologically rather a "good" sign, since he needs some area in which he can release tension resulting from the otherwise too strenuous psychologic task he takes on himself in regard to sublimation and integration of all psychologically perceived drives within the coherent system of the ego—all this without resorting to "organizing" through repression (plus *k* with plus *p*). Open *e*, open *hy*, in this case, means that the emotions are lived out without difficulty, although on a sublimated level. He is likely to react to ordinary experiences in an emotional way, which again in a profile indicating so much intellectualization, might be considered as favorable at least in the sense of indicating that despite the strong drives for intellectual sublimation, this boy is a spontaneous, emotional being. It indicates a freely expressive and not rigid behavior. Subjectively he might feel the disadvantages of this lack of emotional control. He might be easily irritable and emotions might find their way into his thinking processes even on occasions when they have a disturbing effect on intellectual concentration.

Now that we have analyzed the one outstanding "not-fitting" vector, we can continue by interpreting the vectors as they appear in succession on the profile, since the rest of the test pattern reveals a usual correlation among the factors and the vectors; yielding in every respect the "typical" picture of the intellectually sublimating person. Whatever gives the uniquely individual character or coloring of a personality has to be looked for always in the correlations which are *not* usual, in the vector which is the *least* fitting within the general pattern of the profile. In the present case, we found this most individual coloring in the fact that this boy *is* spontaneous and might have difficulties in intellectual concentration, despite all his conscious drives toward sublimation and integrated behavior.

The Sexual vector shows the greatest fluctuation within the whole profile, the minus *h*, minus *s* configuration changing into a minus *h*, open *s*, although it was just the *s* which was more strongly minus than the *h* in the first profile. This can be taken as an indication that handling aggression is problematic for this boy. He vacillates between a more passive and a more openly aggressive behavior. Yet even in the case of acceptance of an "aggressive" role (the second profile with open *s*) one can be sure that "aggression" in this case means active and energetic sublimation, fighting for his ideas, and not aggression in an antisocial form. Minus *h* with open *s* is a typical configuration for what one could call "masculine" sublimation, meaning thereby that subjects with this reaction in the sexual vector are likely to live out their "need for masculinity" in a desexualized form of professional work of an active sort (as against the passive "receptive" type of sublimation which goes more with minus *h and* minus *s)*. The interesting aspect of this minus *h,* open *s* configuration is that by indicating both desexualization and living out masculine tendencies in a sublimated form it has slightly opposing meaning depending on the sex of the subject. It is given by masculine women who sublimate their masculinity in professional work, while in the case of men, it means rather the fact that the subject is avoiding complete identification with the masculine component of sexuality, even though these subjects cannot be described as "feminine" in their behavior. For some reason they seem to have conflicts about "masculine" aggression on the primarily sexual level, but are well able to sublimate their doubtlessly existing need for such behavior in professional work, in which then they are usually successful. This "dual" and conflicting behavior is indicated by the fact that this is a "dissociated" sexual picture, showing that the two partial and opposing components of sexuality have been treated very differently, which, as we know, is always the sign of a poor amalgamation of the basic sex drives, expected to show some fusion in sexually well-functioning individuals. In the case of one of the factors being loaded, the other open, both component drives of sexuality seem to be operating strongly in the personality; however, they exert their effects from different layers of the personality.

In the case of the present *S* vectorial constellation, on the second profile of T.R., the configuration indicates that the feminine, tender part of sexuality is strongly experienced as such (strongly, because of its dissociated appearance from the *s* factor), yet he more or less consciously represses it from open manifestation and overemphasizes his masculine aggression, which, on the other hand, is hindered from healthy sexual manifestation due to its lack of fusion with the *h,* thus being channelized into other nonsexual forms of behavior. The presence of minus h guarantees that even in case of overemphasizing this masculine aggression, it will have no antisocial effects. The correctness of this interpretation in the present case is borne out by the fact that open s appears in the second test after a negative s in the first; thus the conflict between masculine and feminine identification is indicated in two independent ways: once within one profile by the disproportionate loading of the two "twin" factors, and then by the change taking place in the s factor from the first to the second testing. I have analyzed this constellation to this extent because I wanted to point out in a concrete case the difference, as far as behavior is concerned, in the two subjects in whom we found dissociation in the Sexual vector, yet dissociation in different directions, and correspondingly, with diametrically opposite behavioral consequences, even though both boys were unbalanced in their sexuality.

The Ego vector, on the other hand, is well balanced in both profiles, particularly in the second, where the "counter-balancing one" squares appear under the plus k as well as under the plus p factor. The fact that the k factor, without showing any changes in direction, does increase with two choices (one more in plus and appearance of one in the minus on the second profile) is a further indication that the second profile corresponds to a state of better integration within the ego than was shown in the first. It is of interest to note that this better state of ego integration occurs when the minus s in the sexual factor disappears. It might indicate that the drive for sublimated identification with the masculine role can be better integrated within the ego, than can his acceptance of his tendency toward "feminine" passivity (minus s). These types of changes are characteristic for the so-called "normal" or "healthy" individuals, who by no means are expected to be beings without conflicts and without fluctuations within the state of tension in their various drives; yet they are expected not to show extreme changes from one testing to the other which on the profiles would be indicated by the complete "mirror" changes of the factorial as well as vectorial constellations (see chapter on classification of changes).

The ego pictures in both profiles of T.R. indicate that this boy wants to accept himself the way he is; he intends to be "emotional" (plus p) as well as "intellectual" (plus k); he wants to cathect objects of the environment, yet keep up his self-sufficient narcissistic integrity. This, as has been said in discussing the plus k, plus p configuration, results by necessity in an extremely tense situation within the ego, which by the person might be experienced as a critical situation which cannot be kept up for long periods of time because of the psychologic contradictions inherent in simultaneous and complete identification with these two opposing ego drives, yet which to a high degree precludes any seriously pathologic symptoms within the ego just because of the mutually mitigating effect of these two drives, and because the whole process and conflict is conscious to the person to such a great extent that most of the pathologic effect of the drives becomes absorbed.

The one possible pathologic implication of this tense ego constellation, that of preschizophrenia, can be excluded because the change in the ego vector shows that this boy, instead of being likely to "break down," shows rather a potentiality for increasing the effect of the organizational power (increasing his k) within the ego, and increasing it in the most desirable way, by showing at least a slight tendency toward dividing his attitude, not forcing himself so much to carry out the most difficult task of accepting and organizing every emotional content on the conscious level. The second profile indicates an incipient willingness to withdraw some of his psychic energy from constant introspection, or in other words, to be slightly less con-

cerned with the state of his own ego, thus having more
energy at his disposal to be invested in more concretely
realistic aspects of the world. In the case of the plus *k*,
plus *p* configuration in the *Sch* vector, the lack or presence
of the counterbalancing one squares under each factor, seem
to make a great deal of difference in respect to the realistic
efficiency of the person. Although sublimation is indicated in every variation of this specific ego picture, yet
without the subject's ability to leave some of his ego within
the sphere of the unconscious (unconscious as indicated by
the presence of minus reactions in the *Sch* vector) the drive
toward sublimation is often exhausted before it could have
manifested itself in any constructively tangible products of
sublimation. In the case of our present subject, we can
assume that he is on the way to change from an inflated
adolescent in the height of intellectual and emotional
"Sturm und Drang" period, into a really productive, sublimating adult.

The configurations and the changes taking place in the
Contact vector support this interpretation of the subject's
being in a "transition" period of emotional and social
adjustment. Plus-minus *d*, plus-minus *m* on the first profile
changes into minus *d*, plus-minus *m* in the second profile.
The change from a totally ambivalent attitude in regard
to evaluating the objects of the environment, toward a
slightly less ambivalent attitude, takes place simultaneously
with the change toward a state of better organization within
the ego. The configuration within the *C* vector on the
first profile indicates an ambivalence—or vacillation—in
regard to whether or not environmental objects should be
valued highly, and sought for actively, or whether or not
there should be attempts to gain gratifications on a completely abstract, and in this sense, unrealistic level. As we
have mentioned in our discussion of this configuration of
the *d* and *m* factors, this total ambivalence in the *C* vector
is usually not experienced by the subject as a hopeless con-

flict, but the opposing attitudes toward the objects and values of the world manifest themselves rather in the succession of small time units, resulting in an inconsistent behavior. On the second profile we find a more definite stand-point in regard to evaluating the importance of material objects of the world. On the second profile, the C vectorial configuration approaches the pattern of ·minus d, plus m, indicating a depreciation of the materialistic values, with increasing importance of the idealistic, nontangible values. As has been said in the general section about this configuration as well as in discussion of our first case (T.T.), this constellation usually indicates a good and optimistic attitude toward the environment, with gratifications obtained on a sublimated level. However, even though this configuration is implicit in the second profile of T.R., the presence of the minus part of the m factor is an indication that this boy experiences frustration in regard to his need to cling to some person for the sake of obtaining love and support. In discussion of the meaning of the plus-minus m position, it has been mentioned that this m factorial constellation, if recurring within a series bearing otherwise favorable signs for sublimation, is usually caused by the basic bisexual characteristics of the subject's sexual constitution, the conflict in the m factor indicating that neither clinging to a person of the opposite sex or to one of the same sex is completely satisfactory. We might further assume that the excessive drive toward sublimation and the extreme cathexis of the own ego-processes is also in some way in causal connection with this basic conflict of bisexual organization. The change taking place within the sexual vector and the configuration of the h and s factors in the second profile support this hypothesis.

In conclusion we can say that these two profiles reflect an intensively sublimating and socialized individual. Intellectual or artistic professions are practically certain in the event of such profiles. T.R.'s personality reflects an extremely differentiated and complex level of organization. He seems to be in a transition period from a more conflicting and adolescent-like stage towards a better organized and less ambivalent stage of productive adulthood. Basic conflicts are indicated in the area of sexuality, the "feminine" and "masculine" components of sexuality lacking amalgamation, thus being experienced as mutually incompatible forces rather than different aspects of the same basic drive. More specifically, this boy shows inconsistency in regard to passive, recipient, or active manipulative behavior. He is able to identify and carry out the role corresponding to the latter, however, only after having deflected sexual libido from the primarily sexual goal; in other words, through sublimation. Despite being successful in this respect, he experiences frustration in regard to his object relationships, which, however, does not cause serious symptoms because of his ability to derive gratifications of a sublimated nature.

The following facts of the personal history of this boy should be mentioned in order to furnish comparative findings to our test interpretation. At the time the test was taken he was an enthusiastic and most successful medical student. Ever since his childhood, he was considered to be quite brilliant intellectually, without, however, being an overly "good" child. Studying and getting the best grades came easily to him, without his having to concentrate hard on his schoolwork. He was aware of this ability, and expressed frequently his fears that people generally overestimated him, and he felt that sooner or later he would have to disappoint those (primarily his parents) who expected him to develop into somebody "exceptional" in his later life, since he did not feel the strength to exert really hard work requiring long-range concentrated efforts. He was afraid that he would never be able to narrow his interests sufficiently to be really successful in one specific field. His range of interest and actual knowledge varied widely, from mathematics and physics to languages, literature, history, psychology, and a number of activities including bicycling, hiking, dancing, going to parties, etc. Despite his apparent "success" in social gatherings, this was a field in which he felt insecure. He was afraid that girls would not like him unless he went out of his way to act really "masculine." He forced himself to make numerous dates and to do everything boys of his age were supposed to do, however without enjoyment. He changed his girl friends frequently because—in his own words—he became "bored" in going out with the same girl for any length of time. His behavior was usually gay and happy, yet he felt basically lonesome in the company of boys and girls of his own age. On the other hand, he was able to derive intensive satisfaction from reading, writing, studying, or working on a specific theoretical problem. His parents were both intellectual professional people, his father a chemist, his mother a pediatrician, which he later became himself. Both his parents loved him, their only child, but he was aware that their marriage was unhappy—or no marriage beyond formality—and that without consideration of him both parents would have been divorced. His attitude toward his parents was that of love and understanding, almost frighteningly mature even at early puberty when he realized the complete independence of the lives of his father and mother. He did not condemn either of them, but consciously tried to make them happy. His anxieties had roots in his feelings that he might disappoint them. His parents treated him as an adult at a very early age, being unusually sincere with themselves as well as with each other and with the child. Consequently the child identified himself with both of them, this double identification serving possibly as a psychologic basis for his later conflicts about being feminine or masculine in behavior.

The identification was made even more complex by the fact that his mother was strongly "masculine" and his father strongly "feminine" in personality. Given this home background, it would be hard to imagine anybody developing a healthier sexual pattern than this boy did. At the time the profiles were taken, he was considering the possibility of going into psychoanalysis, with the probable view of becoming a psychoanalyst himself; however, he felt that for a while he would wait and try to "bring order" within himself in which task I think he succeeded very well. When he left town I did not see him for years until recently I met him once more. He had become a practicing pediatrician, married, the father of a child, and gave every indication of one who was rather satisfied with his life. He spontaneously talked about the times of his greatest emotional and intellectual upheaval (when the tests were administered) and stated that, although conflicts still exist, he felt reasonably happy, enjoyed his work and his family. Undoubtedly there was some bitterness in talking about himself as a "regular" practitioner who, in supporting a family, had little time for research. I wondered about the changes in his ego vector, but had no opportunity to administer the test.

On the basis of this case, we can point out the factorial correlations in Figure 18 as typical.

Finally the test-series of B.I., a severely confused schizophrenic patient of a state hospital, is presented primarily as an example of one of the most pathologic types of change, such types of change which can *never* be expected to occur either in so-called "normal" or neurotic subjects. It will be of interest to compare the structural features of this series with those of F.T. whose series of ten profiles has been presented in Fig. 5, Chapter VI, in which we discussed the case from the point of view of formalized analysis, on the basis of purely quantitative computations and the diagnostic tables of drive formulas presented in the appendix of Szondi's *Experimentelle Triebdiagnostik.*

First let us inspect the finding reached on the basis of quantitative scoring methods, in the present series of B.I. The ratio of all his open reactions over all his plus-minus reactions corresponds to the value of 2.2. This is approxi-

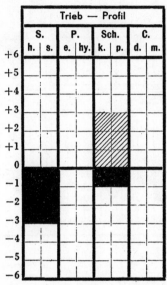

FIG. 18. Typical picture of sublimating individual who intends to face and intellectualize his emotions without stifling them (opposite to figure 16).

mately twice the value obtained in the case of F.T. (1.08). On the basis of this ratio we can say about B.I. only that he may be expected to be much less self-controlled and considerably more prone to "act out" in his behavior than F.T. The type of his "acting out," even with respect to whether it is within the range of normal spontaneous or psychotic symptoms, cannot be decided on the basis of this one ratio.

Furthermore, the scoring sheet indicates that B.I. belongs in the category, or "drive-class," of C_{m-}, which means that

DIAGNOSIS: schizophrenia
mixed type

Name: B. I.   Alter: 32   Beruf:

Szondi-Test
Blatt mit zehn Triebprofilen

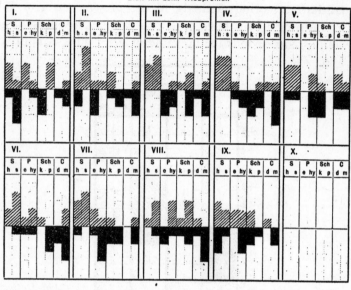

1947	S		P		Sch		C		Σ	Σ	Σ
Nr.	h	s	e	hy	k	p	d	m	0	$\pm$	0 u. $\pm$
I.	+	−	+	⊘	−	+	⊘	−	2	⊘	2
II.	±	+(!)	−	⊘	+	−	⊘	−	2	1	3
III.	+	+	−	−	0	±	⊘	−	2	1	3
IV.	+	+	⊘	−	−	−	⊘	−	2	⊘	2
V.	+	+	⊘	±	−	⊘	±	−	2	2	4
VI.	+	+	⊘	+	⊘	−	−	−	2	⊘	2
VII.	+	+	+	−	−	−	⊘	−	1	⊘	1
VIII.	⊘	+	−	+	⊘	±	⊘	−	3	1	4
IX.	±	+	+	±	±	⊘	⊘	−	2	3	5
X.											
Σ 0	1	⊘	3	2	3	2	7	⊘	18		
Σ ±	2	⊘	⊘	2	1	2	1	⊘		8	
T. sp. G.	3	⊘	3	4	4	4	8	⊘			26
Latenzgrösse	S = 3. S+		P = .!. e		Sch = 0		C = 8. m⁻				

1. Tendenzspan-
nungsquotient $= \dfrac{\Sigma\,0}{\Sigma\pm} = \dfrac{18}{8} = 2.2$

2. Triebformel:

Symptomatische:	d_8
Submanifeste bzw. sublatente:	hy_4, k_4, p_4, h_3, e_3
Wurzel-Faktoren:	$S_0^+ \quad m_0^-$

3. Latenzproportionen:
$$\frac{Cm^-}{8} : \frac{Ss+}{3} : \frac{P}{1} : \frac{Sch}{0}$$

4. Triebklasse: $Cm-$

Copyright 1947 by Verlag Hans Huber, Bern

FIG. 19. B. I., A SCHIZOPHRENIC PATIENT.

it is the Contact Vector in which the two twin factors are handled the most disproportionately, the d factor giving symptomatic reactions in eight out of nine profiles (seven open and one plus-minus), while the m factor is in minus position throughout the nine profiles. Accordingly, we would expect that the most critical need in this man is the frustrated need of oral clinging. Whatever open symptoms we might find in him we assume most are basically motivated unconsciously, first by this frustrated need to cling to somebody passively for love and support, and second by his drive towards aggressive manipulation of his environment (s being the other factor without any symptomatic reaction, and appearing eight times out of nine in plus position).

Turning to the appendix of Szondi's *Experimentelle Triebdiagnostik,* we consult Psychodiagnostic Table XVIII, which gives us the formulas for the "drive-class" C_{m-}. In this table the one formula which is most similar to (but not identical with) the constellation of the factors in our present "formula," is indicated as being most characteristic for manic patients. As will be seen from the case history, our patient does have a great number of symptoms which are of "manic" character. Yet, his hospital diagnosis was that of schizophrenia, with mixed symptoms of hebephrenic and excited catatonic features. The reason that in this case the "drive-formula" has not really indicated the schizophrenic disturbance is that the most characteristic test symptom of schizophrenia, the mirror-like reversal of factors from one testing to the next, does not show up as a "symptomatic reaction" in this type of tabulation, since sudden changes from the plus to the minus reaction are not tabulated as symptomatic—as are only the open and plus-minus reactions. This does not mean, of course, that this type tabulation of series should not be done; it does remind us, however, of the importance of interpreting always the qualitative changes taking place in the factors and vectors, as indicated on the graphic profiles (or one can transpose the graphic squares into numbers, in which case it might be easier to obtain a quick overview of the factorial changes within a long series without losing the detailed qualitative data).

The qualitative approach to interpretation of the present series yields the following findings:

First, the general incoherence of the configuration of the total series is obvious.

a. One is struck immediately by the number of loaded plus or minus reactions in various factors which have no counter-balancing one square in the opposite direction.

b. The first profile shows an almost complete dissociation of the respective twin-factors in each vector. This should be mentioned because the first profiles in any series seem to have a specific significance from the point of view of diagnosing behavior.

c. Disproportionate loading of the vectors is apparent throughout the series, particularly in profiles V and VIII. In profile V it should be noted that the open factors are actually one hundred per cent open, which is practically never obtained (in two factors of the same profile) in nonpsychotics.

d. Next, one should observe the complete "mirror"-changes taking place from one testing to the other (the tests having been administered daily). Most frequent are these changes in the *Sch* vector. From profile I to II the minus k with plus p changes into plus k with minus p. From profile V to VI, minus k with open p changes to open k with minus p. From profile VIII to IX, open k with plus-minus p changes into plus-minus k with open p. As we have pointed out before, changes are expected in the series of any subject, and even in cases of relatively well-functioning individuals we might get a complete turning over of a vectorial configuration within the course of a whole series. Yet in the case of "normals," this turning over is a gradual process, occurring through a number of "transitory" steps, and not into such complete mirror reflections of the previous vectorial picture, from one day to the next.

This degree of inspection of the present test series is enough for the formulation of the following statements: This subject is *not* well-functioning, and has pathologic symptoms which are more serious than any form of neurosis. He has a basically disbalanced personality, without any steady control mechanisms. His ego is seriously disintegrated (not simply regressed) and he has no consistent attitude in regard to the use of any particular ego mechanism. States of complete adualistic fusion into his environment alternate with pictures of rigid compulsiveness, giving the most narcissistic reaction of emotional detachment, followed by reaction indicating the most acute need to fuse into and love persons in his environment. Consequently his behavior must be seriously erratic and unpredictable.

The "mirror-changes" in the *Sch* vector indicate the presence of a schizophrenic process; however, in order to evaluate the relative importance of the undoubtedly existing process in the framework of the total personality pattern, we have to inspect the occurrences taking place in the other vectors. There is only one great change in the Sexual vector, taking place from profile I to II, from plus *h* with minus *s,* to plus-minus *h* with strongly (five plus) plus *s.* The Paroxysmal vector shows considerable changes in each successive profile. Yet, a complete vectorial "mirror"-change is seen only once, from profile VII to VIII, plus *e* with minus *hy* changing into minus *e* with plus *hy.* There is such a complete "mirror"-change in the *P* vector also, between the configurations of profile II and IV, changing from minus *e* with open *hy* into open *e* with minus *hy.* However, profile III shows the transitory step of minus *e* with minus *hy*, thereby diminishing some of the pathologic significance of this change.

Thus, we can conclude that the pathologic significance of the changes within the *Sch* vector are greater than those of the *P* vector, although changes in the latter are undoubtedly indicative of the existence of pathologic paroxysmal symptoms.

There are relatively few changes in the Contact vector. The *m* factor is in minus position all through the nine profiles, the *d* factor is seven times open, once minus, and once plus-minus. On the basis of our general principles for interpretation of a series of profiles, we have to conclude that an actual pathologic process is not taking place within this area; however, we must look for an underlying motivational factor corresponding to the steady minus *m*. Furthermore, underlying factors are represented in the relatively stable plus *h* and plus *s*.

Thus we must conclude that this man shows most acute symptoms within the Schizophrenic vector. In the framework of such a completely disorganized profile, in which is shown no possibility for sublimation (because all factors constantly change with the exception of plus *h*, plus *s*, open *d*, and minus *m*), and in which are indicated the worst possible relationship to objects of his environment (plus *s*, open *d*, minus *m*), the most probable diagnosis is actual schizophrenic psychosis. Besides schizophrenic symptoms there must be some serious paroxysmal type of disorder, yet real epilepsy can be excluded on the following basis: in case of grand-mal seizures, one would expect occasional draining of the *s* factor. The ego picture of epileptics is expected to be primitive, reflecting a poorly structured infantile ego, yet not showing those types of "mirror"-changes which imply that the core of the process takes place within the ego functions and not through the motor system proper (as in the case of grand-mals).

On the basis of the steady minus m and the loaded plus s, one also must think of antisocial behavior. Actually, there are no signs which would contradict the hypothesis that this man has serious antisocial tendencies; however, the general pattern of changes indicates that this can not be his main diagnosis. Criminal behavior alone could not account for the changes in either the Sch or the P vectors. Yet the criminal syndrome of plus s, minus e, minus p, and minus m is clearly there in profiles II and III. Again it should be remembered that the first profile in a series has specific importance for manifest behavior, and B.I. gives minus s and plus e in his first profile.

Thus, despite the obvious indications for paroxysmal and antisocial behavior, the most pathologic area remains that corresponding to the patient's ego; in other words, the schizophrenic process seems to be acutely the most characteristic of his pathologic behavior. The next step is decision of the form of schizophrenia. The paranoid form (as the most characteristic feature) is contraindicated by the great inconsistency of the k factor. Systematized forms of paranoid delusions could not persist with this much inconsistency within the ego processes. The lack of minus s is another counterindication against systematized paranoic symptoms. The great changes in the Paroxysmal vector indicate a great deal of motoric excitement which would be in accord either with the excited stage of catatonic symptoms or with hebephrenic symptoms. The steady plus h, plus s, open d, and minus m choices support the latter hypothesis, since these are factor correlations characteristic of manic psychotic symptoms (which is also our conclusion or the basis of the formalized analysis of the series), and hebephrenic patients are known to show somewhat similar symptomatology to manic psychotics.

Thus the final diagnosis would be schizophrenia, with excited catatonic and erratic hebephrenic features. Paroxysmal behavior and antisocial tendencies are to be expected in this patient. Prognosis is very poor because of the complete disorganization of the personality; the steady plus h with plus s suggesting that the patient was most probably a primitive and nonsublimating type of individual, even before his actual breakdown. The open d, minus m indicates a completely aggressive and negativistic attitude toward his environment: there is no more object attachment and no positive ways to seek gratification for his strongly frustrated oral need for clinging.

I want to conclude with one more remark concerning methodology. In the event we are confronted by a series of profiles as inconsistent and disbalanced as this, interpretation cannot proceed in any detailed elemental manner. One may not begin with interpretation of the positions of the single factors, vectors, or even whole single profiles, since the essence of the entire series lies in *changes,* and the fact that the series *is* inconsistent. Once this essence has been grasped, and the diagnosis of psychotic disturbance has been made, we can go into more careful observation and comparison of the type of changes taking place in the various vectors in order to reach a differential diagnosis. However, every interpretation following the first realization of psychotic disturbance is narrowed down in its meaning to pathologic interpretation. For example, there is no point in the interpretation, on the basis of the first profile, of B.I.'s behavior as "ethical" (plus e) and self-controlled (minus k), when the changes on the next profile indicate the diametric opposite of these characteristics. Similarly, plus h with plus s—usually a nonsublimating but rather well amalgamated and "healthy" picture of sexuality, certainly can not be interpreted as such, if none of the other factorial constellations indicates any possibility for a satisfactory object relationship, or, in analytic terms, a satisfactory handling of the libido. It indicates only, in this most pathologic context, that this is a man with strong sexual and aggressive impulses ready to be discharged.

In other words, interpretation must always be flexible. First, the interpreter has to inspect the series as a whole; he has to get a "feeling" for the general structural characteristics as well as for the type of changes taking place. In this manner, he can decide about the probability of the four main categories: well-functioning individual; neurotic; psychotic, or antisocial. Detailed interpretation of the vectors, profiles, syndromes, etc., follows this first general inspection, the choice among the various possible meanings of a given constellation being defined by the general pattern of the whole series. Interpretation which does not follow this "from the whole to the parts" approach, can sometimes take a much longer time, resulting in a great number of partial interpretations, which are hard to integrate into a coherent personality characterization. The statements might even be wholly correct and fitting to the subject in question, yet ultimately fail to impel the feeling that the interpretation adequately has described a living, human individual.

The most important points of the case history of patient B.I. are the following: at the time the tests were administered, B.I. had been in a state hospital for two years. He was committed by the court to which he was brought as a result of his commission of robbery several times. His psychotic behavior was immediately obvious at his hearing. He had a continuous silly laughter, and was obviously hallucinating, being unable to give any coherent answer. He was an illegitimate child, brought up in an orphanage until he was six (frustrated need to cling—minus *m*!) at which age he was taken by his mother. The mother at that time lived with a sadistic and alcoholic man. At the age of ten, the boy left his mother and wandered into another city. He had various odd jobs, changing his work almost every week. He spent a few years in a reformatory. After his release, he continued his restless life, wandering as a vagrant, doing nothing in particular.

In the hospital his behavior was most erratic. He fluctuated between manic elation and rages during which he attacked his room mates physically. He hallucinated a great deal, having auditive, visual, but mainly tactile hallucinations. He frequently felt that he was being touched in a sexual way (strong plus h, plus s) and enjoyed the touch, which was usually the reason he gave when asked the cause of his elated moods. He also had a great variety of incoherent delusional symptoms. He talked about "all his women" (about 500 in number) who usually slept with him. He said he was glad to be a man, because a woman has to be "split in two" when she bears a child. (This is an interesting projection of his own experience of being "split.") He talked about his plans to become a boxer once he was released (plus s), or to become a general who would order his soldiers to kill millions of people. Sometimes he had religious delusions, and spoke of himself as the founder of innumerable churches.

He felt extremely strong and healthy (plus h, plus s) but he had to take care of himself to remain so. Every night, he felt that he had to lie in a certain position on his right side in order to keep strong and to live a hundred years. Sometimes he worried whether he really did not change his position during the night (syndrome of hypochondriac anxiety, indicated by the minus hy with minus k).

He had delusions and actual symptoms of pyromania, having attempted several times to set the hospital on fire (paroxysmal epileptoid equivalent).

The comparison of the series of profiles of B.I. and that of F.T. (fig. 5) shows diametric opposite structural features in every respect, just as the severe compulsive rigidity of F.T. was diametrically opposite to the most erratic psychotic behavior of B.I.

In the first ten profiles of F.T. there was no "mirror"-change in any of the vectors. There was not even a single turning over from a plus to a minus reaction, or the reverse, in any of the factors. The absolute number of plus-minus reactions has been 25 as against the eight plus-minus reactions of B.I. This alone indicates an over-controlled behavior, with lack of spontaneity in F.T. The possible diagnosis of psychosis could be immediately eliminated on the basis of the high number of ambivalent reactions, particularly with a steady ambivalent k factor, and the general consistency of the reactions. Criminal behavior can be eliminated on the same basis, adding also the presence of the steady minus s, and the plus part of the e and the m factors. Next, one would have to decide whether this subject is a well-controlled, psychologically healthy person, or whether he is an over-controlled neurotic. The fact that ambivalence is found consistently in the e, the k, and the m factors, decides definitely for the latter diagnosis, particularly with the practically always drained p factor.

By now we know that minus k with open p, and plus-minus k with open p, is the characteristic reaction of subjects who fight against accepting their need to cathect objects and who fight compulsively against their own emotions. Plus-minus k, with open p, has been pointed out as the typical reaction of persons who want to free themselves from an emotional tie, but who nevertheless remain in this stage of fighting against their own drives instead of really freeing themselves. An escape into forced sublimation would be a possible solution for this Sch configuration; however, the unhappy object relationship as indicated by the open d with plus-minus m, and plus d with plus-minus m configuration, precludes the hypothesis that this man is able to find satisfaction on a sublimated level (minus d, plus m, or open d, plus m would be expected in this case). Furthermore, the steady minus s without any counter-balancing one plus s, in the case of a 32 year old man, is certainly more than just the indication for a healthy but passive behavior. Particularly when it is associated with steady plus or open *h*, as in the case of F.T., does it show pathologically submissive and masochistic characteristics.

Finally the ambivalent and steady loading of the *e* factor indicates a continuous fight for keeping up controlled behavior while, at the same time the steadily drained *hy* shows that something is acted out continuously. Considering all the indications for constrictive control (plus-minus *e*, plus-minus *k* with open *p*) and the repressed aggression as indicated by the steady minus *s*, the logical conclusion is that this man can act out continuously nothing but a sort of exhibitionistically compulsive repetitive symptom. His case history has been presented in connection with the formalized analysis of this series. Here I wanted to come back briefly to this case in order to show how, on the basis of the qualitative interpretation of the vectorial and factorial constellations, we would have arrived at the same conclusion in diagnosing this man as a severe compulsion neurotic. The monotony of this series, with all the signs of constrictive control and repressed aggression, is in striking contrast to the complete disorganization of all the controlling mechanisms with complete lack of repressing aggression in the case of our previously presented schizophrenic patient.

THE PRESENTATION of these few interpretations closes this introduction to the Szondi method. Although the illustrative profiles are limited, it is to be hoped that they are adequate to facilitate interpretation of other profiles not included. Actually, the variety of factorial combinations is almost infinite; as in the case of any other projective technic, the real process of learning, although aided by books, can be acquired only through many years of experience in working with the method, and through starting with cases for which additional clinical material is available. A second book concerning clinical application of the Szondi test, with ample case material, will follow soon.

Author Index

General Index

Loaded reaction, 27
Logic, 180
Love-object, 152, 257–58, 279
  loss of, 191
  of minus *k* with minus *p* subject, 228
  and open *hy*, 108
  secondary, 205
  specificity of, 253

m, 12
m factor, 23, 131–66
  and Contact vector, 66
Mania, 132–34, 140–41
  incipient, 160
  minus *k* in, 202
  plus *h* with plus *s* in, 81
Manic-depressive psychoses, 165
  open *e* with open *hy* in, 117
Manic process, 231
Manic psychosis, 132–34, 202
  minus *e* with plus *hy* in, 111
  minus *k* with minus *p* in, 229
  open *d* with plus *m*, 310
  open *hy* in, 108
  plus *k* in, 197
Manic rage, 231
  minus *k* with minus *p* in, 229
"Marginal" character, of young people, 239
"Martyr" characters, 303
"Masculine" aggression, 319
"Masculinity," 86
Masochism, 269, 296–98
Masturbation, minus *e* with minus *hy*, 114
Materialism, 149
Maturation, 225
Mechanism
  energy-consuming, 153
  of introjection, 215, 217
  self-regulating, 112
Medical student
  profiles of, 315
  case illustration of, 314–26
Melancholia
  differentiated from mourning, 121
  Freud's theory on psychodynamics of, 220
Men
  plus *h* with minus *s* in, 84
  See also Adults
Mental disorder
  genetic origin of, 1
Methodology, 334–35
Minus *d*, 124–27, 292–93

Minus *d* with minus *m*, 151–53
Minus *d* with plus *m*, 146–48, 292–93, 323
Minus *d* with plus-minus *m*, 322
Minus *e*, 93–94, 310
Minus *e* with minus *hy*, 112–14
Minus *e* with open *hy*, 310, 316–18
Minus *e* with plus *hy*, 110–12
Minus *h*, 70–71, 320
Minus *h* with minus *s*, 82–83
Minus *h* with open *s*, 318–19
Minus *h* with plus *s*, 85–86
Minus *hy* 103–6, 300
Minus *k*, 198–202, 312
  in symptom formation, 181
Minus *k* with minus *p*, 224–32, 253
Minus *k* with open *p*, 232, 283, 337
Minus *k* with plus *p*, 238–42
Minus *m*, 138–42, 311, 335
Minus *p*, 178–82
Minus *s*, 75–78, 337–38
  and ego integration, 320
"Mirror-changes," 330–31, 332
Mirror reaction, 43–44
Mirror reversal, 62
Money, 125–26
  identification with feces, 120
Mother fixation, 125
Motor sphere, 98–99
Motor symptoms, emotions and, 102
Motor system, 168, 198
Motoric tension, 73
Mourning, 220
  differentiated from melancholia, 121
Multiorientation of libido, 153–54
Murderers. *See* Criminality
Music, 195–96
Musicians
  minus *h* with minus *s* in, 82
  minus *k* with minus *p* in, 229
  open *d* with plus *m*, 158
  plus *m* in, 137
  plus *s* in, 75
Mutism, 187

Narcissism, 191, 194
  infantile form of, 209
  and *k* factor, 188–89
  secondary, 190
  in open *k* subjects, 207
  plus *k* with plus *p* subject, 254
  in plus-minus *k* with plus *p* subject, 245
  primary, 205, 207, 267
  secondary, 205
Narcissistic-exhibitionistic drives, 292
  "sign" for, 291